Windsor Farm

108610

Developing Minds

PROGRAMS FOR TEACHING THINKING

Revised Edition, Volume 2

W9-BUA-996

Edited by
Arthur L. Costa

Association for Supervision and Curriculum Development
Alexandria, Virginia

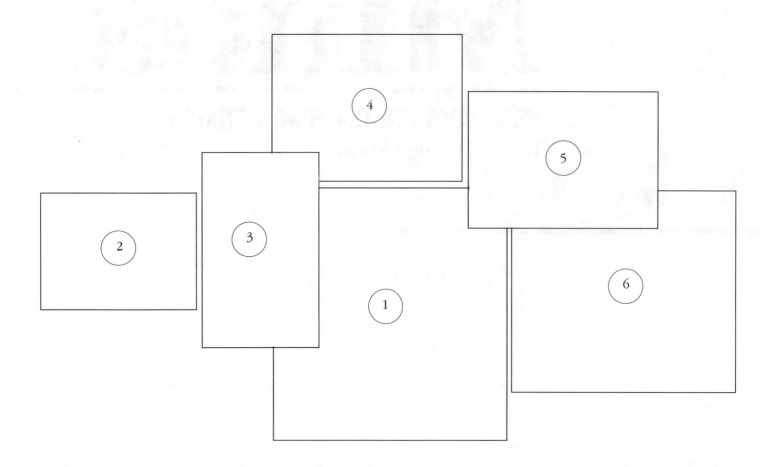

Cover Photos: Photos 3–5 Copyright © by Susie Fitzhugh.

Copyright © 1991 by the Association for Supervision and Curriculum Development. All rights reserved. No part of this publication may be reproduced or transmitted in any form or by any means, electronic or mechanical, including photocopy, recording, or any information storage and retrieval system, without permission in writing from the publisher. The contents of this publication may, however, be reproduced if they are intended solely for nonprofit, educational use.

Ronald S. Brandt, *Executive Editor*
Nancy Modrak, *Managing Editor, Books*
Julie Houtz, *Senior Associate Editor*
Ginger Miller, *Associate Editor*
Carolyn Pool, *Associate Editor*
Cole Tucker, *Editorial Assistant*
Gary Bloom, *Manager, Design and Production Services*
Stephanie Kenworthy, *Assistant Manager, Production Services*
Keith Demmons, *Graphic Designer*
Valerie Sprague, *Desktop Typesetter*

ASCD publications present a variety of viewpoints. The views expressed or implied in this publication are not necessarily official positions of the Association.

Printed in the United States of America

Price: $10.95
ASCD Stock No.: 611–91027
ISBN: 0-87120-181-X

Library of Congress Cataloging-in-Publication Information:

Developing minds/edited by Arthur L. Costa.
    p.   cm.
    Rev. ed. of: Developing minds, 1985, published in one volume.
    Includes bibliographical references and index.
    Contents: Vol. 1. A resource book for teaching thinking—v.
  2. Programs for teaching thinking.
    ISBN 0–87120–180–1 (v. 1): $24.95—ISBN 0–87120–181–X (v. 2): $10.95
    1. Thought and thinking—Study and teaching. 2. Cognition in children.
LB1590.3.D48   1991
    371.2'078—dc20
                                             91–3069
                                             CIP

Developing Minds
Programs for Teaching Thinking

Introduction

The vast majority of problems, decisions and situations which confront us daily are those which do not have just one answer. Several solutions are usually possible. Logic suggests that if one can mentally generate many possible solutions, the more likely it is that an optimum solution will be reached. This is a creative process—the formation of new and useful relationships.

—Richard E. Manelis

Educators considering the selection and installation of one or more of the available cognitive curriculum programs are often confused by the vast array of alternatives. Each program serves a different purpose and audience, is lodged in a different theoretical home, and produces different outcomes.

Because of this overload of complexity, educators are tempted to make simplistic decisions based on cursory examinations or political urgency, financial economy, or ease of installation. Sometimes schools have shunned the decision and have chosen to develop their own programs.

An example of this complex decision is the need for staff development—a very costly consideration. Some programs require a massive commitment of time and money for staff development. Other programs, which consider staff development to be helpful but not essential, could be installed on the basis of the power of the materials themselves, the helpfulness of the teacher guides, or the need for only minimal inservice. Still other programs regard staff development as critical and essential to employing the program with elegance, integrity, and philosophical consistency. These programs are based on the belief, expressed by Francis R. Link, that there can be "no curriculum development without staff development," that there is no change without change in teacher perception, skill, and knowledge. For some schools, however, ease of installation with a minimum of staff development may be a priority for adoption.

This volume is a companion to *Developing Minds: A Resource Book for Teaching Thinking.* It (1) describes many of the major programs designed to develop the intellect, (2) identifies the audience for whom each program is intended, (3) distinguishes among the several theoretical and philosophical assumptions on which each is based, (4) provides any research or evidence of the success of the program in achieving its intended goals, and (5) supplies names and addresses of contacts for more information. The last chapter displays how several of the programs focus on similar outcomes.

1

Balancing Process and Content

Marilyn Jager Adams

The world is changing rapidly. We cannot even guess what specific knowledge and skills will be critical to any one of our students in the future. As responsible educators, therefore, we must give students more than knowledge: we must develop in them both the acumen to decide, for themselves, what else they need to know and the abilities to acquire that information accurately and efficiently. And we must arm students with more than skills: beyond knowing how, they must *understand* how; they must be prepared to think about when, why, why not, and how else.

In short, students must learn to think. Can direct instruction in thinking skills help them to do so? Research on human learning and memory suggests that it may (Adams 1989; Resnick 1987)—depending on how it is presented and extended.

Learning, Memory, and Transfer

Human memory is nothing like a piecemeal catalog of knowledge. Learning does not consist of packing away a simple list of whatever distinct or nameable concepts one deems worthy of memorization. Instead, the human mind absorbs whole situations. Using any familiar parts as its building blocks, the mind constructs its own detailed and highly structured representation of every experience. In this way, a very real part of the schema we eventually develop about any concept consists of information about its peripheral details and the contexts in which it has occurred (McClelland and Rumelhart 1986).

Such extended information about concepts is important to our ability to understand what we see and hear. For example, if I commented on Fido's beautiful coat, you would assume that I was talking about his fur—not his Burberry jacket. In the same conversation, I might ask you for suggestions on his diet, tips on getting rid of his fleas, or strategies for keeping him from snacking on the neighbors' garbage. If you are a dog lover, you might have ready responses to each.

As the example illustrates, schemas organize and fill out the scant information we typically receive about the world. They greatly constrain our inferences and expectations, and they strongly bias and even delimit the set of responses that we bring to each situation. If you knew nothing at all of dogs, the above conversation might have been quite brief. If Fido turned out to be my son instead instead of my dog, you would want to reconsider your answers—as well as your opinion of me. In the same way that an appropriate schema is crucially helpful, an inappropriate one is likely to be of no help at all—or worse.

Just as schemas bundle together information that has been related in one's experience, they also conceptually segregate information that has not. In the interest of cognitive coherence, this too is of crucial service. To illustrate, imagine that you are reading about John Dean and the Watergate fiasco. Not once as you read along do you confuse "John" with King John, Pope John, John Cage, or John who was in your 4th grade class. On reading that John was a Baptist, you do not take him to be John the Baptist; you do not even consider the possibility.

The point is that when you are thinking within any particular schema, your thoughts rarely wander to another, no matter how suggestive the cues. As it thus protects you from spurious associations and the mental chaos that would result therefrom, the partitioning of knowledge by schemas is clearly beneficial. In the interest of teaching for transfer, however, it carries a very unfortunate side effect: it inhibits you from jumping between schemas even when doing so would give you the most productive edge on a problem.

It should not be surprising, then, that transfer effects tend to be weak when thinking skills are taught in conjunction with some particular content area. If the thinking skills are introduced and developed through specific content, they will, perforce, be remembered, understood, and—importantly—accessible only in relation to that content. The resulting schema will hang together as a richly interconnected complex of knowledge about the topic. Here and there, embedded within it, will be the thinking skills that were taught alongside. From any other domain, it may be possible to access these skills through explicit and pointed analogy; depending on how tightly they are encoded in terms of the content, it also may not. In any case, their spontaneous transfer cannot be expected.

This may seem a strong argument for teaching thinking through the abstract materials of "content-free" approaches. After all, if the skills are developed in the abstract, shouldn't they be conceptually neutral and, therefore, equally generalizable to all applicable problem domains?

Although the argument sounds good, there must be something wrong with it. The disappointing transfer effects of the content-free curriculums are repeated in miniature across scores of training and transfer studies in the psychological literature.

Can a curriculum really be content-free? The answer is no. The content of a curriculum is the medium of instruction. It is the materials to which the to-be-developed skills are applied and through which they are defined and exercised. In terms of content, the difference between content-oriented and content-free curriculums is not whether or not they have it; it is whether the content they do have consists of traditional classroom matter or, say, abstract graphic designs. Most important, and whichever the case, the content of the course defines the context within which the thinking skills will be retained and through which they may be recalled.

The Dilemma and Its Solution

With an eye toward choosing the optimal approach to teaching thinking skills, the horns of the dilemma are now clearly defined:

(1) If the goal of the course is to develop a schema that is fundamentally about thinking, then the course should consistently and unambiguously be about thinking. To the extent that it is instead centered on mathematics or biology or the Civil War, so too will be the thinking skills that it was intended to develop.

(2) If the goal of the course is to maximize transfer, the materials or content through which the lessons are developed should reflect as diverse and broadly useful a range of problem types and content as is possible. If the course materials are divorced from real-world situations, the lessons they are designed to instill must also be.

The significance of this dilemma lies in recognizing that transfer is the primary goal of a course on thinking. Indeed, if the processes don't transfer, they cannot even be called thinking. They can be called learning, or memory, or habit, but not thinking. The purpose of a course on thinking is to enhance students' abilities to face new challenges and to attack *novel* problems confidently, rationally, and productively.

In keeping with the first half of our dilemma, evaluations of efforts to teach thinking skills indicate that success is most often associated with those that include explicit and consistent labeling of the principles and processes along with direct instruction in the whens, whys, and hows of their application. In keeping with the second half of our dilemma, success is further associated with those experiments that exercise taught principles and processes across a diverse range of content and problemtypes (see Adams 1989).

Courses on thinking skills differ significantly in the extent to which such range is programmed into their sequence and materials. On the other hand, the positive effects of thinking skills instruction are also heightened when teachers transport the principles, processes, and terminology to the other subjects (Savell, Twohig, and Rachford 1986). Although this tendency is often treated as a confounding factor in formal evaluation efforts, theory urges that it be strongly and methodically supported wherever thinking skills programs are earnestly undertaken. The most important consideration in establishing effective instruction in thinking skills is less likely to be which program you choose than the convincingness with which you and your colleagues can extend its lessons and utility to the rest of the curriculum.

Summary

If I have reinvented the content-process debate through this discussion, I have also laid it bare. Process is about interpretation and understanding. Content is about knowledge. Knowledge without the ability to explore its relations is useless. And cognitive theory makes clear that understanding without knowledge is not merely impractical but psychologically impossible.

Thinking skills curriculums are expressly about process. As such, they offer an incomparable means of providing direct instruction on general and powerful principles and modes of thought. Yet the power of a course on thinking skills lies in extending and interlacing the processes thus developed with other aspects of the students' schooling and their daily lives.

REFERENCES

Adams, M. J. (1989). "Thinking Skills Curricula: Their Promise and Progress." *Educational Psychologist*, 24: 25–77.
McClelland, J. L., and D. E. Rumelhart. (1986). *Parallel Distributed Processing, Vol. 2: Psychological and Biological Models*. Cambridge, Mass.: MIT Press.
Resnick, L.B. (1987). *Education and Learning To Think*. Washington, D.C.: National Academy Press.
Savell, J. M., P. T. Twohig, and D. L. Rachford. (1986). *Empirical Status of Feuerstein's "Instrumental Enrichment" (FIE) as a Method of Teaching Skills*. (Tech. Rep. No. 699). Arlington, Va.: U.S. Army Research Institute.

2

Structure of Intellect (SOI)

Mary N. Meeker

Understanding one's own magical mystery is one of the teacher's most important assets if he is to understand that everyone is thus differently equipped.

—Buckminster Fuller

Guilford's theory of intelligence, the Structure of Intellect (SOI), was first applied in 1962 in Los Angeles County as a measure of human intellectual abilities. Many administrators have regarded SOI as a program primarily for the gifted because its first use was to identify intellectual abilities that differentiated gifted students in California.

But all students have intelligence. The SOI answers "what kind" instead of "how much." That is, the SOI-LA assessments determine 26 intellectual abilities in all kinds of students. Educators and psychologists can obtain a complex documentation of at least 96 of the 120 kinds of thinking abilities (Meeker and Bonsall 1962, 1969; Meeker and Meeker 1975), including preparation abilities that lead to higher-level critical thinking abilities. Since 1962 SOI has been used to:

- Teach thinking skills and abilities to all age groups.
- Teach creativity (divergent production).
- Teach reasoning and higher-level critical thinking skills (evaluation) and abilities.

- Identify SOI learning abilities that are necessary for learning academics and teach them to students who have not yet developed these abilities.

In 1962, I applied the SOI theory to analyses of the Binet and WISC tests and derived a profile of intelligence by basing these IQ tests on a theory of intelligence (rather than on their probability-based foundation). This profile enabled psychologists to determine in which areas students were gifted and which of their abilities seemed underdeveloped (Meeker and Bonsall 1962).

By 1974 we had validated 26 (of the known 96) factored abilities necessary for successful learning. This research led to the development of various SOI learning abilities tests. The first norming (Form A) was stratified economically and ethnically for 2,000 students at each grade level.

Relationship of SOI Abilities to Higher-Level Thinking Abilities

If we are to design curriculum to develop higher-level thinking abilities, it is necessary to differentiate between *basic* and *higher-level* critical thinking abilities. Just as basic reading differs from advanced reading, basic thinking abilities also differ from critical thinking abilities. The developmental aspects of scope and sequence are shown in

---

FIGURE 1

SOI-LA Test—Reliabilities

	Test — Retest		Alternate
	Form-A	Form-B	Form
Overall	**.93**	**.92**	**.91**
Figural-learner	.79	.79	.77
Symbolic-learner	.90	.90	.89
Semantic-learner	.87	.87	.85
General comprehension	.87	.88	.85
Memory	.78	.76	.74
Analytic problem-solving	.81	.81	.80
Evaluation	.75	.75	.74
Creativity	.60	.66	.63
Reading	.90	.90	.88
Ready-readiness	.81	.78	.75
Reading-concept use	.89	.86	.85
Arithmetic	.85	.85	.85
Mathematics	.76	.76	.76

Figures 3 and 4 (R. Meeker 1983). Each shows how reasoning abilities are differentiated between the two fundamental curriculums for language arts and arithmetic-math-science, and how basic learning abilities are differentiated (and fundamental) for advanced critical thinking and reasoning abilities. The top portion of each figure lists the learning abilities required to achieve mastery of basic reading (Figure 2) and basic arithmetic (Figure 3).

Start at the top of the chart in Figure 3, which shows the sequence of foundational abilities involved in learning each discipline, which, if developed, leads to curriculum mastery for knowledge. These SOI abilities lay the basic foundation for sequencing the learning abilities; once mastered, they allow the student's learning of higher-level reasoning or critical thinking abilities. The scope of critical thinking will be determined by the knowledge of subject matter.

Figure 3 lists six reading and language arts foundation abilities. If any one is undeveloped, specific reading problems occur. (The Teacher's Guide explains how to use SOI test results.) Once these abilities are developed, students can develop the intermediate abilities, which lead to accomplishment of the critical thinking activities requiring verbal (semantic) intelligence. Figure 3 defines specific kinds of thinking abilities.

Just as IQ tests are global and nonspecific, a general, unspecified critical thinking program does not provide information about kinds of thinking or their requisites. For this reason, we need a road map for teaching higher-level thinking abilities and an assessment method to chart diagnostically where students are and where we have taken them. It is unconscionable to allow students to fail in critical thinking programs because the teacher has not assessed whether the students have the basic intellectual abilities to participate.

Figure 4 lists the sequence of abilities required for bringing students to critical thinking competency, which builds on arithmetic and mathematics knowledge. Once students have mastered the foundational abilities necessary for learning basic arithmetic, they can perform successfully in mathematics, provided they have also developed the intermediate spatial abilities. Figure 4 lists the kinds of thinking abilities students need for competency in computer literacy, algebra, mechanical drawing, sciences, and geometry. By mastering the contents of these disciplines, students are prepared to develop the abilities necessary for critical thinking: analytic

---

FIGURE 2
Abilities Identified as Being Necessary For Success in Reading and Arithmetic*

READING (Foundational abilities):

_____ **CFU**—Visual closure

_____ **CFC**—Visual conceptualization

_____ **EFU**—Visual discrimination

_____ **EFC**—Judging similarities and matching of concepts

_____ **MSU (visual)**—Visual attending

_____ **MSS (visual)**—Visual concentration for sequencing

READING (Enabling skills):

_____ **CMU**—Vocabulary of math and verbal concepts

_____ **CMR**—Comprehension of verbal relations

_____ **CMS**—Ability to comprehend extended verbal information

_____ **MFU**—Visual memory for details

_____ **NST**—Speed of word recognition

WRITING:

_____ **NFU**—Psycho-motor readiness

ARITHMETIC:

_____ **CFS**—Constancy of objects in space (Piaget)**

_____ **CFT**—Spatial conservation (Piaget)**

_____ **CSR**—Comprehension of abstract relations**

_____ **CSS**—Comprehension of numerical progressions

_____ **MSU (auditory)**—Auditory attending

_____ **MSS (auditory)**—Auditory sequencing

_____ **MSI**—Inferential memory**

_____ **ESC**—Judgment of arithmetic similarities

_____ **ESS**—Judgment of correctness of numerical facts

_____ **NSS**—Application of math facts

_____ **NSI**—Form reasoning (logic)**

**pre-math abilities

CREATIVITY:

_____ **DFU**—Creativity with things (figural-spatial)

_____ **DSR**—Creativity with math facts (symbolic)

_____ **DMU**—Creativity with words and ideas (semantic-verbal)

*See ERIC 11-0-2822 for confirmatory studies.

FIGURE 3
SOI Abilities to Basic Learning Skills
Through Curriculum to Critical Thinking

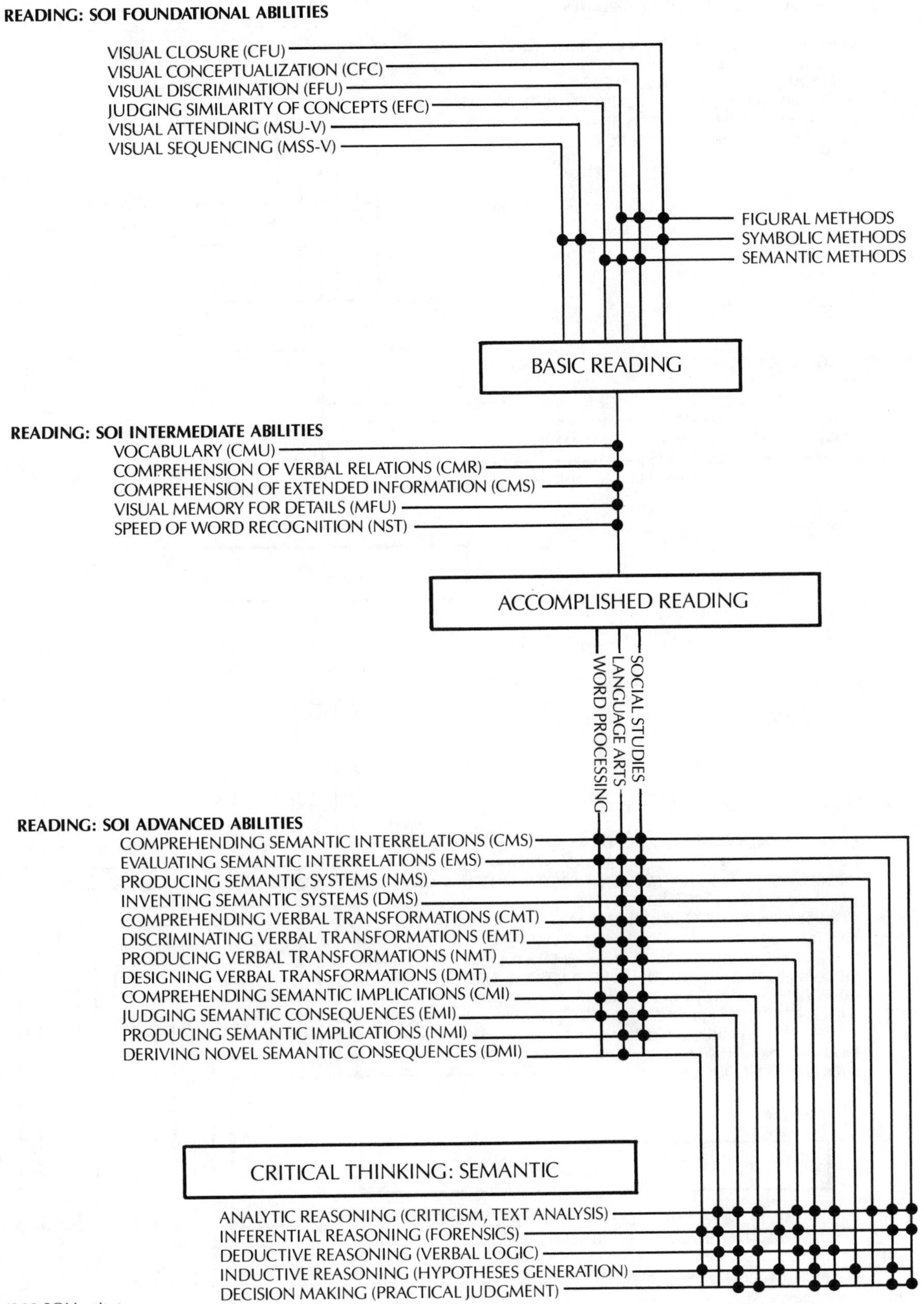

READING: SOI FOUNDATIONAL ABILITIES

VISUAL CLOSURE (CFU)
VISUAL CONCEPTUALIZATION (CFC)
VISUAL DISCRIMINATION (EFU)
JUDGING SIMILARITY OF CONCEPTS (EFC)
VISUAL ATTENDING (MSU-V)
VISUAL SEQUENCING (MSS-V)

FIGURAL METHODS
SYMBOLIC METHODS
SEMANTIC METHODS

BASIC READING

READING: SOI INTERMEDIATE ABILITIES

VOCABULARY (CMU)
COMPREHENSION OF VERBAL RELATIONS (CMR)
COMPREHENSION OF EXTENDED INFORMATION (CMS)
VISUAL MEMORY FOR DETAILS (MFU)
SPEED OF WORD RECOGNITION (NST)

ACCOMPLISHED READING

SOCIAL STUDIES
LANGUAGE ARTS
WORD PROCESSING

READING: SOI ADVANCED ABILITIES

COMPREHENDING SEMANTIC INTERRELATIONS (CMS)
EVALUATING SEMANTIC INTERRELATIONS (EMS)
PRODUCING SEMANTIC SYSTEMS (NMS)
INVENTING SEMANTIC SYSTEMS (DMS)
COMPREHENDING VERBAL TRANSFORMATIONS (CMT)
DISCRIMINATING VERBAL TRANSFORMATIONS (EMT)
PRODUCING VERBAL TRANSFORMATIONS (NMT)
DESIGNING VERBAL TRANSFORMATIONS (DMT)
COMPREHENDING SEMANTIC IMPLICATIONS (CMI)
JUDGING SEMANTIC CONSEQUENCES (EMI)
PRODUCING SEMANTIC IMPLICATIONS (NMI)
DERIVING NOVEL SEMANTIC CONSEQUENCES (DMI)

CRITICAL THINKING: SEMANTIC

ANALYTIC REASONING (CRITICISM, TEXT ANALYSIS)
INFERENTIAL REASONING (FORENSICS)
DEDUCTIVE REASONING (VERBAL LOGIC)
INDUCTIVE REASONING (HYPOTHESES GENERATION)
DECISION MAKING (PRACTICAL JUDGMENT)

Copyright 1962 SOI Institute

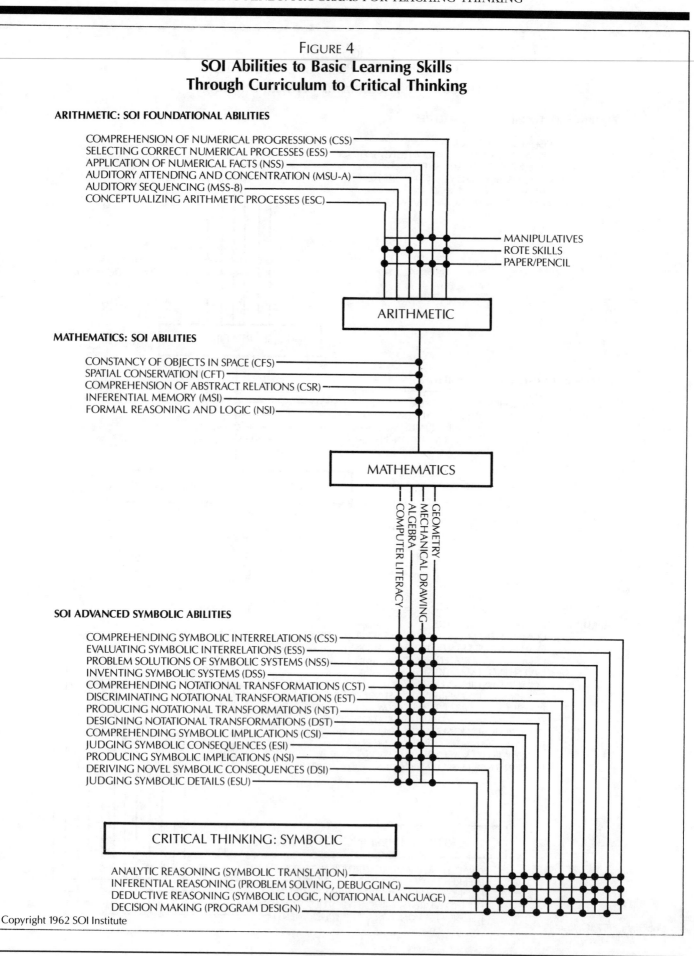

FIGURE 4

SOI Abilities to Basic Learning Skills
Through Curriculum to Critical Thinking

ARITHMETIC: SOI FOUNDATIONAL ABILITIES

COMPREHENSION OF NUMERICAL PROGRESSIONS (CSS)
SELECTING CORRECT NUMERICAL PROCESSES (ESS)
APPLICATION OF NUMERICAL FACTS (NSS)
AUDITORY ATTENDING AND CONCENTRATION (MSU-A)
AUDITORY SEQUENCING (MSS-8)
CONCEPTUALIZING ARITHMETIC PROCESSES (ESC)

MANIPULATIVES
ROTE SKILLS
PAPER/PENCIL

ARITHMETIC

MATHEMATICS: SOI ABILITIES

CONSTANCY OF OBJECTS IN SPACE (CFS)
SPATIAL CONSERVATION (CFT)
COMPREHENSION OF ABSTRACT RELATIONS (CSR)
INFERENTIAL MEMORY (MSI)
FORMAL REASONING AND LOGIC (NSI)

MATHEMATICS

GEOMETRY
MECHANICAL DRAWING
ALGEBRA
COMPUTER LITERACY

SOI ADVANCED SYMBOLIC ABILITIES

COMPREHENDING SYMBOLIC INTERRELATIONS (CSS)
EVALUATING SYMBOLIC INTERRELATIONS (ESS)
PROBLEM SOLUTIONS OF SYMBOLIC SYSTEMS (NSS)
INVENTING SYMBOLIC SYSTEMS (DSS)
COMPREHENDING NOTATIONAL TRANSFORMATIONS (CST)
DISCRIMINATING NOTATIONAL TRANSFORMATIONS (EST)
PRODUCING NOTATIONAL TRANSFORMATIONS (NST)
DESIGNING NOTATIONAL TRANSFORMATIONS (DST)
COMPREHENDING SYMBOLIC IMPLICATIONS (CSI)
JUDGING SYMBOLIC CONSEQUENCES (ESI)
PRODUCING SYMBOLIC IMPLICATIONS (NSI)
DERIVING NOVEL SYMBOLIC CONSEQUENCES (DSI)
JUDGING SYMBOLIC DETAILS (ESU)

CRITICAL THINKING: SYMBOLIC

ANALYTIC REASONING (SYMBOLIC TRANSLATION)
INFERENTIAL REASONING (PROBLEM SOLVING, DEBUGGING)
DEDUCTIVE REASONING (SYMBOLIC LOGIC, NOTATIONAL LANGUAGE)
DECISION MAKING (PROGRAM DESIGN)

Copyright 1962 SOI Institute

reasoning, inferential reasoning, deductive and inductive reasoning and decision making.

A Plan for a Critical Thinking Curriculum

There are differences between critical thinking abilities and learning abilities and between the kinds of critical thinking abilities required for a verbal curriculum and for a quantitative curriculum. There are also developmental differences in the sequence and levels of difficulty of those abilities. The *developmental* aspects of presenting critical thinking abilities are shown in Figure 5.

Educators are always faced with choosing the kind of program best suited to the needs of their students and their budgets. This brief description of the Structure of Intellect attempts to show the complexity of critical thinking abilities and the importance of separating verbal and quantitative preparation. SOI allows us to start even our youngest students on the ladder of developing higher-level reasoning and critical thinking abilities. More important, because SOI as-

sessments are teacher-group administered, they allow administrators to evaluate the effectiveness of any change in the curriculum by providing assessment information both before and after the change has been made.

The negative aspect of SOI assessments and instructional materials usually centers around their comprehensiveness. To use SOI requires two days of training and retraining: (1) teachers need training in diagnostic procedures, and (2) SOI materials require specific rather than general methodology.

The advantage of using SOI is that it defines 90 thinking abilities ranging from the basic foundational level to advanced higher-order thinking abilities. The greatest payoff is increased academic achievement as measured by standardized achievement tests. The spillover into improved self-concept is an affective bonus.[1]

SOI *is* complex and precise. It is this precise clarity that makes it such a powerful tool for education.

FIGURE 5
Developmental Aspects of Presenting Critical Thinking Abilities

SUBJECT MATTER	REASONING ABILITY	SOI TEACHING MODULES	GRADE
Language Arts/Reading	Basic		
	Concept formation	CFC	Primary
	Differentiating concepts	EFC	Primary
	Comprehending verbal relations	CMR	Primary
	Comprehending verbal systems	CMS	Elementary
	Enrichment		
	Memory for implied meanings	MMI	Elem.-H.S.
	Judging verbal implications	EMI	Elem.-H.S.
	Problem solving	NST	All
	Interpreting verbal meanings	NMR	H.S.
	Using analogical ideas	NMI	Elem.-H.S.
	Creative writing	DMU	All
	Creative interpretation	DMT	High School
	Creative grammatics	DMS	Elem.-H.S.
Arithmetic, Mathematics, Science Preparation	Basic		
	Comprehending space	CFS	All
	Conserving abstracts in spatial perspectives	CFT	All
	Deduction/formal logic	NSI	Elem.-H.S.
	Inductive reasoning	ESS	Elem.-H.S.
	Decision making	ESC	All
	Enrichment		
	Discriminating notational transformations	EST	High School
	Producing notational transformations	DST	High School
	Comprehending inferences	CMI	High School
	Judging symbolic results	ESI	High School
	Producing symbolic implications	NSI	High School
	Creative consequences	DSI	High School

REFERENCES

Guilford, J. P. (1977). *Way Beyond the IQ*. Great Neck, N.Y.: Creative Synergetic Associates.

Meeker, M., and M. Bonsall. (1962). "The NSWP." Los Angeles County Department of Education, Research, and Guidance.

Meeker, M. (1969). *The SOI: Its Uses and Interpretations*. Columbus, Ohio: Charles Merrill.

Meeker, M., and R. Meeker. (1975). *Teachers' Guide to Using SOI Test Results*. Vida, Oregon: SOI Systems.

Meeker, M., R. Meeker, and G. Roid. (1984). *The Basic SOI Test Manual*. Los Angeles: WPS.

Meeker, R. (1983). Report prepared for California State Superintendent of Schools and presented to the Urban Task Force of Superintendents, Puerto Rico, Havana.

NOTE

[1] Other documents that may be of interest to readers include a sample computer analysis that charts a student's intellectual profile of 26 SOI abilities and a chart that depicts the relationship of SOI abilities to school curriculum programming. Both are available from the SOI Institute (see box for address and telephone).

Structure of the Intellect (SOI)

Developer:	Mary Meeker (based on Guilford's S.I. Theory)
Goal:	Equip students with the necessary intellectual skills to learn subject matter and critical thinking.
Sample skill:	NMI: coNvergent production of seMantic Implications (choosing the best word)
Assumptions:	• Intelligence consists of 120 thinking abilities that are a combination of *operations* (such as comprehending, remembering, and analyzing); *contents* (such as words, forms, and symbols); and *products* (such as single units, groups, relationships). • Twenty-six of these factors are relevant to success in school. • Individual differences in these factors can be assessed with the SOI-LA tests and improved with specifically designed SOI materials and computer games.
Intended audience:	All students and adults.
Process:	Students use materials (some three-dimensional) prescribed for them based on a diagnostic test. Computer software gives analyses and prescriptions.
Time:	Varies, but can be 30-minute lessons twice a week until abilities are developed on post-assessment.
Available from:	SOI Institute, P.O. Box D, Vida, OR 97488. Telephone: 503-896-3936.

3

Instrumental Enrichment

Frances R. Link

There is no curriculum development without staff development.

—Frances Link

Improving the overall cognitive performance of the low-achieving adolescent demands a broad strategy of intervention that focuses on the *process* of learning rather than on specific skills and subject matter. Instrumental Enrichment is such a program: a direct and focused attack on those mental processes, which, through absence, fragility, or inefficiency, are to blame for poor intellectual or academic performance.

The core of the Instrumental Enrichment program—which was developed by Reuven Feuerstein, an Israeli clinical psychologist—is a three-year series of problem-solving tasks and exercises that are grouped in 14 areas of specific cognitive development. They are called instruments rather than lessons because in themselves they are virtually free of specific subject matter. Each instrument's true goal is not the learner's acquisition of information but the development, refinement, and crystallization of those functions that are prerequisite to effective thinking (see Figure 1). In terms of behavior, Instrumental Enrichment's ultimate aim is to transform retarded performers, to alter their characteristically passive and dependent cognitive style to that of active, self-motivated, independent thinkers.

The Instruments

The instruments provide sufficient material for one-period lessons given two to five days a week. Although a three-year sequence is recommended, the program may be implemented in two years, depending on the class curriculum and students' needs. Instrumental Enrichment is not intended to replace traditional content areas, but as a sup-

plement to help students get the most out of all opportunities to learn and grow, and to make bridges to all subject areas. A three-year program is outlined here. A two-year program is under production.

In the first-year curriculum, students use the following instruments:

Organization of Dots—helps students find the relationships—shapes, figures, and other attributes—among a field of dots, much the way we pick out constellations in the night sky. In this way, students begin developing strategies for linking perceived events into a system yielding comprehensible information that can be a basis for understanding and logical response.

Orientation in Space I—promotes the creation of specific strategies for differentiating frames of reference in space, such as left, right, front, and back.

Comparison—fosters precise perception, the ability to discriminate by attribute (equal/unequal, similar/dissimilar), and the judgment necessary to identify and evaluate similarities and differences.

Analytic Perception—addresses the ability to analyze component parts in order to find how they relate to each other as well as how they contribute to the overall character of the whole they compose.

In the second-year curriculum, students use these instruments:

Categorization—helps students learn the underlying principles and strategies for creating conceptual sets and categories, a vital prerequisite for higher mental processing.

Instructions—emphasizes the use of language as a system for both encoding and decoding operational processes on levels of varying complexity. Exercises focus on critiquing instruction, rewriting instructions to supply missing relevant data, and creating instructions and directions for others to follow.

FIGURE 1
Instrumental Enrichment Cognitive Functions

I. GATHERING ALL THE INFORMATION WE NEED (INPUT)
   1. Using our senses (listening, seeing, smelling, tasting, touching, feeling) to gather clear and complete information (clear perception).
   2. Using a system or plan so that we do not skip or miss something important or repeat ourselves (systematic exploration).
   3. Giving the thing we gather through our senses and our experience a name so that we can remember it more clearly and talk about it (labeling).
   4. Describing things and events in terms of where and when they occur (temporal and spatial referents).
   5. Deciding on the characteristics of a thing or event that always stays the same, even when changes take place (conservation, constancy, and object permanence).
   6. Organizing the information we gather by considering more than one thing at a time (using two sources of information).
   7. Being precise and accurate when it matters (need for precision).

II. USING THE INFORMATION WE HAVE GATHERED (ELABORATION)
   1. Defining the problem, what we are being asked to do, and what we must figure out (analyzing disequilibrium).
   2. Using only that part of the information we have gathered that is relevant, that is, that applies to the problem and ignoring the rest (relevance).
   3. Having a good picture in our mind of what we are looking for or what we must do (interiorization).
   4. Making a plan that will include the steps we need to take to reach our goal (planning behavior).
   5. Remembering and keeping in mind the various pieces of information we need (broadening our mental field).
   6. Looking for the relationship by which separate objects, events, and experiences can be tied together (projecting relationships).
   7. Comparing objects and experiences to others to see what is similar and what is different (comparative behavior).
   8. Finding the class or set to which the new object or experience belongs (categorization).
   9. Thinking about different possibilities and figuring out what would happen if we were to choose one or another (hypothetical thinking).
   10. Using logic to prove things and to defend our opinion (logical evidence).

III. EXPRESSING THE SOLUTION TO A PROBLEM (OUTPUT)
   1. Being clear and precise in our language to be sure that there is no question as to what the answer is. Putting ourselves into the "shoes" of the listener to be sure that our answers will be understood (overcoming egocentric communication).
   2. Thinking things through before we answer instead of immediately trying to answer and making a mistake, and then trying again (overcoming trial and error).
   3. Counting to ten (at least) so that we do not say or do something we will be sorry for later (restraining impulsive behavior).
   4. Not fretting or panicking if for some reason we cannot answer a question even though we "know" the answer. Leaving the question for a little while and then, when we return to it, using a strategy to help us find the answer (overcoming blocking).

Temporal Relations—addresses chronological time, biological time, and other temporal relations. Students learn to isolate the factors involved in evaluating or predicting outcomes—time, distance, velocity—and to find the interrelationships among those factors.

Numerical Progressions—promotes the ability to perceive and understand principles and formulas manifested in numerical patterns.

Family Relations—promotes understanding of how individual roles in hierarchical organizations define the network of relationships that are encountered in daily life and work.

Illustrations—encourages spontaneous awareness that a problem exists, analysis of why it exists, and projection of cause-and-effect relationships.

In the third-year curriculum, students are introduced to four instruments:

Transitive Relations and Syllogisms—fosters higher-level abstract and inferential thought. *Transitive Relations* deals with drawing inferences from relationships that can be described in terms of "greater than," "equal to," or "less than." *Syllogisms* deals with formal propositional logic and aims at promoting inferential thinking based on local evidence. Students learn to critique analytic premises and propositions.

Representational Stencil Design—requires students to analyze a complex figure, identify its components, and then recreate the whole mentally in color, shape, size, and orientation.

Orientation in Space II—complements earlier instruments by extending students' understanding of relative positions from a personal orientation to the stable, external system represented by the points of the compass.

Mediated learning experience may be viewed as the means by which nascent, elementary cognitive sets and habits are transformed into the bases for effective thinking. Consequently, the earlier and the more often children are subjected to mediated learning experiences, the greater will be their capacity to efficiently perceive, understand, and respond to information and stimulation in and out of school.

Teacher Training

Whatever the particular focus of an instrument, its larger purpose is always the further development of students' conscious thought processes and their discovery of practical applications of those processes in and out of school. In this effort, teachers play the crucial role as mediating agents.

Teacher training involves a minimum of 45 hours of inservice annually, plus on-the-job use of exercises in the classroom, if possible, while training is in process. Training programs are custom designed to fit the inservice schedules of school systems.

Instrumental Enrichment

Developer:	Reuven Feuerstein
Goal:	To develop thinking and problem-solving abilities in order to become an autonomous learner.
Sample skills:	Classification/comparison, orientation in space, recognizing relationships, following directions, planning, organizing, logical reasoning, inductive and deductive reasoning, synthesizing.
Assumptions:	• Intelligence is dynamic (modifiable), not static. • Cognitive development requires direct intervention over time to build the mental processes for learning to learn. • Cognitive development requires *mediated* learning experiences.
Research:	Empirical data exist to document improvement in cognitive functions; improvement in self-concept; improvement in reading, writing, and mathematics subjects after two years of implementation.
Intended audience:	Upper elementary, middle, and secondary levels.
Process:	Students do paper-and-pencil "instruments," which are introduced by teachers and followed by discussions for insight to bring about transfer of learning. The teacher becomes the mediating agent. The cognitive tasks in the instruction materials are not subject-specific but parallel the subject matter being taught by the teacher.
Time:	Two to three hours a week (plus bridging to subject matter and life skills) over a two- to three-year period.
Available from:	Curriculum Associates, Inc., 1211 Connecticut Avenue, NW, Suite 414, Washington, DC 20036. Telephone: 202-293-1760. (For teaching training, contact Frances R. Link.)

4

Thinking to Write: Assessing Higher-Order Cognitive Skills and Abilities

Frances R. Link

Since 1956, when Jerome S. Bruner, Jacqueline J. Goodnow, and G. A. Austin published their seminal text, *A Study of Thinking*, researchers have made significant progress in uncovering exactly what mental processes lie beneath the terms "thinking" and "learning." Finding strategies that provide evidence for the transfer of learning has also been a primary goal of the research on thinking, but the development of these strategies and of strategies for placing the student in control of learning how to think are still in the embryonic stage.

Much of this research has concentrated on the relationship between cognition and language. Although research in this area is in a state of transition, one of the most common theories is that language and cognition have a kind of reciprocal relationship. The most logical place to test such a theory is the classroom, where practitioners have a natural environment in which to explore the possible relationships between language and cognition.

It's time that we encourage curriculum workers and teachers to swing away from elaborate statistical methods or tight experimental designs and take advantage of much more realistic studies of an individual child or "observational" studies of groups of students. The teacher then becomes the key person involved in collecting and documenting changes in behavior and evidence for transfer of learning. In "Thinking to Write," the Student Work Journal—a "mediated writing experience"—is an important evaluation instrument. It enables the teacher and the student to analyze narrative

thinking. Students learn to monitor their own performance and become aware of their ability to learn how to learn, thus gaining insight into their own cognitive processes. And one extraordinary side effect of the Work Journal has been improved writing and oral language skills.

The Work Journal as an Evaluation Instrument

Writing and speaking are powerful tools in thinking, learning, and evaluating cognitive processes. Over the years, however, there seems to be less and less class time devoted to writing activities. The Student Work Journal is a tool that encourages continuous writing in all classrooms.

The Work Journal differs from a personal diary or unstructured journal in two ways: it is intended to be shared orally and to produce evidence of how writing becomes a facilitator rather than an inhibitor of thought. This notion is as important for teachers as for students. The invention of "mediated" or guided, structured writing experiences used in the Student Work Journal reduces student writing anxiety and allows teachers to assess students' understanding of concepts, principles, and strategies used in problem solving, and to evaluate their organizational skills, summative behavior, and awareness of the mental processes used in structured writing experiences. Each mediated writing experience has one or more cognitive demands. It may require students to compare, to provide relevant details, or to give evidence of planning or bridging by making connections and transforming knowledge, as shown in Figure 1 (an example of a Student Journal page).

Copyright © 1990 by Frances R. Link.

FIGURE 1

Thinking to Write
Evaluation Procedures

SEEING PATTERNS   **MEDIATED WRITING EXPERIENCE 13a**

1.   Think about a school, community, or national election in which the outcome might be uncertain.
2.   Write a sentence describing this election, including when and where it will take place.
3.   Write a sentence explaining something about either the candidates or the issues that would make predicting the outcome difficult.
4.   How do you think that voter surveys or polls inform the voters?
5.   Write a concluding sentence telling how you think surveys enable us to make predictions.

Title: Date:

Word List
cause
cycle
effect
election
equality
feminism
forecast
history
integration
issue
numbers
officers
opinion
optimistic
pattern
political
poverty
predict
president
reason
secretary

AREAS OF COGNITIVE FOCUS 13a

Gathering relevant information
Conceptualizing
Engaging in critical analysis
Locating events in time and space
Making predictions
Using logical evidence

EVALUATION QUESTIONS

1.   Did the student give details of event, time, and place?
2.   Was evidence given for the difficulty of predicting?
3.   Could the student conceptualize the effect of surveys on voting?

©1987 Curriculum Development Associates, Inc.

The links between writing tasks, strategies, and metacognitive elements may become increasingly evident to the learner and to the teacher. The journal helps the student and teacher to assess understanding and the ability to "transfer" strategies and understanding to new situations. The evidence makes clear for them what is known and not

---

Thinking to Write

Developer:	Frances R. Link, President, Curriculum Development Associates, Inc.
Goal:	To provide a school-based evaluation system that focuses on teaching thinking, writing, and problem solving.
Sample skills:	The evaluation system addresses cognitive functions and operations of higher-order thinking, such as those implicit in: planning, strategies for problem solving, decoding and encoding information and symbols, setting priorities, logical reasoning, and concept development.
Assumptions:	The curriculum, the learner, and the teacher are the architects of school assessment and evaluation studies. Thinking abilities and skills are the core of the curriculum. The assessment system acts as a positive force to improve teaching, to better learning, and to inform curriculum change.
Intended audience:	Nine-year-olds through college students.
Process:	In "Thinking to Write," the evaluation for the record includes documentary evidence in the form of student work journals, teacher journals of classroom observations and case studies, classroom videotapes, pre- and post-profiles of changes in student cognitive behavior, test essays to assess transfer of learning.
Time:	Journal writing once a week.
Source:	Curriculum Development Associates, Inc., 1211 Connecticut Ave., NW, Suite 414, Washington, DC 20036. Telephone: 202-293-1760.

known. It documents intellectual growth. Thus, writing produces performance criteria in a narrative form. The "mediated" writing experience demands that the learner be aware of his or her feelings, self-motivation, need to plan, thinking processes, and strategies for knowing how to know and for managing problems to be solved.

All students need to be encouraged to think reflectively. This is an important goal of each mediated writing experience. When journal entries are read aloud in the classroom, each student is encouraged to elaborate on what has been written. Elaboration develops and extends narrative thinking and serves as both a reflective and an active self-assessment experience, with the student in control. The student is reflecting on goals, on content, on his or her own feelings, and on the strategies used to produce the writing. This often triggers the use of former knowledge and always seems to promote increased use of vocabulary to express an emotion, a concept, a strategy, or a generalization. It's a method that allows students, rather than just teachers, to reflect critically on their work.

The evaluation process recommended for the "Thinking to Write" program integrates assessment and instruction as the program integrates thinking and writing skills. The process embodies several basic principles, regarding assessment from a cognitive point of view:

• The instruments document thinking and writing ability.

• Student involvement is as important as teacher involvement.

• Varied procedures are available to personalize and individualize the assessment.

• The results provide feedback to students for learning and to teachers for teaching.

The process includes nine assessment instruments; five are essential to the success of the program for assessing writing as related to thinking, and four are supplemental, but

---

FIGURE 2
Thinking to Write
Evaluation Procedures

Essential Procedures for Evaluating Writing	Timing
• Self-evaluation of essay by students	• First 3 topics, then as needed
• Self-rating of cognitive development by students	• Beginning and end of semester
• Rating of cognitive development by teacher	• Beginning and end of semester
• Test essay by teacher	• Middle and end of semester
• Student interviews by students, teachers, or others	• Any time

Additional Procedures for Documenting Cognitive Growth	Timing
• Teacher work journals	• Middle to end of semester
• Documentation of critical incidents	• Continuing
• Videotapes of classes	• Any time
• Teacher Interviews	• Any time

strongly recommended, to assess overall cognitive development. These instruments are outlined in Figure 2.

We need to become less timid about helping students gain insight through their own ability to evaluate and transform thought into language. And we need to test the assumption that when the learner controls and directs the learning process, thinking and learning will result in motivation to transfer strategies and knowledge to new situations. Writing, specifically student-composed narrative in the form of cognitively oriented journal tasks, promises to become the most important and insightful method of assessing higher-order thinking.

5

Expand Your Thinking

David Hyerle

The mind of man is capable of anything—because everything is in it, all the past as well as all the future.
—Joseph Conrad

Applying Thinking Skills to Content Learning to Use Graphic Organizers

Important ideas and relationships often go unseen by students because verbal tools alone do not clearly communicate the overall patterns of how people are thinking.

For example, I was recently working with a social studies teacher in a middle school classroom. The teacher took me aside and said, "Look, I have written everything out on the board, even the main idea, and I have told students over and over again what I mean. Why can't they understand?" With her permission, I went to the board and began, with the class, to visually map out the relationships between concepts, using classification "trees" and other maps for showing the pattern of her main idea, supporting propositions, and specific details. These visual representations created a connected, whole picture of what the teacher had tried to verbally communicate to students. The maps thus helped students to translate the *sequence* of her spoken and written sentences into the pattern of her thinking. Students could then *see* what she meant.

Over the past decade, educators have taken positive steps toward teaching for and about thinking by investigating different views of thinking, defining thinking skills, focusing on teacher questioning, and asking students to verbalize and reflect on their thinking. Yet a core question remains: How can we help students—on their own—to flexibly apply thinking skills to content learning?

Let me suggest one response: Connected, graphic representations can supplement the use of verbal and numeric symbols for communicating our thinking in the classroom. All participants in the classroom can use practical visual tools—graphic organizers—for applying abstract thinking skills to content learning and teaching. Students can learn how to visually represent and connect information in linear, holistic, and analogical patterns. Students then have the additional tools for reflecting on the pathways of their thinking and for improving their thinking abilities. Graphic representations also enable teachers to see and assess students' maps of prior knowledge, to present new content information in connected ways, and to evaluate students' content learning by seeing the development of students' thinking over the course of instruction.

Expand Your Thinking (Hyerle 1989b) is a program that introduces students to these graphic tools for applying thinking skills in content learning. Students work through the program in cooperative pairs to learn how thinking maps can be used to organize, communicate, and share their thinking. They are shown that "expanding your thinking" means both applying "thinking maps" to content learning and sharing their thinking with other students. Teachers are supported by a guide that shows how they can expand their teaching repertoire by using thinking maps *and* by practicing "teaching for thinking" strategies, which are an integrated part of the directions for each student activity.

Together, students and teachers can use *Expand Your Thinking* as a starting point for using thinking maps to create different mental models of the same content information. They can efficiently share these differences and at the same time make connections between similar thoughts. As Jones, Pierce, and Hunter (1988) state: "A good graphic representation can show at a glance the key parts of a whole and their relations, thereby allowing a holistic understanding that words alone cannot convey" (p. 21).

Drawing the Lines: Toward a Connective View of Knowledge and Thinking

Students who work through the *Expand Your Thinking* program use thinking maps to draw the lines that represent specific thinking skills and patterns of thought. They also question, in a fundamental way, how they make sense of things by connecting and creating patterns of content information. This practical use of thinking-skills maps is based on an underlying, theoretical view of knowledge and thinking as *the active making of mental connections*. It is also through this connective view of knowledge that the so-called "lower order" or "micro-logical" thinking skills, such as classification, are presented to students.

A recent challenge for educators is trying to describe the relationship between lower- and higher-order thinking. On one side, educators who reject the direct teaching of discrete lower-order thinking skills. On another side are those who cringe when higher-order content questions are asked of the students who have not shown proficiency with "lower-order" thinking skills. What is the problematic line between lower- and higher-order thinking? The problem, as I see it, is that the "lower-order" skills are being presented to students as primarily rote, analytic tools for processing "given" information and not for deeply questioning how knowledge is being made through these processes. The outcome is that these skills are often taught in isolation as disconnected, strictly analytic tools for thinking, to the near exclusion of holistic thinking.

One reason for the overemphasis on analysis has been the influence of a traditional view of knowledge, called "logico-deductive." In this theory of knowledge, skills such as labeling and classification are seen as atomistic processes. Words and numbers are understood as unquestioned labels that correspond unambiguously to things in the world, and each thing represented understood as fitting into a preexisting, "natural" category that has a clearly defined boundary. Yet, as biologist Stephen Jay Gould points out, *applying* the skill of classification is of a higher order:

Taxonomy is a fundamental and dynamic science dedicated to exploring the causes of relationships and similarities among organisms. Classifications are theories about the basis of natural order, not dull categories compiled only to avoid chaos (Gould 1989, p. 98).

Despite the dynamism revealed by Gould, the processes of classification and many other such analytical skills are found at the bottom of nearly all models of thinking skills. Because these skills are presented as low level, the understanding of the skills is not often richly developed by students nor applied in connected, holistic ways. Research released over the last ten years by leaders in the fields of biology

(Gould 1981; Mayr 1989), psychology (Gardner 1983), cognitive linguistics (Lakoff 1989; Lakoff and Johnson 1980), moral development (Gilligan 1982), philosophy (Putnam 1988), and education (Perkins 1986) reveals that the logico-deductive view of knowledge, though important and useful, is not the only view of knowing and thinking. These researchers and educators point toward other ways to conceive of knowledge and the processes of thinking.

One view of knowledge may be called "connectivism" (Hyerle 1989a) and is based on a perspective that knowledge is actively constructed as people represent and *connect* a variety of forms of sensory information. Through this process, knowledge is "remade" between human beings and remains open to reinterpretation. Knowledge viewed as connective is patterns of information—

• linked together by unclear mental boundaries, such as boundaries between categories;

• constructed through communication in a social context;

• represented by a range of signs, symbols, and images and by idealized mental models and theories; and

• supported by conceptual metaphors.

Through connectivism, we attempt to see the complexity of a problem in context, while honoring different points of view and learning from them. Though we may draw on past regularities for information, we recognize that knowledge is not given: Knowledge is made. Knowledge viewed as connective is an interpretive process of thinking about the mental relationships we create between things. In a most fundamental way, it is from a connectivist view that we begin to deeply investigate these "things" we call boundaries and relations.

What do we mean when we say that boundaries and relations are things? Are not the water's edge and the land's end one and the same? Is the shoreline a part of the land or of the sea, or is it a line in its own right? . . . *A person must draw that line somewhere*. . . . The world is really a dynamic operation; only by means of symbols can the mind deal with it "as if" it were a static structure (Upton 1961, p. 31).

This insight, by the late Albert Upton, Professor Emeritus at Whittier College, shows that we are constantly using word symbols to represent "things," making distinctions between and connecting these symbols, and thereby creating mental boundary lines. An essential benefit of using graphic organizers as tools for improving students' thinking abilities is that we are asking students to *draw that line*, then to see and question the connections they are making between things. These lines connect things as we creatively analyze relationships, such as between categories, between parts of whole objects, or between sequences in an event. The boundary lines that students establish between things—first in their minds and then on a page—are mental models of how they think.

What is "higher-order" and "critical" about these lower-order connections is that once students begin to investigate seemingly simple mental boundaries they will be more likely to see greater complexity, dissolve hardened opinions and idealized dichotomies, and open up to different points of view. For example, if a young student attempts to draw a line between night and day, the student may see that the lines are fuzzy areas we call sunrise and dusk. Similarly, another student may see people in the world as either "good" or "bad"; but drawing the line and fully investigating each classification may reveal a deeper understanding of humankind. In reality, relationships between things and people are often fuzzy and complex. In our minds, all too often, even the most fundamental connections between things are idealized as clear and absolute; thus, the complex nature of mental relationships remains hidden from sight.

A Connective Model of Thinking Skills and Maps

Expand Your Thinking builds toward a view of knowledge as connective and is based on a practical model of thinking processes and maps described in the following pages. This model was initially developed by Upton, who viewed the cognitive act of thinking as a dynamic union of the analytical "taking apart" and the creative "synthesis" of things—through representations. His first book for students, *Creative Analysis* (Upton and Samson 1963) is based on this model. By using *Creative Analysis*, Upton's students at Whittier College learned about basic patterns of thought and how to verbalize and graphically organize these patterns. Though Upton was relatively uninterested in IQ scores, *all* of the 280 students who went through his freshman course over an eight-month period gained in their scores using a standardized intelligence test as the pre-post measure. The average IQ score increased 10.5 points. This statistically significant change in IQ scores was reported in the *New York Times* (Hechinger 1960) at a time when there were few alternative definitions of "intelligence."

The Upton model is neither hierarchical nor process oriented in its theory or application. Unlike most models, this is not a set of procedures for problem solving, but rather a view of patterns of thinking processes that are related—and a corresponding set of maps. Upton's model is most useful when perceived as a set of tools for thinking and when used in response to the needs and objectives of students. The model, which is presented in *Expand Your Thinking*, includes six thinking processes:

- Thing-making

- Qualification
- Classification
- Structure analysis
- Operation analysis
- Seeing analogies

Thing-Making

As a semanticist, Upton stressed the importance of having students become aware of how we represent physical or mental "things" using signs, symbols, and images in context. Most of the time we use symbols such as words or numbers—and, now, computer languages. Upton and his colleague, Richard Samson, called this symbolizing process *Thing-making*. Often this process is understood as lower order and mechanical. It is usually called "naming" or "labeling," using nouns. Yet one of the higher order challenges that our students face is to develop a dynamic view of symbols—what I call *symboliteracy*—through which they must actively remake and interpret things in context using symbols. Consider how we continually ask students to "put" some "thing" in context, such as a vocabulary word, to find the meaning.

The Circle Map in Figure 1, my recent addition to Upton's model, is used as a visual tool for putting things in context. The "thing" represented is written or drawn in the center circle and contextual information is shown in the outside circle. Each circle represents how we create mental boundaries when we try to define something. This basic map can be expanded by drawing a frame around the outside of the two circles, to represent the frame of reference for defining something in context. The visual frame and the circles provide reflective tools for asking: What is your cultural background, and what are your life experiences and your religious, political, social, and emotional points of view that influence how you make sense of something in context? Using this map helps students to see that *how* they represent and define something is influenced by context and their own background experiences.

Qualification

When we are trying to define and make sense of something, we are drawing on our sensations of the world. Upton called this process *Qualification*. When describing a person, a character in a story, or a naturally occurring element, we draw on our five senses—and our emotions—to project or attribute qualities to things, and to abstract qualities from things. Some qualities are more tangible, such as sensory qualities of hot and cold, whereas other qualities are less tangible, such as the emotive quality of sculpture. The Bubble Map in Figure 2 is used to represent the process of

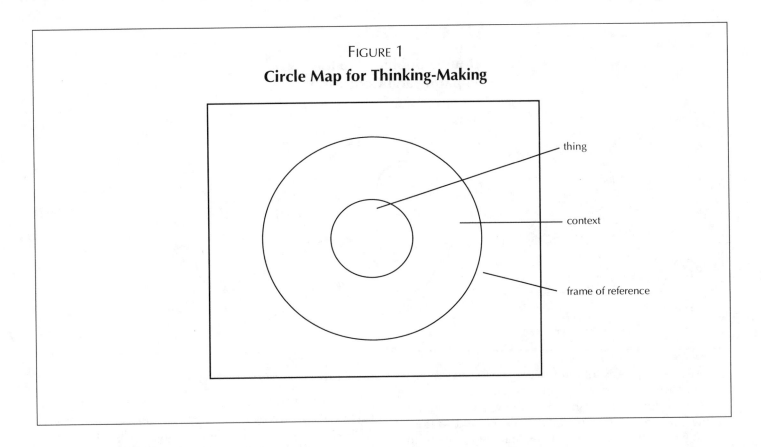

FIGURE 1

Circle Map for Thinking-Making

thing

context

frame of reference

abstracting from and projecting qualities onto things, and to identify sensory, logical, and emotional qualifications we are making. Notice that the circle in the middle is the thing being qualified. The lines extending outward each represent the abstraction/projection process, and the outside circles are used as abstracted place holders for adjectives and phrases.

This map can be expanded for the process of comparing and contrasting the qualities of two things using the Double-Bubble Map (Figure 3). The middle circles are the perceived common qualities of the two things being compared, while the outside circles describe the unique qualities of the two things, respectively.

Classification

Because we are constantly making sense of things in context, we also investigate relationships between multiple things and qualities that we perceive. We try to see the connected mental webs, or patterns of relationships that create "context" and support our inferences. Upton drew from the work of those who closely study our physical world—such as biologists—to identify three patterns of thinking. These scientists create taxonomies or classifications of things, study the anatomy or physical structures of things, and interpret the physiology or operation of things.

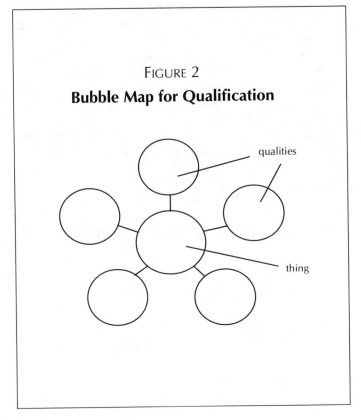

FIGURE 2

Bubble Map for Qualification

qualities

thing

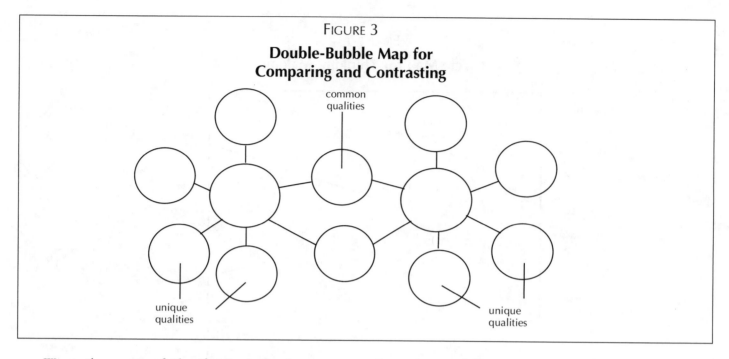

FIGURE 3
**Double-Bubble Map for
Comparing and Contrasting**

common
qualities

unique
qualities

unique
qualities

We use the process of *Classification* in the classroom as a way to see the main idea and supporting details of a reading passage, to study cultural groups in the world, to organize writing, to sort information in computers, and to create taxonomies in the sciences. What is interesting about this process is that things rarely exist in absolute categories, and not all classification systems are hierarchical. Not all things in a group necessarily share all of the same qualities. There are gray areas and overlapping categories. Classification systems, then, are created by and between humans through our perceptions, actions, and communication in the world.

The familiar Tree Map (Figure 4), is just one of the maps used for applying the skill of classification. This map represents a top-down pattern for sorting information, with the general term on the top, and specific groups and specimens below.

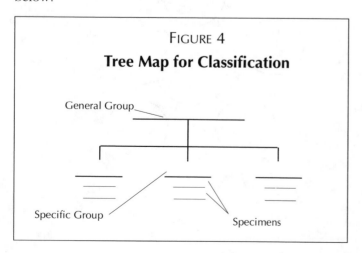

FIGURE 4
Tree Map for Classification

General Group

Specific Group

Specimens

Structure Analysis

Another way of seeing patterns is by noticing the physical boundaries between things, or part-whole relationships, such as in Upton's "shoreline" example cited previously. Upton called this process *Structure Analysis*. We use this process to understand spatial relationships, such as the setting of a play, the dimensions of geometric figures, the parts of the human body, even the geopolitical landscape. Much in the same way that categories do not exist absolutely in the world, Upton also believed that boundaries are represented by humans when we freeze an otherwise dynamic world.

The Brace Map (Figure 5) is used for looking for part-whole relationships. On the left side, the "whole" thing is drawn or written above the line. The braces represent the physical joints between parts, and the lines are the place-holders for major "parts," followed by the subparts. This map can be expanded infinitely to smaller (atomic) or larger (universal) parts of the whole.

Operation Analysis

If the world is a dynamic operation, then the process Upton called *Operation Analysis* is an expression of this view. Operation Analysis is the process of interpreting changes or sequences. We ask our students to interpret such things as directions, sequences in math or computer programs, timelines in history, and the plot lines of literature. The familiar Flowchart Map (Figure 6) is a useful starting point for thinking about different kinds of operations. This basic flowchart shows that an operation may have many

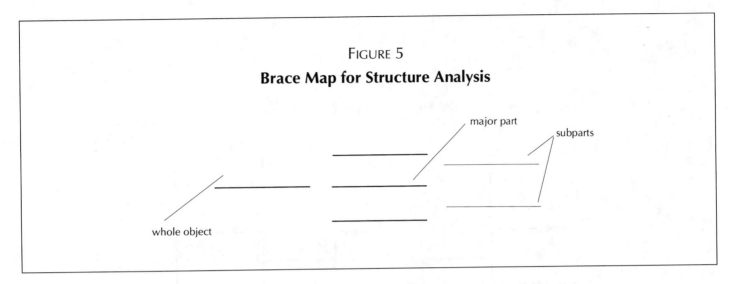

FIGURE 5

Brace Map for Structure Analysis

major part

subparts

whole object

stages and substages. When students draw the rectangles, they create a juncture between one stage and another, depending on their point of view. As the operations are seen to be more complex, feedback loops can be added through a "systems" approach (Roberts 1983).

A flowchart can be expanded into the Cause-Effect Map (Figure 7), useful for investigating cause-effect patterns of thinking. Of course, when students examine human interactions in the social sciences, the changes in history or of characters in a novel, and physical changes, they discover that each discipline has different cause-effect dimensions that can be thought about and displayed using different forms of this basic map.

Seeing Analogies

Central to Upton's model is a process of thinking that shows connections between representing and qualifying things, as well as relationships and interactions. It is the process of seeing similarities between relationships, what Upton called *Seeing Analogies*. Through our ability to create analogies, we are able to transfer information from one "body" of "knowledge" to another. This also enables us to communicate abstract ideas—such as in science and politics—by using conceptual metaphors. Metaphors are commonly thought of as poetic tools, yet this form of analogical thinking is one of the foundations for the human conceptual system (Lakoff and Johnson 1980).

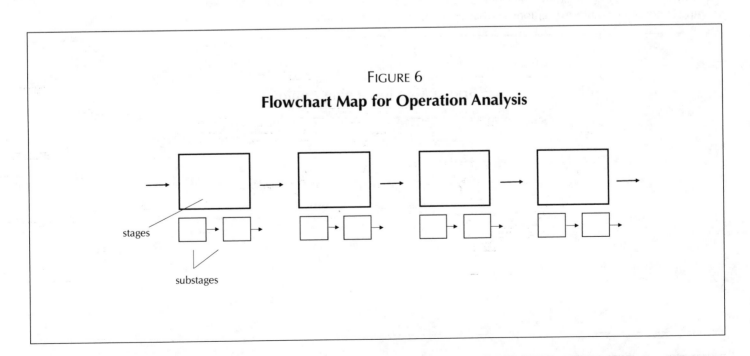

FIGURE 6

Flowchart Map for Operation Analysis

stages

substages

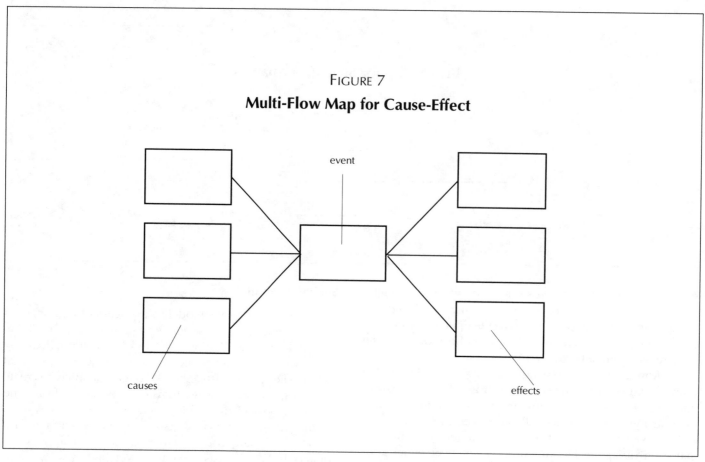

FIGURE 7

Multi-Flow Map for Cause-Effect

The Bridge Map (Figure 8) represents the pattern of Seeing Analogies: The line of the bridge represents the "relating factor" that is transferred across relationships. The relating factor is the common relationship that a student finds to exist between two or more pairs of things. Students can expand this map to create multilevel analogies and to investigate conceptual metaphors.

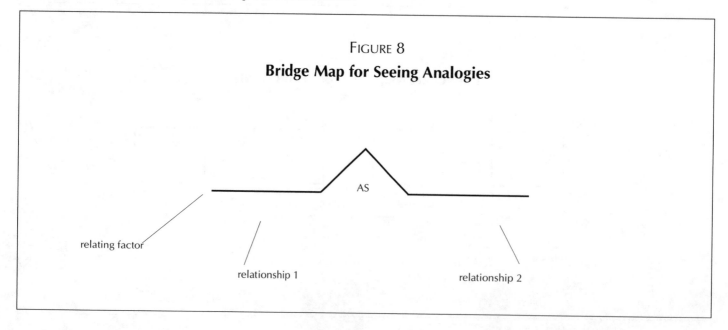

FIGURE 8

Bridge Map for Seeing Analogies

Each line, circle, or square of these thinking maps represents a relationship or boundary; such graphics provide a consistent visual vocabulary for creating maps and for thinking on a high order about fundamental acts of cognition. In addition, the pattern and name for each map together create a key image for using the skill: circles for representing things in context, bubbles for intangible qualifying, trees for top-down classifying, braces for structuring, flowchart arrows for operating, and bridges for making analogies. These visual-verbal maps are metacognitive tools: By drawing that line or circle between words, and questioning the type of boundaries being drawn, students are displaying and applying connected ways of thinking and knowing.

Expand Your Thinking

A Student Resource

The purpose of the *Expand Your Thinking* program is to introduce upper elementary and middle schools students to the six thinking processes and corresponding maps and then to apply this model to content learning. The program consists of a resource workbook for students and an extensive teacher's guide. The activities in this program help teachers to:

• Introduce students to thinking skills using thinking maps;

• Show how the skills can be applied to content learning using the thinking maps; and

• Structure the learning environment in a cooperative format.

The student workbook is called a *resource* for several reasons. First, the text is written directly to students so that they can read and reread important information without having to depend on the teacher. Second, clear definitions of maps and skills are highlighted within each chapter, and a one-page summary of the six skills and maps is provided as a reference. Third, instructions are provided to students, showing how to construct each thinking map. Finally, activities showing how to apply these maps to specific content areas are clearly designated according to disciplines. Ideally, the workbook is used as a resource by students throughout the year.

The *Expand Your Thinking* program takes approximately 40 class periods to complete. There are eight parts to the student workbook: introductory chapter for defining and applying the model to thinking about a concrete object, one chapter each of the six skills and maps, and a concluding chapter for applying the model to creating a new use for a common object. Each chapter provides about seven activities.

Figure 9 presents an overview of the "Qualification" chapter, an example of a typical chapter sequence. The activities are usually one page in length, and range in completion time from 20 minutes to two full periods of class time—much more time if the additional applications are completed.

FIGURE 9

Overview of Sample Chapter Activities

Chapter 2: Qualification Using the Bubble Map

Activity	Title	Description
A	What is the Skill of Qualification?	Introducing and defining Qualifications using the Bubble Map to describe an apple; students also create their own Bubble Map.
B	Making Sense of the World	Practice qualifying objects from daily life using the Bubble Map to organize sensory impressions.
C	Character Traits	Applying the Bubble Map to the analysis of two character descriptions (language arts).
D	Comparing and Contrasting	Applying the Double-Bubble Map to compare and contrast two characters, followed by a creative writing assignment.
E	Qualities and Subjects	Practice using the Double-Bubble Map by comparing and contrasting information (science, geography, and mathematics).
F	What Are the Reasons For Your Opinions	Applying the Double-Bubble Map to thinking about personal reasons for liking and disliking things; topic: television vs. reading.
G	The Science of Snack Food	Applying the Bubble Map to creating a nutritional snack food, followed by a writing assignment (science).

Each chapter of *Expand Your Thinking* has activities devoted to practice using the maps across multiple disciplines (as in activity E in Figure 9). Other activities focus on in-depth applications in one content area (as in activities C, D, and G). Content applications from the other chapters include: using the Circle Map for reading comprehension, using the Tree Map for organizing information in science, using the Brace Map for identifying geographic boundaries between countries, creating a Flowchart Map for showing how a law is made, and using a multilevel Bridge Map to connect historical information.

Most activities ask students to discuss and add to their maps while in cooperative pairs. Asking students to use visual thinking maps to think about information, and then to verbalize their thinking in pairs helps to create an environment in the classroom through which students are individually expanding their thinking abilities while learning from each other.

A Teacher's Guide to Creating a Thinking Classroom

There are many ways for teachers to promote the improvement of students' thinking. The design of the teacher's guide for *Expand Your Thinking* directly supports teachers in three of these areas by showing how to:

• Introduce thinking skills to students through the use of thinking maps;

• Integrate thinking skills instruction into content teaching; and

• Integrate ten interactive teaching strategies into classroom practice.

Each student page is reproduced in the teacher's guide, with suggested responses showing how each map may be completed. For every student activity there are instructions for the teacher that include a statement of purpose, directions and procedures, and applications to content area teaching.

The heart of this teacher's guide is a section called "Creating a Thinking Classroom." This section includes the ten "teaching for thinking" strategies that teachers can use to facilitate students' thinking, as classified using the Tree Map (Figure 10). These ten strategies are fully described, and then embedded within the teacher's guide for each student activity. As an example, for an activity using a Tree Map to classify different types of transportation vehicles for a social studies report, students are asked to draw maps showing different ways the information could be organized. The objective of this activity is to reveal that their purpose for writing influences how they may classify and therefore organize information. Included in the teacher's directions are three of the strategies for facilitating students' thinking: wait time, metacognitive questions, and justifying your answer.

Teachers are also advised to frequently describe these teaching strategies to their students before, during, or after use. This repetition helps students to become conscious of facilitation skills that they can use with each other, and the strategies support the creation of a thinking classroom.

Beyond Expand Your Thinking: Staff Development Through Curriculum Redesign

Expand Your Thinking can be implemented without a major commitment to staff development, yet with an introductory workshop, the foundation is set for long-term staff development based on the redesign of curriculum materials.

An introductory, half- or full-day workshop is suggested, though not required. The focus during this introduction is on applying thinking skills using the maps and teaching strategies. Extensive training is not required; with the detailed lesson plans and the visual support of mapping, teachers are not in the position of immediately having to create lessons that bridge between an abstract thinking-skill activity and a content application.

Applying Thinking Skills

Beyond the *Expand Your Thinking* materials are staff-development opportunities at three levels. (These three levels, with minor modification, are also available for teachers in schools and districts who want to learn how to use thinking maps for applying thinking skills to content learning independent of published materials.) The umbrella name for the staff development offerings is "Applying Thinking Skills." These training sessions are structured so that teachers work together in small working groups to focus on applying thinking skills and maps in their classrooms—in all three levels of Applying Thinking Skills, as follows:

• *Tools for Thinking* (1 day): This introduction can be attended by teachers who are going to implement *Expand Your Thinking* or by teachers who want a basic-level training in the use of thinking maps. While the focus is introductory, by the end of the day teachers have created materials for use in the classroom.

• *Thinking Skills and Content Area Teaching* (3 days): By the end of this seminar, teachers in working groups have created a series of lessons for immediate use in the classroom. These lessons are based on using thinking maps and the ten "teaching for thinking" strategies. All of the transformed curriculum materials created by the groups are reviewed, and feedback suggestions are provided.

• *Curriculum Design for Teaching Thinking* (5 days): This institute is an extended version of the Seminar design.

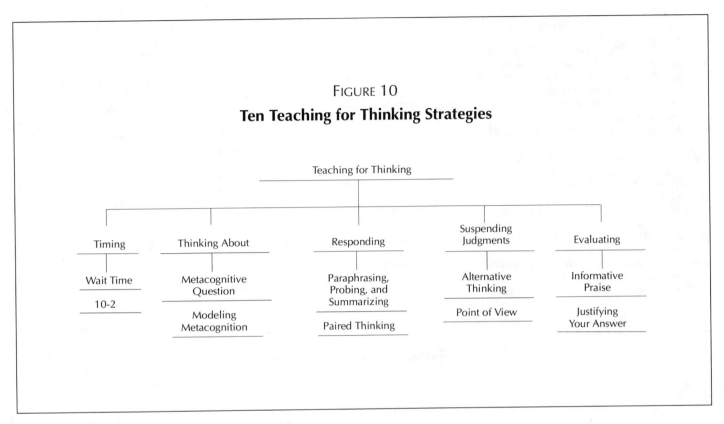

FIGURE 10

Ten Teaching for Thinking Strategies

By the last session, teachers in working groups have redesigned a complete curriculum unit and some of the materials have been piloted. These units integrate the use of thinking maps; teaching strategies; and, when appropriate, assessment tools using maps. These rough-draft units are then reviewed and feedback suggestions provided.

The emphasis shifts from how to use thinking maps and teaching strategies in the classroom in the introductory training, toward the redesign of curriculum materials, including basals, in the 3- and 5-day sessions. A school or district can initiate a staff development program at any of these levels, with or without implementing *Expand Your Thinking*.

Teachers as Authors of Curriculum

Teachers come to staff development days with the expectation of taking something new back to the classroom that they can use. As shown in the three levels of staff development, the key to each session is that teachers use the thinking skills maps to renew their own curriculum materials and add to their teaching repertoire. In the seminar and institute settings, teachers are asked to bring materials that they will be using with their students so they have the opportunity to take renewed materials back to the classroom. As a follow-up to the institute, an additional option is available for finalizing the redesigned materials. The materials can be edited,

printed, and compiled in a *Teacher's Resource Manual*. This material can be duplicated and shared within a school and disseminated across a district. This finished product of staff development is a resource that supports the long-term commitment to teaching for and about thinking, provides practical materials for use by teachers, and honors those groups of teachers who have worked together to expand their teaching repertoire.

*   *   *

Expand Your Thinking is a program primarily used for teaching students how to apply thinking skills to content learning, using thinking maps. The long-term goal is to enable students to work together as they consciously apply thinking maps to learning. With the addition of staff development in "Applying Thinking Skills," a second long-term goal is set to enable teachers to work together as they learn to use thinking maps in their daily teaching by redesigning the materials they already use in their classrooms. Through these programs, students and teachers are seeing how to connect and express their thinking, using maps and strategies; and teachers have the opportunity to transform how *and* what they teach.

REFERENCES

Costa, A. L., and L. F. Lowery. (1989). *Techniques for Teaching Thinking*. Pacific Grove, Calif.: Midwest Publications.

Gardner, H. (1983). *Frames of Mind: The Theory of Multiple Intelligences*. New York: Basic Books.

Gilligan, C. (1982). *In a Different Voice*. Cambridge: Harvard University Press.

Gould, S. J. (1981). *The Mismeasure of Man*. New York: W. W. Norton.

Gould, S. J. (1989). *Wonderful Life*. New York: W. W. Norton.

Hechinger, F. (June 27, 1960). "Student I.Q.'s Rise in California Test." *The New York Times*.

Hyerle, D., (1989a). *Designs for Thinking Connectively*. Unpublished Manuscript, Position Paper, University of California–Berkeley.

Hyerle, D. (1989b). *Expand Your Thinking*. Stamford, Conn.: Innovative Sciences.

Jones, B., J. Pierce., and B. Hunter. (December 1988–January 1989). "Teaching Students to Construct Graphic Representations." *Educational Leadership* 46, 4: 20–25.

Lakoff, G. (1989). *Women, Fire, and Dangerous Things*. Chicago: University of Chicago Press.

Lakoff, G., and M. Johnson (1980). *Metaphors We Live By*. Chicago: University of Chicago Press.

Mayr, E. (1989). *The Growth of Biological Thought*. Cambridge: Harvard University Press.

Novak, J. D., and B. D. Gowin. (1984). *Learning How to Learn*. Cambridge: Cambridge University Press.

Perkins, D. N. (1986). *Knowledge as Design*. Hillsdale, N.J.: Lawrence Erlbaum.

Putnam, H. (1988). *Representation and Reality*. Cambridge: Massachusetts Institute of Technology Press.

Roberts, N. (1983). *Computer Simulation: A Systems Dynamics Modeling Approach*. Reading: Addison Wesley.

Upton, A. (1961). *Design for Thinking*. Palo Alto, Calif.: Pacific Books.

Upton, A., and R. Samson. (1963). *Creative Analysis*. New York: E. P. Dutton.

Expand Your Thinking

Developer:	David Hyerle (based on the work of Albert Upton)
Goals:	Training students to use graphic organizers as tools for applying thinking skills to content learning through working in cooperative pairs.
Sample skills:	Using flowcharts for sequencing and cause/effect reasoning, classification tree maps for main idea and supporting evidence, bubble maps for descriptions and comparison/contrast, bridge map for seeing analogies, circle map for defining things in context, brace map for seeing structural relationships.
Assumptions:	• Knowledge is connected, patterned information that often is linked together by unclear mental boundaries and mental models. • Thinking (creative and analytical) and learning are facilitated by having students use graphic organizers to visually connect and represent information. • Communication of thinking is facilitated when students cooperatively share their thinking with others, using graphic organizers.
Intended audience:	Regular program: grades 5–7.
Process:	Students work in cooperative pairs throughout most of the program. Students are introduced to an integrated model of six fundamental thinking processes and corresponding graphic organizers for applying each process. Within each skill chapter, students first apply each "thinking map" to common, everyday information; then to basic information from different content areas; and, finally, in greater depth within a specific content area activity.
Resource:	*Expand Your Thinking*, by David Hyerle (1989).
Time:	Varies with individual schedules; one period per week is suggested.
Available from:	Innovative Sciences, Inc., 300 Broad Street, Park Square Station, P.O. Box 15129, Stamford, CT 06901-0129. Telephone: 800-243-9169.

6

The CoRT Thinking Program

Edward de Bono

Creativity involves breaking out of established patterns in order to look at things in a different way.

—Edward de Bono

A major trend may be developing in education toward the direct teaching of thinking as a skill. I intend in this article to answer two basic questions related to this trend. First, what is thinking? And second, how can we teach thinking directly? My answers spring from 16 years of experience in the field. During this time I developed an instructional program on thinking skills that is now used by several million school children in many different countries and cultures.

Of course, some educators believe that thinking is simply a matter of innate intelligence. Two corollaries follow this belief: (1) we do not have to do anything specific to help highly intelligent individuals learn how to think, and (2) there is little we can do to help less intelligent individuals learn how to think. Thus those who hold this belief rest content. Yet many highly intelligent individuals often seem to be rather ineffective thinkers. Such people are often good at reactive thinking and puzzle solving—but less able to think about topics that require a broader view. They may show cleverness, but not wisdom.

I prefer to see the relationship between intelligence and thinking as similar to the relationship between a car and its driver. Engineering determines the innate potential of the car, but the skill with which the car is driven must be learned and practiced. Thus I would define thinking as "the operating skill with which intelligence acts upon experience."

What, then, is the relationship of information to thinking? It seems obvious to me that God can neither think nor have a sense of humor. Perfect knowledge precludes the

need to move from one arrangement of knowledge to a better one. Thus, perfect knowledge makes thinking unnecessary. Nonetheless, educators often seem to believe that we can attain such perfect knowledge. However, even if it were possible to absorb perfect knowledge about the past, we can only have a very partial knowledge about the future. Yet as soon as a youngster leaves school, he or she will be operating in the future. Every initiative, decision, or plan will be carried out in the future and thus will require thinking, not just sorting and resorting of knowledge. I have coined the term "operacy" to stand along literacy and numeracy as a primary goal of education. Operacy is the skill of doing things, of making things happen. The type of thinking that my program (which I will describe later) teaches is very much concerned with operacy.

In short, information is no substitute for thinking, and thinking is no substitute for information. The dilemma is that there is never enough time to teach all the information that could usefully be taught. Yet we may have to reduce the time we spend teaching information, in order to focus instead on the direct teaching of thinking skills.

The relationship between logic and thinking is likewise not a linear one. The computer world has a saying, "Garbage in-garbage out." In other words, even if the computer is working flawlessly, this will not validate a given outcome. Bad logic makes for bad thinking, but good logic (like the flawless computer) does not ensure good thinking. Every logician knows that a conclusion is only as good as the premises. Mathematics, logic (of various sorts), and—increasingly—data processing are excellent service tools. But the deeper we advance into the computer age, the greater the need to emphasize the perceptual side of thinking, which these tools serve.

Meanwhile, emotions, values, and feelings influence thinking in three stages. We may feel a strong emotion (e.g., fear, anger, hatred) even before we encounter a situation.

Copyright © 1990 by Mica Management Resources Inc.

More usually, there is a brief period of undirected perception, until we recognize the situation. This recognition triggers emotion, which thereafter channels perception. The trained thinker should be operating in the third mode: perception explores the situation as broadly as possible, and, in the end, emotions determine the decision. There is no contradiction at all between emotions and thinking. The purpose of thinking is to arrange the world so that our emotions can be applied in a valuable manner.

The relationship of perception to thinking is, to my mind, the crucial area. In the past, far too many of our approaches to thinking (e.g., mathematics, logic) have concerned themselves with the "processing" aspect. We are rather good at processing but poor in the perceptual area.

What do I mean by perception? Quite simply, the way our minds make sense of the world around us. Language is a reflection of our traditional perceptions (as distinct from the moment-to-moment ones). Understanding how perception works is not so easy. But this is a crucial point—one that has a direct effect on the way we teach thinking.

Imagine a man holding a small block of wood. He releases the wood, and it falls to the ground. When he releases it a second time, the wood moves upward. This is strange and mysterious behavior. The third time he releases the wood, it remains exactly where it is—suspended in space. This is also mysterious behavior. If I were now to reveal that, in the second instance, the man was standing at the bottom of a swimming pool, then it seems perfectly natural for the wood to float upward. In the third instance

the man is an astronaut in orbit; thus, it is perfectly natural for the wood to remain suspended, since it is weightless. Behavior that seemed strange and unaccountable suddenly seems normal and logical—once we have defined the "universe" in which it is taking place.

The traditional universe of information handling is a "passive" one. We record information through marks on paper or marks on magnetic tape. We can handle and process that information. The marks on the surface of the paper or tape and the information itself do not alter, unless we alter them.

An "active" system is totally different; here the information actually organizes itself into patterns. We human beings have self-organizing information systems. I first wrote about them in 1969 in my book, The Mechanism of Mind (de Bono 1969). I showed then how such systems work, and I suggested how the structure of a nerve network would produce such pattern-making effects. My hypothesis has since been simulated by computer, and the nerve network functions substantially as I had suggested (Lee and Maradurajan 1982). In the world of information handling, the concept of self-organizing information systems is now coming to the fore (Hopfield 1982). Such systems are quite different from our usual computers.

Once we enter the "universe" of active, self-organizing systems, then the behavior of such things as perception and creativity becomes quite clear. The processes are no longer mysterious. Just as happened with the block of wood, phenomena that seemed to be unaccountable are suddenly seen to be explicable—once we have identified the ap-

---

CoRT (Cognitive Research Trust)

Developer:	Edward de Bono
Goal:	Teach thinking skills useful to everyone in and out of school.
Sample skills:	PNI—Positive, Negative, Interesting CAF—Consider All Factors
Assumptions:	• Lateral thinking, unlike vertical thinking, is not necesssarily sequential, is unpredictable, and is not constrained by convention. • It is not necessay to be right at every stage of the thought process or to have everyting rigidly defined. • Intelligent people are not necessarily skillful thinkers.
Intended audience:	Ages 8 to 22, all ability levels.
Process:	Students practice "operations" following "lesson notes." Teachers present and monitor the exercises.
Time:	One lesson 35 minutes or longer per week for 3 years.
Comments:	Evaluation results suggest that the program leads students to take a broader view of formally posed problems.
Published by:	Science Research Associates (SRA), A Division of the Macmillan/McGraw-Hill School Publishing Company, 155 N. Wacker Drive, Chicago, IL 60606-1780.
Training available through:	Science Research Associates, 2030 Addison St., Suite 400, Berkeley, CA 94704. Telephone: 415-841-7715. FAX: 415-841-6311

propriate universe.

The function of a self-organizing system is to allow incoming experience to organize itself into patterns. We could loosely compare these patterns to the streets in a town. The self-organizing system is immensely efficient; it allows us to get up in the morning, cross a road, recognize friends, read and write. Without such a pattern-making and pattern-using system, we would spend about a month just in crossing a road.

However, the advantages of a patterning system are also its disadvantages. "Point-to-point thinking" is a good example. In this kind of thinking, we follow a pattern from one point to the next—and then follow the dominant pattern from the next point onward. In an experiment that I conducted jointly with the Inner London Education Authority (unpublished material Cognitive Research Trust), I asked 24 groups of 11-year-olds to discuss the suggestion that "bread, fish, and milk should be free." Although many of the children came from deprived backgrounds, 23 of the 24 groups opposed the idea of free bread, fish, and milk. The point-to-point thinking that led to this stand went as follows: (1) the shops would be crowded; (2) the buses going to the shops would be crowded; (3) the bus drivers would demand more money; (4) the drivers would not get more money, and they would go on strike; (5) other people would go on strike as well; and (6) there would be chaos—so giving away bread, fish, and milk is a bad idea. Thus, point-to-point thinking can lead us astray, as we miss the forest while fixating on the trees.

However, direct teaching of thinking can offset the disadvantage of a patterning system. At the end of a pilot project on the teaching of thinking in Venezuelan schools, for example, we held a press conference. A journalist attending that conference claimed that all attempts to teach thinking are really a form of brainwashing in western capitalist values. The journalist happened to be wearing spectacles. So I removed her spectacles and asked what she used them for. She told me that she used the spectacles in order to see things more clearly. I then explained that the perceptual tools we were teaching in the lessons on thinking served the same purpose. The tools enable youngsters to scan their experiences so that they can see things more clearly and more broadly. A better map of the world is the result. These thinkers can still retain their original values and choices, however. Giving spectacles to nearsighted individuals enables them to see three glasses on a table - containing wine, orange juice, and milk. The individuals still exercise choice as to which drink each prefers. In the same way, our instructional program cuts across cultures and ideologies. The program is used in industrialized nations, such as Canada and Great Britain, and in developing nations, such as Venezuela and Malaysia; it will soon be used in Cuba, China, and Bulgaria—as well as in Catholic Ireland.

My point is that, in terms of perception, we need to achieve two things: (1) the ability to see things more clearly and more broadly, and (2) the ability to see things differently (i.e., creativity or "lateral thinking" (de Bono 1970). As I have said, perception takes place in an "active" information system. Such systems allow experience to organize itself into immensely useful patterns, without which life would be impossible. But, as I said above, the very advantages of the patterning system are also its disadvantages. We must overcome these disadvantages and improve perception in two ways: in breadth and in creativity or lateral thinking (both of which fall under the heading of "change").

Let me turn now to the second question that I posed at the beginning of this article. How can we teach thinking as a skill? Such teaching is not tomorrow's dream. In Venezuela, for example, 106,000 teachers have been trained to use my program. My program is also in use in many other countries—including Australia, the United States, and Israel, as well as those nations I have mentioned previously.

The program of which I speak is called CoRT. (The acronym stands for Cognitive Research Trust, located in Cambridge, England). I have already outlined the theoretical foundation for the design of this program. The lessons themselves focus on the perceptual aspect of thinking. The design of the tools takes into account the behavior of self-organizing patterning systems.

The design criteria for a practical instructional program should include the following elements:

• The program should be usable by teachers who represent a wide range of teaching talents, not just by the highly gifted or the highly qualified, (The 106,000 Venezuelan teachers were not all geniuses.)

• The program should not require complicated teacher training, since it is difficult to generalize such programs. (The CoRT program can be used by teachers with no special training or with only simple training.)

• The program should be robust enough to resist damage as it is passed along from trainer to trainer—and thence from new trainer to teachers and, finally, to pupils.

• The program should employ parallel design so that if some parts of the program are badly taught and other parts are skipped or later forgotten, what remains is usable and valuable in its own right. (This contrasts with hierarchical design, in which a student must grasp a basic concept before moving on to the next concept layer; failure at any concept layer in a program on this type makes the whole system unworkable.)

• The program should be enjoyable for both teachers and youngsters.

• The program should focus on thinking skills that help a learner to function better in his or her life outside of school, not merely to become more proficient at solving puzzles or playing games.

Before considering ways of teaching thinking, we must confront a prior question: Should thinking be taught in its own right? Certain practical considerations affect the answer to this question. For example, there are no gaps in the school schedule as it now exists. Thus, it seems to make more sense to insert thinking skills into an existing subject area. English makes a good home, because a natural synergy exists between thinking and the expression of thought in language. In addition, the teaching style is often more open-ended in English classes than in some other subject areas. However, the CoRT program has been used effectively by science teachers, by music teachers, and even by physical education teachers.

Despite these practical considerations, I believe that we should have a specific place in the curriculum that is set aside for the teaching of thinking skills. This formal recognition is essential so that pupils, teachers, and parents all recognize that thinking skills are being taught directly. In time I would certainly hope that the skills taught in the "thinking lessons" would find their ways into such subject areas as geography, history, social studies, and science. However, the first step is to establish "thinking" as a subject in its own right.

This brings me to the central problem: transfer and content. Does a generalizable skill of thinking exist? Many theorists think not. They believe instead that there is thinking in mathematics, thinking in science, and thinking in history—but that in each case the rules are different, just as the rules for *Monopoly* differ from those in chess. I do not see this as a point of view with which I must either agree or disagree totally. Clearly, subject idioms exist. Nevertheless, it is possible to establish both habits of mind and specific thinking techniques that can be applied in any subject area. For example, the willingness to look for alternatives is a generalizable thinking habit. And deliberate provocation is a technique that can be applied to generate ideas in any situation.

Because we cannot succeed in teaching generalizable thinking skills through the use of specific content materials, some theorists believe that such skills cannot exist. But there is another way of looking at the situation: the view that generalizable thinking skills exist but cannot be taught using specific content. My experience has led me to the latter view. As I have already noted with regard to the "discussion method" of teaching thinking skills, little transfer of such skills seems to take place from one situation to another. Given the mechanics of perception and attention, this is hardly surprising. If the subject of a discussion is interesting, then, by definition, attention follows this interest. But this attention is not focused on the metacognitive level; that is, participants are not thinking about the *thinking* that they are using to discuss the subject. Moreover, it is very difficult to transfer a complex action sequence from one situation to another. That is why the CoRT program deliberately focuses on "tools" that can be transferred.

I have noticed among U.S. educators a tendency to try to teach thinking through content materials. This approach seems—to its proponents—to have two merits. First, this approach makes it easier to introduce thinking into the curriculum, because the material must be covered anyway (and it is already familiar to the teacher). Second, this approach seems to be killing two kinds of birds with one stone: teaching thinking and teaching content. But this approach is not effective. I am afraid that the nettle must be grasped. Either one wishes to teach thinking effectively or merely to make a token gesture. Attending to content distracts from attending to the thinking tools being used. Theory predicts this outcome: you cannot build meta-patterns on one level and experience patterns on another level at the same time. Experience backs up this expectation. Wherever there has been an attempt to teach thinking skills and content together, the training in thinking seems to be weaker than when those skills are taught in isolation.

So what is the CoRT method? It is best to illustrate this method with an example.

I was teaching a class of 30 boys, all 11 years of age, in Sydney, Australia. I asked if they would each like to be given $5 a week for coming to school. All 30 thought this was a fine idea. "We could buy sweets or chewing gum. . . . We could buy comics. . . . We could get toys without having to ask Mum or Dad."

I then introduced and explained a simple tool called the PMI (which I will describe later). The explanation took about four minutes. In groups of five, the boys applied the PMI tool to the suggestion that they should be given $5 a week for coming to school. For three to four minutes they talked and thought on their own. At no time did I interfere. I never discussed the $5 suggestion, other than to state it. I did not suggest that the youngsters consider this, think of that, and so forth. At the end of their thinking time, the groups reported back to me: "The bigger boys would beat us up and take the money. . . . The school would raise its charges for meals. . . . Our parents would not buy us presents. . . . Who would decide how much money different ages received? . . . There would be less money for a school minibus."

When they finished their report, I again asked the boys to express their views on the suggestion of pay for attending school. This time 29 of the 30 had completely reversed their opinion and thought it a bad idea. We subsequently learned that the one holdout received *no* pocket money at home. The important point is that my contribution was minimal. I did not interact with the boys. I simply explained the PMI tool, and the boys then used it for their own—as *their* tool. My "superior" intelligence and broader experiences were not influences. The boys did their own thinking.

The PMI is a simple scanning tool designed to avoid the point-to-point thinking that I mentioned earlier. The thinker looks first in the Plus direction (good points), and then in the Minus direction (bad points), and finally in the interesting direction (interesting things that might arise or are worth noting, even if they are neither good nor bad). Each direction is scanned formally, one after another. This formal scan produces a better and broader map. Thinking is used to explore, not merely to back up a snap judgement. The thinker then applies judgement to the better map. The PMI is the first of the 60 CoRT lessons.

For the rest of this particular lesson on thinking, I might have asked the boys to apply the PMI in various ways (e.g., one group doing only "Plus" or "Minus" or "Interesting") to a number of thinking items, such as: Should all cars be colored yellow? Would it be a good idea for everyone to wear a badge showing his or her mood at the moment? Is homework a good idea? Note that the items are not related. Moreover, the group would be allowed to spend only two or three minutes on each. This is quite deliberate and essential to the method.

The items are switched rapidly so that attention stays on the PMI tool and not on the content. Once skill in the use of tool is developed, students can apply the PMI to other situations in other settings. One girl told us how she used the PMI at home to decide whether or not to have her long hair cut. Some children report that they have used the PMI with their parents, in discussing such major decisions as moving to a new town or buying a car. This is the sort of transfer that the CoRT program aims to achieve.

The PMI is a scanning tool, not a judgment tool. If a thinker spots 10 "Plus" points and only two "Minus" points, this does not necessarily mean that the idea is a good one. Like all scanning, the PMI is subjective, depending on the thinker's perspective. One boy said, as a "Plus" point, that yellow cars would be kept cleaner. Another boy stated this as a "Minus" point—because he had to clean his dad's car and would therefore have to perform this chore more often. Both were right.

The PMI is designed to be artificial, memorable, and easy to pronounce. At first, some teachers rejected "PMI" as pointless jargon. They preferred to encourage or exhort the youngsters to look at the good points and the bad points in any situation. The youngsters probably did so—at that moment. However, without the artificial term "PMI" to crystalize the process and to create a meta-pattern, the exhorta-tion does not stick. One teacher told me how he used the term "PMI" and how his colleague was soon convinced of the value of the term "PMI."

One girl said that she initially thought the PMI a rather silly device, since she knew how she felt about a subject. But she noted that, as she wrote things down under each letter (she was doing a written exercise instead of the usual oral approach), she became less certain. In the end, the points she had written down did cause her to change her mind. Yet, she had written down the points. That is precisely the purpose of a scanning tool.

It is important that the description of thinking and the design of tools are two totally different things. It is possible to describe the process of thinking and to break it into components. But then one is tempted to turn each component into a tool, on the premise that, if the components are taught, thinking skills must surely be enhanced. However, teaching someone how to describe a flower does not teach him or her how to grow a flower. The purpose of analysis and the purpose of an operating tool are separate and distinct.

The CoRT tools are designed specifically as operating tools. Such a design has two components: (1) the tool must be easy to use, and (2) it must have a useful effect. Abstract analyses and subdivisions of the thinking process may be intellectually neat, but this does not guarantee usability or effectiveness. My many years of experience, working with thousands of executives and organizations in different countries, have given me some insight into those aspects of thinking that have practical value. I have also worked with scientists, designers, lawyers, and many others who are involved in the "action world" of thinking, as distinct from the "contemplative world."

The CoRT program has 6 sections, each consisting of 10 lessons: CoRT I (breadth), CoRT II (organization), CoRT III (interaction), CoRT IV (creativity), CoRT V (information and feeling), and CoRT VI (action). All teachers who use the program should teach CoRT I. (Some teachers use only the 10 lessons of CoRT I.) Thereafter, the sections can be used in any order. For example, a teacher might use CoRT I, CoRT IV, and CoRT V. The last section (CoRT VI) is somewhat different from the other sections, in that it provides a framework for a staged approach to thinking.

I believe that thinking is best taught to 9-, 10-, and 11-year-olds. Youngsters in the middle grades really enjoy thinking and motivation is very high. They have sufficient verbal fluency and experience to operate the thinking tools. The curriculum is more easily modified in the middle grades to include thinking as a basic subject. But the CoRT materials have also been used with children younger than 9 and with students ranging in age from 12 to adult.

So basic is thinking as a skill that the same CoRT lessons have been used by children in the jungles of South America and by top executives of the Ford Motor Company, United Kingdom. The lessons have been taught to students ranging in I.Q. from below 80 to above 140. The lessons have also been used with groups of mixed ability.

David Lane, at the Hungerford Guidance Centre in London, found that the teaching of thinking to delinquent and violent youngsters brought about an improvement in behavior, as measured by a sharp fall in the number of disciplinary encounters these youngsters had with supervisors (personal communication from David Lane). William Cooley and Edna Cooley, in preliminary work at an institution for young offenders, found similar changes (Cooley and Cooley forthcoming). They recounted how one youth, on the verge of attacking an officer with a hammer, brought to mind a thinking lesson concerned with consequences—a quietly put the hammer down. I mention these changes in behavior for two reasons. First, I believe that the true test of teaching thinking is the effect of such teaching on behavior. Second, we do not really have any adequate way of measuring thinking performance. Standardized tests are largely irrelevant, because they do not allow us to observe the thinker's composite performance.

John Edwards taught the CoRT program in lieu of a portion of the science syllabus to a class in Australia. Using an analysis-of-discourse approach to measurement, he found that the trained students did significantly better at thinking than untrained peers; the trained students even seemed to do better in science, although they had less instructional time devoted to that subject (Edwards). It is not difficult to show that pupils who have had training in thinking produce a wider scan when they are asked to consider some subject. In Ireland, Liam Staunton found that, before CoRT training, individuals produced an average of four sentences on a topic, whereas after CoRT training, they produced an average of 47 (personal communication from Liam Staunton). We are currently analyzing data from the Schools Council project in England.

I prefer that CoRT users carry out their own tests and pilot projects. Tests carried out by designers of a program are of limited value for two reasons: (1) the conditions of teaching are ideal (and often far removed from those prevailing in schools where the program will be used), and (2) such studies always contain an element of bias.

It is impossible, however, to measure the soft data: the confidence of those who have had training in thinking, the focus of their thinking, their willingness to think about things, the effectiveness of their thinking, their structured approach and breadth of consideration. Teachers often sum up these factors as "maturity," in commenting about those children who come to their classroom after some training in thinking.

I would expect four levels of achievement in the acquisition of thinking skills through the use of CoRT program:

• *Level 1.* A general awareness of thinking as a skill. A willingness to "think" about something. A willingness to explore around a subject. A willingness to listen to others. No recollection of any specific thinking tools.

• *Level 2.* A more structured approach to thinking, including better balance, looking at the consequences of an action or choice (taking other people's views into account), and a search for alternatives. Perhaps a mention of a few of the CoRT tools.

• *Level 3.* Focused and deliberate use of some of the CoRT tools. The organization of thinking as a series of steps. A sense of purpose in thinking.

• *Level 4.* Fluent and appropriate use of many CoRT tools. Definite consciousness of the metacognitive level of thinking. Observation of and comment on the thinker's own thinking. The designing of thinking tasks and strategies, followed by the carrying out of these tasks.

In most situations, I would expect average attainment to fall somewhere between levels 1 and 2. With a more definite emphasis on "thinking", this would rise to a point between levels 2 and 3. Only in exceptional groups with thorough training would I expect to find average attainment at level 4.

Perhaps the most important aspect of the direct teaching of thinking as a skill is the self-image of a youngster as a "thinker," however. This is an operational image. Thinking becomes a skill at which the youngster can improve. Such a self-image is different from the more usual "value" images: "I am intelligent" or "I am not intelligent" (I do not get on well at school, and school is a bore). Value images are self-reinforcing. So are operational images—but the reinforcement goes in the opposite directions at the other end. In other words, the less intelligent students find repeated evidence of their lack of intelligence, but they also notice those occasions when they do manage to come up with good ideas.

REFERENCES

Copley, W., and E. Copley. (Forthcoming). *Practical Teaching of Thinking.*

de Bono, E. (1969). *The Mechanism of Mind.* New York: Simon and Schuster.

de Bono, E. (1970). *Lateral Thinking.* New York: Harper & Row.

Edwards, J. Unpublished paper. Queensland, Australia: James Cook University.

Hopfield, J. (September 1982). "Brain, Computer, and Memory." *Engineering and Science.*

Lee, M. H., and A. R. Maradurajan. (1982). "A Computer Package of the Evaluation of Neuron Models Involving Large Uniform Networks." *International Journal of Man-Machine Studies* 189-210.

7

IMPACT

S. Lee Winocur

The IMPACT (Improving Minimal Proficiencies by Activating Critical Thinking) program seeks to improve student performance in basic skill subjects by infusing critical thinking instruction into the content areas. In addition to the major goal of improved student achievement on district tests of basic competency, project objectives include improved performance of tasks that require critical thinking and independent judgment and, on standardized measures of reading and mathematics, improved instruction through staff inservice education and trained coordination of program installation.

Program Components

The IMPACT curriculum includes three essential features of effective instruction:

• Skills are clearly identified and placed in a hierarchical sequence of cognitive development.

• Skills are presented in a lesson-plan format designed to provide modeling and practice and to systematically identify reinforcement of the thinking processes that are integral to and essential for subject area mastery.

• Ten teacher behaviors that promote critical thinking are identified, practiced, and coached by peers.

Although originally designed as an alternative approach to remedial reading and math in junior and senior high schools, IMPACT can be used in a variety of subject areas with students of varying ability levels in all grades. The learning activities accommodate individual development and differing learning styles and allow all students to experience success as they actively participate in tasks that move from the concrete to the abstract.

Students receive classroom instruction using the IMPACT program two to three hours per week. Small-group and cooperative instruction are emphasized, but large-group and individual instruction are also used. To provide appropriate learning experiences for students who have varying educational backgrounds, interests, and skill achievement levels, the study sheets that accompany each lesson use diverse instructional methodologies and are written at several different levels of vocabulary and task difficulty. Learning activities include group discussion, oral and written reports, team research projects, artwork, and dramatic presentations.

Program Training

Teachers attend an intensive 18-hour training session that focuses on the Universe of Critical Thinking Skills, the theoretical base for implementing critical thinking, the IMPACT lesson design, teaching behaviors, and social interactions that reinforce critical thinking in the classroom. Teachers receive the IMPACT materials only if they successfully complete the training.

Level I training is followed by peer coaching. Teachers practice identified teaching strategies, teach the IMPACT thinking skills, observe one another in the classroom, record the use of each teaching behavior, and review feedback on observation findings.

At Level II, one or more representatives from each district are eligible for training as district-site coordinators, certified to conduct training for other teachers. Regional trainers certified by the project are contracted by the Huntington Beach Union High School District to train in each state. The IMPACT program is sponsored by the National Diffusion Network as a model staff development program and by Phi Delta Kappa. IMPACT's strengths lie in its clear theoretical base, its validated effectiveness, its ease of implementation, and its synthesis of theory.

IMPACT

Developer:	S. Lee Winocur
Goals:	To improve students' performance in content areas by facilitating their acquisition of higher-level thinking skills.
Sample skills:	Classifying and categorizing, ordering, identifying relevant and irrelevant information, formulating valid inductive and deductive arguments, rendering judgments.
Assumptions:	• All students are capable of higher-level thinking. • Thinking skills can be taught. • Thinking skills can be learned. • Thinking skills are basic to the learning process. • Thinking is best introduced in a social context. • Thinking skills must be related to the curriculum.
Intended audience:	All students.
Process:	Students' basic skills improve through learning activities that include a critical thinking component infused into content area lessons through (1) a sequential and cumulative Universe of Critical Thinking Skills designed to help students reason, (2) a model lesson format, and (3) ten teaching behaviors that label and reinforce students' thinking in an interactive environment.
Time:	Two to three hours per week.
Source:	S. Lee Winocur, National Director, IMPACT, Huntington Beach Union High School District, 21412 Magnolia St., Huntington Beach, CA 92646.

Program Materials

The Curriculum Materials Kit provides a language arts handbook and a mathematics curriculum handbook. Each contains 60 teacher-developed lessons focusing on critical thinking skills that directly affect reading, comprehension, and mathematical problem solving. A filmstrip provides motivational experiences and information related to the learning and transfer of logical reasoning to school and everyday life. Home Enrichment Learning Packets reinforce selected skills in critical thinking identified as being the most difficult for students to grasp. These self-paced packets are sent home with students as supplementary materials. Packet topics include Reliable/Unreliable Sources, Cause and Effect, Relationships, Meaning of Statements, Assumptions, and Point of View.

The IMPACT Training Manual explores the program's theoretical base, provides sample lessons and exercises in implementation, examines ten teaching behaviors, and explains the Universe of Critical Thinking Skills. Materials are available to IMPACT graduates through Phi Delta Kappa.

8

Philosophy for Children

Matthew Lipman

The aim of Philosophy for Children is to promote excellent thinking: thinking that is creative as well as critical, imaginative as well as logical, inventive as well as analytical. But to make children think well, we must first make them think. This involves an intellectual awakening, a strengthening of their ability to discriminate the relationships among things—to draw appropriate distinctions and make connections.

Unfortunately, the models of children available on television and in most children's stories do not offer much evidence that children do in fact reflect, consider, deliberate, infer, seek out underlying assumptions, define, or hypothesize, to name a few of the mental activities characteristic of people who think (see Figure 1). Editors of children's readers evidently prefer story characters who have feelings, engage in physical actions, and note facts; references to thinking are considered superfluous. If the stone is flat, it's flat. What difference does it make that Jane *imagines*

it's flat, Tom *infers* that it's flat, Bruce *wonders* if it's flat, Edna *supposes* it to be flat, and so on? In forming a model of thinking children, it *does* make a difference, and this is one objective of Philosophy for Children.

Program Materials and Goals

The following passage is from *Kio and Gus*, a novel for children in grades K–4:

There usually aren't many cars on the road that runs by the corral. Something's coming now, although it's still a long way off. Now I hear the siren! It's an ambulance, and it's speeding very fast. There must have been an accident somewhere.

Just as the ambulance gets near the corral, I hear Brad trying to quiet Tchaikovsky down. The siren terrifies him. Suddenly Tchaikovsky rears up on his hind legs and Kio is thrown on the grass! Face down. Brad and I bend over him. But he just lies there.

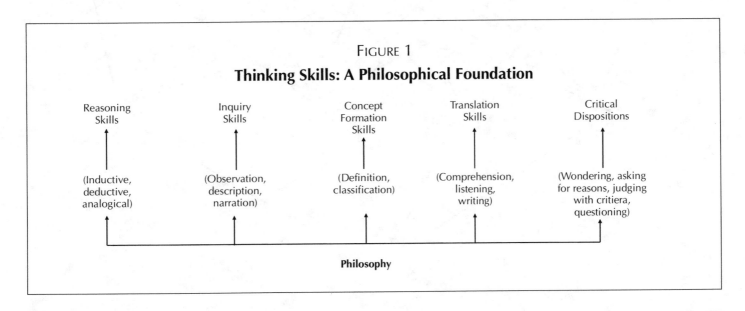

FIGURE 1

Thinking Skills: A Philosophical Foundation

Reasoning Skills	Inquiry Skills	Concept Formation Skills	Translation Skills	Critical Dispositions
(Inductive, deductive, analogical)	(Observation, description, narration)	(Definition, classification)	(Comprehension, listening, writing)	(Wondering, asking for reasons, judging with critiera, questioning)

Philosophy

The ambulance stops and backs up. Two people hurry out, scoop Kio up, put him in the ambulance and drive off. Tchaikovsky stands around nibbling at some grass. It all seems so strange, that an ambulance on its way to the hospital should cause an accident!

Gus, the narrator, is blind. Apparently she has never seen. How much of what she told us could she have perceived directly through her other senses? What could she have inferred? What could she not have observed? What might she have learned from the testimony of others? What might she have inferred from such testimony? How much of her story is description, and how much is explanation? These questions, reworded for young children, are the subject of lively classroom discussion. While the readers cannot perceive what Gus perceived, they can reenact her inferences. This is an example of how children in early elementary school can learn what inferring ("Figuring things out") is and practice it at the same time. Inferring, in turn, is fundamental to a child's ability to acquire meanings. And that ability, in turn, is essential to academic success.

Kio and Gus is one of six novels currently available as part of the Philosophy for Children curriculum; it emphasizes reasoning about nature, especially animals and the environ-

ment. Another K–4 program, *Pixie*, stresses language and reasoning, particularly analogical thinking. Children in grades 5–6 who read and discuss *Harry Stottlemeier's Discovery* learn the principles of reasoning. The remainder of the curriculum requires students to apply the tools of intellectual inquiry acquired in the first three programs to specific subject areas. The *Lisa* program—for grades 7–8—applies them to ethical reasoning. The other two programs are for secondary school students; *Suki* stresses the unification of thinking and writing, and *Mark* takes a reflective approach to the social sciences.

Thus, the early elementary portion of the Philosophy for Children curriculum provides children with a broad array of situations that challenge them to practice their reasoning and inquiry skills; the middle school portion introduces them to the principles underlying such practices; and the later portion enables them to apply their cognitive skills, now sharpened and better understood, to a variety of academic and life situations (see Figure 2). Whatever the grade level, Philosophy for Children is generally taught about two and one-quarter hours weekly for an entire year. It is not unusual

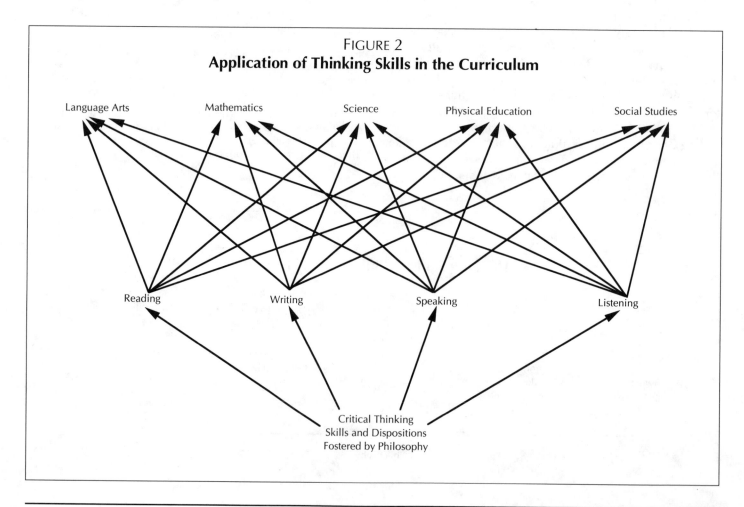

FIGURE 2
Application of Thinking Skills in the Curriculum

Language Arts Mathematics Science Physical Education Social Studies

Reading Writing Speaking Listening

Critical Thinking
Skills and Dispositions
Fostered by Philosophy

Philosophy for Children

Developer:	Matthew Lipman
Goal:	Improve children's reasoning abilities and judgment by having them think about thinking as they discuss concepts of importance to them.
Sample skills:	Drawing inferences, making analogies, forming hypotheses, classification.
Assumptions:	• Children are by nature interested in philosophical issues such as truth, fairness, and personal identity. • Children should learn to think for themselves, to explore alternatives to their own points of view, to consider evidence, to make careful distinctions, and to become aware of the objectives of the educational process.
Intended audience:	Children, kindergarten through high school.
Process:	Students read special novels with inquisitive children as characters, followed by teacher-led discussion using structured discussion plans, exercises, and games.
Time:	Three 40-minute periods per week.
Available from:	Institute for the Advancement of Philosophy for Children, Montclair State College, Upper Montclair, NJ 07043. Telephone: 201-893-4277.

for each program to extend over two years since much class time must be devoted to discussions and exercises.

Characters in the Philosophy for Children novels are shown discussing ideas. When, for example, the practice of taking turns comes up, they look for the underlying principle, which they may identify as *sharing* or *reciprocity.* When the question of what someone's "real name" is arises, they insist on examining what is meant by "real" as carefully as what is meant by "name." In other words, these fictional children display intellectual curiosity about concepts, principles, and ideals. The practice that elementary school children receive in discussing the general concepts philosophy deals with (such as *truth, justice, person, right,* and *education*) prepares them to understand the more specific concepts they will encounter in the secondary school curriculum. To students who are aware that truth is important but unsure just what truth is, the opportunity to discuss the concept is welcomed. Likewise, students who want to be treated "as persons" and who want to know how to treat others that way appreciate an opportunity to discuss what a person is.

Indeed, discussion of the readings is of crucial importance. Philosophical discussions differ from more conventional conversations in that the dialogues seek to conform to the rules of logic and inquiry as the children have learned them. Dialogues disciplined by logical considerations promote better thinking, because logic consists of the criteria through which better and worse thinking are distinguished. Philosophy for Children aims at producing scrupulous readers and reasonable discussants. It also aims at producing children disposed to wonder, inquire, deliberate, and specu-

late. Whether or not the children who do these things know the names of the skills they employ is relatively unimportant; what matters is that thinking becomes something they enjoy doing and do well.

Program Training and Effectiveness

Not every teacher is cut out to teach Philosophy for Children, including some teachers who, by other standards, are highly effective. Philosophical issues are generally problematic and have to be approached with an open mind and a readiness to admit that one doesn't know the answers. A teacher of philosophy must be self-effacing with regard to personal views and exercise patience with students' efforts to think for themselves. The teaching of philosophy demands mutual rather than unilateral respect.

Training in the use of the curriculum materials is indispensable for most teachers. On-site teacher training programs may extend as long as two years. More intensive workshops are also available, including a three-day introductory seminar, which covers one-half of a program.

Evidence supporting the effectiveness of Philosophy for Children has been derived from a series of Educational Testing Service (ETS)-conducted experiments, as far back as 1976, and involving as many as 5,000 students over a one-year period (see Iorio, Weinstein, and Martin 1984; Shipman 1983; Weinstein 1982). Results indicate that 5th, 6th, and 7th grade students in experimental classes gained 80 percent more in reasoning proficiency than did comparable students in control classes. There was also an academic spinoff: experimental students showed a 66 percent greater gain in reading and a 36 percent greater gain in mathematics than control students.

Since it is generally conceded that reasoning is the common ingredient in all academic pursuits, we may infer that improved reasoning ability is the most promising avenue to improved academic performance. Since there is little being done in the way of diagnosing children's reasoning deficiencies with consequent remediation, it's not surprising that student performance on reasoning tests seems to reach a plateau between 4th and 5th grades and remains there at least until college. Given simple but fundamental reasoning tasks, students tend to answer correctly fewer than 75 percent of the questions. Nevertheless, as the 1980–81 ETS experiment (Shipman 1983) demonstrated, a one-year intervention with Philosophy for Children can cut the experimental students' deficiency by a third. It would be wrong to infer that children's creativity is not stimulated by the emphasis on reasoning; a 1984 ETS experiment (Iorio et al. 1984) with 3rd graders showed that the control group's level of appropriate responses diminished over a year's time, while experimental students registered gains of 63 percent and 46 percent on the two test instruments.

A visit to a classroom where Philosophy for Children is being taught competently will reveal the exuberance with which children respond to the opportunity to discuss ideas that matter greatly to them and to think cooperatively in a community of inquiry. By promoting children's questioning and inquiry skills, Philosophy for Children enables them to discover the connections among the apparently fragmentary curriculums that make up the school day. In addition to this much-needed unifying function, the program sharpens the reasoning and concept-formation skills that students sorely need in later years. Indeed, there is no better way of ensuring that schools produce reasonable citizens than to introduce reasoning skills at the beginning of the child's education and to reinforce such skills throughout the remainder of the schooling process.

REFERENCES

Iorio, J., M. L. Weinstein, and J. F. Martin. (1984). "A Review of District 24's Philosophy for Children Program." *Thinking: The Journal of Philosophy for Children* 5, 2: 28–35.

Shipman, V. C. (1983). "Evaluation Replication of the Philosophy for Children Program—Final Report." *Thinking: The Journal of Philosophy for Children* 5, 1: 45–47.

Weinstein, M. L., and J. F. Martin. (1982). "Philosophy for Children and the Improvement of Thinking Skills in Queens, New York." *Thinking: The Journal of Philosophy for Children* 4, 2: 36.

9

The California Writing Project

Carol Booth Olson

The UCI Thinking/Writing Project integrates basic principles of learning theory, current research on the composing process, and practical strategies of the National Writing Project in a developmental approach to fostering critical thinking skills through writing. It is based on the premise that since writing is a complex, critical thinking activity, a training program consisting of lessons that gradually increase in intellectual difficulty and lead students through the levels of thinking will make the "what" in a paper more accessible and allow students to focus on the "how" of composing. Overall, helping students to become better thinkers will enable them to become better writers, and vice versa.

Project Activities and Services

The Thinking/Writing Project involves three main activities:

1. *Curriculum Development*. Teacher/Consultants from the project have created a 300-page notebook, *Thinking/Writing: Fostering Critical Thinking Skills Through Writing*, which contains:

• A rationale for why writing can and should be used as a tool for promoting cognitive growth.

• A thinking/writing taxonomy.

• A description of the sensory/descriptive, imaginative/narrative, practical/informative, and analytical/expository domains of writing.

• Thirty demonstration lessons (for primary, elementary, intermediate, high school, and college and for each level of Bloom's Taxonomy—knowledge, comprehension, application, analysis, synthesis, and evaluation) that provide explicit strategies for teaching each stage of the composing process—prewriting, precomposing, writing, sharing, revising, editing, and evaluation.

• Consideration of how the affective domain relates to the thinking/writing process.

• An explanation of how to create thinking/writing lessons.

• A summary of interviews with university faculty regarding their expectations of the thinking/writing abilities entering freshmen should possess.

• A thinking/writing bibliography.

2. *Teacher Training*. The Thinking/Writing Project offers a variety of staff development programs, which run from three hours to six days and can be tailored to specific teacher and student populations. A typical workshop combines one-third theory with two-thirds practice. Participants are introduced to the thinking/writing model and then experience a demonstration lesson by participating in each stage of the writing process. The project also has sample syllabi available for the following courses: Writing and Critical Thinking, Young Writers' Workshop, the UCI Thinking/Writing Project for Entering Freshmen, the Training of Trainers Project in Thinking and Writing, and Thinking/Writing/Computing.

3. *Evaluation*. In order to evaluate the project's impact on students, several instruments have been developed. The evaluation data and the evaluation design itself are available from the project.

Project Directors

The UCI Thinking/Writing Project is directed by Carol Booth Olson, Co-Director of the UCI Writing Project and Coordinator of Project Radius; it is co-directed by Owen Thomas, Professor of English, Linguistics, and Teacher Education; and John Hollowell, Campus Writing Director. Twenty-seven Teacher/Consultants from the UCI Writing Project, representing all grade levels, are involved in the curriculum development, teacher training, and evaluation components of the project.

For more information write: Carol Booth Olson, UCI Writing Project, Office of Teacher Education, University of California at Irvine, Irvine, CA 92717.

10
Future Problem Solving

Anne B. Crabbe

The trouble with our times is that the future is not what it used to be.

—Paul Valery

The Future Problem-Solving Program offers students a chance to compete with their peers as they learn to think creatively about solutions to predicted problems of the future. The program, which is based on the work of Alex Osborn and Sidney Parnes, was developed in 1974 by E. Paul Torrance, an internationally known expert in creativity. The plan has since expanded from a curricular unit for high school students to an international program that reaches an estimated 200,000 students each year.

Program Objectives

When Torrance created the Future Problem-Solving Program, his primary motives were to encourage youngsters to think creatively and to help them develop richer images of the future. In addition to using the logical and sequential parts of their intellects, Torrance wanted students to develop, exercise, and use their intuition and imagination.

Since its earliest days, the program's objectives, like its scope and audience, have grown. The Future Problem Solving Program now embraces several other objectives, which include helping students (1) increase their written and verbal communication skills, (2) become better team members, (3) develop and improve their research skills, (4) integrate a problem-solving process into their daily lives, and (5) improve their analytical and critical thinking skills. Evidence indicates that the program is fulfilling its objectives.

Program Participants

The regular program has three grade-level divisions: Juniors, grades 4–6; Intermediates, grades 7–9; and Seniors, grades 10–12. A noncompetitive Primary Division is open to students in any grade, although it is designed for students in grades K–3.

The program appeals primarily to gifted students, but the materials and processes are appropriate for children at all ability levels. In fact, Parnes has reported success in using the process with mentally retarded children.

Program Components

Practice Problems

Early in the school year, teams of four students receive a set of practice problems, which are the heart of the program. Each problem begins with a "fuzzy situation" and instructions for steps to be followed. The first practice problem directs students to complete the first four steps of the problem-solving process. The second and third problems add more steps, so that by the third problem students are negotiating the full process developed by Osborn (1963) and Parnes (1967). To complete the process, students must:

1. Research the general topic by reading books and magazines, reviewing audiovisual materials, interviewing experts, visiting agencies, or using other sources of information.

2. Brainstorm possible problems related to the fuzzy situation.

3. Identify from the above list one underlying problem they feel is central to the situation.

4. Brainstorm alternative solutions for the underlying problem as a focus.

5. Develop five criteria for evaluating their alternative solutions.

6. Rank their ten most promising alternative solutions according to all five criteria.

7. Total the scores to identify the best solution and write a few paragraphs describing it.

Team members record the results of these efforts in booklets, which they then mail to trained volunteers for review and scoring; the booklets are returned to the team with comments and suggestions. Teams that have submitted the best work on the third practice problem are invited to compete in State FPS Bowls.

Topics for the three practice problems, as well as the state and national problems, are voted on by the participating students. The topics they select are as varied as they are complex; for instance, ocean communities, robotics, nuclear war, prisons, lasers, nuclear waste, genetic engineering, the greenhouse effect, drunk driving, education, and the militarization and industrialization of space.

State FPS Bowls

Competitions are held each spring in the 40 states having sanctioned FPS Programs. Teams of students come together, most often on a college campus, to participate in competitive problem solving, social activities, and educational presentations. Winning teams, one from each grade-level division, advance to the International FPS Conference, where they represent their state.

International FPS Conference

A four-day international competition is held each June for the best problem-solving teams from around the world: the winners of the 40 State FPS Bowls, teams from the other 10 states (eligible through the Open Division, which is run by the National FPS Office), and teams from foreign countries. This international event offers a full schedule of activities, including competitive problem solving, as well as lots of social and educational experiences.

Scenario Writing Contest

The Scenario Writing Contest challenges students to develop their creative writing talents. Asked to project themselves 25 years into the future, students create short stories related to one or more of the FPS topics of the year. In the year-long program, students may submit three scenarios; each one is evaluated and returned to the author with suggestions for improvements, but only the third scenario is competitive. Or students may opt to submit just one scenario, for the competition. Many of the students who have participated in this activity have shown exceptional writing talent.

Future Problem Solving

Developer:	E. Paul Torrance (based on the work of Alex Osborn and Sidney Parnes)
Goals:	Develop creative problem-solving skills while learning about the future.
Sample skills:	Creative problem-solving process, verbal and written communication, teamwork, research techniques, critical and analytical thinking.
Assumptions:	• Problem-solving skills are necessary to function effectively. • In order to prepare for the future, young people need to consider issues related to the future. • Students can and should be taught to think more creatively.
Intended audience:	Regular program: grades 4–12. Primary division: K–3.
Process:	Students in teams of four follow a multiple-step problem-solving process: gathering information, brainstorming problems from a given situation, identifying the major underlying problem, brainstorming solutions, selecting criteria for evaluating solutions, and evaluating solutions to determine the best one.
Time:	Varies; one hour per week is typical.
Available from:	Future Problem Solving Program, St. Andrews College, Laurinburg, NC 28352.

Community Problem-Solving Division

In the Community Problem-Solving Division, students identify real problems in their own communities, use their problem-solving skills to create solutions to those problems, and implement their solutions. Being able to apply their problem-solving skills to real problems is exciting for students. Their efforts have ranged from stocking a children's library in Fiji to developing (and seeing enacted) a state law for disposing hazardous waste in Utah. Some very creative and very helpful solutions have become reality across the country, thanks to the students in this division. The winning teams at each of the three grade-level divisions receive invitations to participate in the International FPS Conference.

Primary Division

The Primary Division, begun in 1984, is a noncompetitive, instructional program for children in grades K–3. Just like the older students, these youngsters tackle three practice problems for which they create solutions. They send their work to trained evaluators who score their work and return it with suggestions for improvement.

* * *

The Future Problem-Solving Program is a novel teaching approach. Its procedures are formal, and teacher-coaches are required to receive specific training (either in training sessions or from written self-study materials), as are the student participants. After training, teams of students are registered with either the state or national program office. Funding, teacher schedules, parent involvement, transportation, advanced training, and so on are handled according to local district guidelines. The program encourages flexibility in these matters and is a refreshing departure from classroom instruction.

REFERENCES

Osborn, Alex F. (1963). Applied Imagination. 3rd ed. New York: Charles Scriber's Sons.
Parnes, Sidney. (1967). Creative Guidebook. New York: Charles Scriber's Sons.

11

Thinking Skills: Making a Choice

Anne H. Nardi and Charles E. Wales

A problem well stated is a problem half solved.
—Charles Kettering

Schools that plan to teach thinking skills must carefully consider both what to teach and how to teach it. The choice of what to teach should be based on the kind of skills graduates will be expected to use when they go to work in business, industry, or government. Whatever career is pursued, one skill crucially affects success after graduation: that skill is decision making. Other skills that support people's decision-making performance, such as creative thinking, critical thinking, and dialectical reasoning, should also be taught, but the process of decision making should be the focal point of what students learn.

What to Teach

Our research shows that the basic decision-making process that all people use includes five thinking operations. Successful decision makers:
- Define the Situation
- State the Goal
- Generate Ideas
- Prepare the Plan
- Take Action

Teachers can determine what to teach about each of these operations by carefully examining the thinking process a person uses when solving a simple problem such as, "What shall I wear today?" The following example shows what needs to be considered. The process begins with the situation.

Guided Design

Developer:	Charles E. Wales with Robert A. Stager and Anne H. Nardi
Goal:	To teach students how to use the process of decision making as they apply the subject matter they are learning.
Sample skills:	Identify and solve open-ended problems; think critically; generate, classify, and explore alternatives; find causes of problems; anticipate potential problems and consequences; and deal with issues of truth, fairness, and differing viewpoints.
Assumptions:	Knowledge is a means, not an end; a necessary but not a sufficient tool for success after graduation. It is the ability to apply knowledge in the process of decision making that is crucial.
Intended audience:	Elementary through college, as well as adult, learners.
Process:	The "complete" decision-making process is modeled step-by-step in slow motion, verbally or with printed instruction-feedback materials. Students use current subject matter as they make decisions. The teacher is a facilitator, mediator, and manager.
Time:	Varies. There should be regular practice in at least one course at every level each term.
Available from:	The Center for Guided Design, Engineering Sciences Building, West Virginia University, Morgantown, WV 26506-6101.

FIGURE 1

A 3rd Grade Problem:
The Car Wreck

Define the Situation

"I hope you have your thinking cap on today because we are going to be detectives. The case involves a car wreck. To find out more, *you'll have to ask me some questions.* By now you should know how to use the 5WH words to generate those questions. Ask away!"

Actors	"*Who* was in the car when it wrecked?"
Props	"*What* kind of car was involved? Were any other things involved?"
Action	"*What* happened before, during, and after the wreck?"
Scene	"*When* did the accident happen?" "*Where* did it happen?" "*What* is that area like?"
Cause	"*Why* did the wreck occur?"
Consequences	"*How* serious was the accident?"

"Those are good questions. Let me tell you what we know. The car was discovered by someone just like you who was riding a bike down a country road where there were both fields and woods. The car had gone off the road and into a ditch, but did not appear to be badly damaged. The engine was still warm and the driver's door was open, but no one was in sight. We don't know why the accident happened or how serious it might be for whoever was in the car."

State the Goal

"That's all we know. Remember—you are going to play detective. *What is the goal of a detective?*"

> "The goal of a detective is to find out what happened and to explain why it happened."

Generate Ideas

"Very good! Our goal is to find out what happened and to explain why it happened. To do that we must first guess why it happened. We must generate some ideas that *might* explain why the car went off the road. These ideas are educated guesses about what might have happened. You know these guesses are called hypotheses. What explanations can you offer? Why do you think this car might have wrecked? What happened to the occupants?"

> **Hypotheses**
>
> "The car had a flat tire and went off the road. Another car came along and took the driver, who was sick or hurt, to a hospital."
> "The car hit or just missed a deer or a cow and wrecked. The driver went for help."
> "A space ship landed in the road and the driver left with the ship."
> "This was the getaway car for a robber who was arrested and taken to jail."

Experiment/Prediction

"Those are very good hypotheses. Now we must generate the idea for an experiment that will test each hypothesis and predict what we expect to find."

Situation. In the first operation the decision maker uses questions based on the five "WH" words (Who, What, When, Where, Why, and How) to define the situation. What I wear today depends on the situation. Are we painting posters? Is it the day for school pictures? The answers to these questions affect each of the operations that follow.

Goal. Good decision makers know that stating the goal is a critical step. A goal not only sets the direction for all succeeding operations, but it is also used to judge both the worth of a plan as it is being prepared and the result of the actions. The goal of today's clothes might be merely to avoid what was worn yesterday, but it could also be to blend in or stand out, to influence others, or to feel very comfortable.

Ideas. Skilled decision makers search for all available options. In our example, the options include all the clothes and shoes a person owns or can borrow.

Plan. Even a relatively simple problem such as this requires a plan. Good decision makers develop a detailed plan for the chosen option. The plan includes a combination of questions, answers, and an evaluation. Some of the questions might be: Are the chosen clothes clean? Torn? Pressed? Do they fit? Do zippers work? Are buttons missing? Skilled decision makers answer these questions, develop a plan, and test that plan mentally to ensure that the goal will be achieved.

Action. The completed plan is translated into action: the decision maker gets dressed. As events unfold, revisions of the plan may, of course, be necessary. And when the day is over, the results are checked to be sure the goal was achieved: Was the outfit just right? This information is stored for use in future decision-making situations.

How to Teach

Because of the way schools are organized, educators tend to think in terms of subjects and some will want to treat decision making in that way. They may decide to offer "thinking" in a new, required course, just as they did with values clarification when it was a popular topic. Decision making cannot be treated that way because it is not just another subject, it is a *process.* Decision making transcends course and discipline boundaries; it relates different subject matter fields and makes them useful. That's why decision making must be directly and explicitly taught at all levels and integrated throughout the curriculum. Practice over time is a critical dimension—students need time to understand and internalize the process.

Our research shows that the process of decision making can be taught at any level of education, from kindergarten to graduate school, in any subject. The difference between these levels is not in the process being taught, but in the

sophistication learners bring to each operation and the subject matter base they draw upon. In kindergarten a problem might be how to get into a car safely. A 1st grader might be asked to consider the process involved in mailing a message to someone who lives far away. The result might be a flowchart that describes the process. In the 3rd grade, students might learn how these five decision-making operations are used to conduct an investigation of a car wreck. Part of the dialogue that might take place in that class is shown in Figure 1.

Decision making is a complex process so teachers must prepare appropriate materials before they enter the classroom. The first task is to select an open-ended problem situation that grows from the subject matter and calls for students to use some of the major concepts they are studying. The second task is to prepare an outline of the solution. Since there are no right answers in decision making, the teacher's outline may not include all of the responses the students will make. This is no problem as long as all of the operations are included in the teacher's outline. Without an outline, teachers are likely to omit operations from the process. Experienced decision makers appear to omit steps because much of their thinking is subconscious. It occurs so rapidly inside their heads that they are unaware of everything they consider. Thus, while experienced people actually use all five operations, they are likely to be poor models for those who want to learn the process. A carefully prepared outline helps to solve that problem.

In the first few primary grades, students should learn how to use the five operations both to change the consequences of a situation and to explain why a situation exists. The problems they face should be simple, the decision making verbal. The teacher should visibly record both the operations and the students' responses so that everyone can see the process. When their writing skills are sufficiently developed, students should do the recording, either on the chalkboard or at their seats.

Eventually, students should work in small groups and produce their own outlines. The focus on the process of decision making and the five operations provides an appropriate structure for collaborative learning activities. At the end of such an activity, if time permits, students may be asked to write a report on the class exercise or some parallel problem.

More complex problems that involve all of the operations should be introduced in later grades and used throughout the secondary program. A proven teaching strategy that provides the needed step-by-step guidance at any level is called *Guided Design* (Wales, Nardi, and Stager 1987). This approach is based on printed instruction-feedback pages prepared in advance by the teacher. These pages go beyond an outline and actually model the decision making of a fictitious group.

The first instruction in a set of *Guided Design* materials presents the problem situation and asks students to list the five "WH" questions they want answered. Students work in groups of five or six so they have to deal with the alternatives that come from different values and divergent viewpoints. When each group has agreed on its questions, the teacher checks the work to be sure it goes in an appropriate direction. If the response is reasonable, the teacher gives each student a feedback page that includes a list of the questions that might have been asked and some of the needed information. Alternately, the students may be asked to get the answers from their textbook, other people, or the library.

After the students consider a new viewpoint, they move on to the next instruction, which asks them to state the goal they hope to achieve. An example of that instruction is shown in Figure 2. In this secondary school module Sherlock Holmes and Dr. Watson are conducting an investigation that they hope will explain why a young lady's electric light suddenly went out. When the students complete their goal statement the teacher gives each person the next page, which includes both the feedback and the new instruction shown in Figure 3. The students' new task is to *Generate Ideas*, to generate hypotheses that might explain why the light went out. Their responses might include a burned-out bulb, a lightning strike, an intruder, or . . . . After the most likely hypothesis is selected, the experiment that will confirm or deny it is planned.

FIGURE 2
A Sample Guided Design Instruction

Instruction 2   STATE THE GOAL

Holmes stroked his chin and paced as he contemplated what the young woman told him. Was she telling the truth or was she lying? Why would she lie? Holmes' thinking was interrupted by Watson who said, "You did the right thing my dear, coming here. I'm sure we can get your light back on."

"Eventually I hope to do that, Watson, but that's not my goal at the moment."

What is the great detective's goal?

This pattern continues as the students think their way through the complete decision-making process. As they work, they learn how to think critically, draw inferences, devise analogies, explore alternatives, and make value judgments. Students also learn the crucial role that facts and concepts play in decision making and why everyone must continue to learn throughout life.

These are important gains, but perhaps the most significant reasons to integrate subject matter and decision making are (1) that students gain a renewed respect for facts and concepts, and (2) that students' motivation to learn and the amount they remember increases. Information is no longer just something to be remembered until the next test, but one of the tools that can be used to solve present and future problems. The potential gain was clearly

---

FIGURE 3
A Sample Guided Design Page

Feedback 2   GENERATE IDEAS

"My goal," Holmes said, "is the goal of every researcher, my goal is to '*explain*' something by finding a cause-and-effect relationship."

> Successful decision makers know there are two roles they might play: Researcher or Practitioner.
>
> The *Practitioner* wants to change the consequences of the situation. If the problem is darkness, the practitioner wants the opposite, the mirror image of that, the goal is to have light. Watson plays that role here.
>
> The *Researcher* wants to answer the why question. If the problem is that we don't know why the light went out, the researcher's goal is the mirror image of that, to find a cause-and-effect relationship that *explains* why it went out. That's Holmes' goal.

Instruction 3.1   GENERATE IDEAS

"Very good, Holmes," Watson said, "but I'd still like to get the light back on for this young lady."
"In due time, Watson. But first we must generate some hypotheses, we must make some educated guesses as to why the light might have disappeared."
If you were working with Holmes and Watson, *what hypotheses would you suggest?*

demonstrated by one research study that compared the performance of college students during the five years before and the five years after a two-semester "thinking" course was added during the freshman year (Wales 1979). The number of students who graduated increased by 32 percent and the grade point average at graduation increased by 25 percent. Could similar gains be made at your school? We won't know until schools begin to teach the process of decision making.

REFERENCES

Wales, C. E., A. H. Nardi, and R. A. Stager. (1987). *Thinking Skills: Making A Choice.* Morgantown: West Virginia University Center for Guided Design.

Wales, C. E. (February 1979). "Does How You Teach Make A Difference?" *Engineering Education* 69, 5: 394–398.

12
Odyssey:
A Curriculum for Thinking

Elena Dworkin Wright

*O*dyssey: A Curriculum for Thinking combines knowledge from current cognitive research with the methods of direct instruction. The overall goal of the program, which is intended for regular heterogeneously grouped classes in elementary and middle schools, is to enhance students' ability to perform a wide variety of intellectually demanding tasks. These include careful observation and classification, deductive and inductive reasoning, the precise use of language, the inferential use of information, hypothesis generation and testing, problem solving, inventiveness, and decision making.

Some lessons concentrate on increasing students' ability to use the knowledge they already have, whereas other lessons teach ways to acquire knowledge, including conventional classroom content. In either case, the lesson objectives are achieved through the application of such strategies as making classification hierarchies and generating alternative points of view. Applying these strategies across diverse problem domains is a critical part of internalizing the mental structures. These applications also reinforce transfer of the formal, abstract procedures to the sorts of personal and classroom challenges students will face beyond the program.

The *Odyssey* approach to the teaching of thinking is deliberately eclectic. Program materials reflect the more persuasive aspects of a number of theories of epistemology and cognitive development. Some lessons involve a Socratic inquiry approach, while others are based on a Piagetian-like analysis of cognitive activities. Still others emphasize exploration and discovery in a way reminiscent of Bruner. The overall design reflects the multi-faceted nature of intellectual performance and a focus on long-term effects that will transfer to content area subjects as well as activities beyond school.

Scope of Materials

Odyssey materials include five teacher guides, each with its own student book. The entire program is also available in blackline master format as Teacher Resource Books. The books are listed below in the recommended order of use.

1. *Foundations of Reasoning* introduces students to the processes of gathering, organizing, and interpreting information in systematic and critical ways. The processes introduced lead to analyzing and synthesizing information that students then use to formulate and verify hypotheses.

2. *Understanding Language* extends analytical skills to the domain of vocabulary. Just as the *Foundations of Reasoning* lessons helped students learn to analyze and describe objects in terms of configurations and characteristics, these lessons help students learn to analyze and describe dimensions of meaning and the impact of written text. This analysis and description involves choice, organization, and sequencing of words, sentences, and paragraphs.

3. In *Problem Solving*, students learn to visualize problems with the help of drawings, graphs, diagrams, tables, simulation, and enactment. They also learn systematic use of trial and error and how to extract the clues from a problem statement.

4. *Decision Making* begins with activities designed to create an awareness of the opportunities for decisions and their importance every day. Students learn to predict logical outcomes of alternatives and to gather and sort information for relevance, consistency, and credibility. Ultimately, students learn to use a preference analysis strategy and to weight dimensions of complex decision situations.

5. *Inventive Thinking* introduces the concept of design and teaches three strategies for understanding a design:

description, comparison, and experimentation. Students evaluate, improve, and invent designs. They also learn to apply the three strategies to more abstract designs involving procedures and theories.

Lesson Design

Each of the lessons has four sections:

1. RATIONALE—why the lesson is included in the course.

2. OBJECTIVES—what the lesson is intended to accomplish. Examples are:

- To increase skills in spatial orientation.
- To make students aware of the power of a strategic approach to problem solving.
- To introduce the relationships of contradiction and implication.
- To teach the rules of antonymy.
- To show the importance of both negative and positive instances in testing hypotheses.
- To introduce a systematic procedure for choosing among options whose preferability differs along several dimensions.
- To teach a general strategy for analyzing any design.

3. TARGET ABILITIES—a list of things the student should be able to do after completing the lesson, such as:

- Use a diagram to understand the meaning of a statement.
- Interpret a story from different characters' points of view.
- Identify pairs of assertions in which one assertion implies another.

- Test hypotheses about the essential characteristics of a class.
- Generate negative antonyms by adding or subtracting the appropriate prefix.
- Evaluate a procedure.
- Analyze a decision situation to determine what alternatives exist.

4. CLASSROOM PROCEDURE—a detailed plan for conducting classes, which teachers can use without additional training. Plans for conducting the class include suggested teacher questions and possible student responses. Teaching lessons model how to elicit information from students so that the students discover for themselves efficient and inefficient ways of using the strategies. Most important, the model lessons convey how to achieve active student participation throughout the course. The models use different teaching strategies to teach the processes of divergent, synthetic, and inductive thinking, as well as convergent, analytic, and deductive thinking.

* * *

The *Odyssey* materials were developed by Harvard University and Bolt Beranek and Newman Inc. for Venezuela's Project Intelligence.[1] *Odyssey* has been widely used in upper elementary and middle school classrooms. A 1981–82 evaluation found that gains made by classes using the experimental materials ranged from 1.15 (Cattell Test) to about 2 (Target Abilities Test) times those achieved by control classes.

Odyssey

Developers:	A team of educators and researchers from Harvard University, Bolt Beranek and Newman, Inc., and the Venezuelan Ministry of Education
Goal:	To teach a broad range of generalizable thinking skills.
Sample skills:	Careful observation, classification, precise use of language, analogical reasoning, hypothesis generation and testing; linear and tabular representation for problem solving; and evaluation of reliability, consistency, and relevance of data.
Assumptions:	• The performance of intellectually demanding tasks is influenced by various types of factors: abilities, strategies, knowledge, and attitudes. • Some, perhaps all, of these factors are modifiable. • The teaching approach should ensure student participation and intellectual involvement.
Intended audience:	Upper elementary through middle school students.
Process:	The emphasis is on discussion and student engagement in problem solving, reasoning, decision making, creative activities. Some paper-and-pencil exercises. Student introspection on own thought processes.
Time:	Three to four 30-minute lessons per week.
Available from:	Charlesbridge Publishing, 85 Main Street, Watertown, MA 02172.

NOTE

[1]For further details about Project Intelligence, see the Project's *Final Report* (Harvard University 1983); Adams 1984; Nickerson, Herrnstein, de Sanchez, and Swets 1986; and Nickerson, Perkins, and Smith 1985.

REFERENCES

Adams, M. J. (Winter 1984). "Project Intelligence." *Human Intelligence International Newsletter.* 8.

Harvard University. (October 1983). *Project Intelligence: The Development of Procedures to Enhance Thinking Skills. Final Report.* Submitted to the Minister for the Development of Human Intelligence, Republic of Venezuela.

Nickerson, R. S., R. J. Herrnstein, M. de Sanchez, and J. A. Swets. (November 1986). "Teaching Thinking Skills." *Journal of the American Psychological Association* 41, 11.

Nickerson, R. S., D. Perkins, and E. E. Smith. (1985). *Teaching Thinking.* Hillsdale, N.J.: Lawrence Erlbaum.

13
Learning to Learn

Marcia Heiman

The pleasures arising from thinking and learning will make us think and learn all the more.

—Aristotle

Learning to Learn (LTL) is a system of critical thinking skills that students apply directly to their work in academic courses. It was originally designed for use with educationally disadvantaged college students. Externally validated studies have shown that LTL results in significant, long-term improvements in academic performance across the curriculum and retention in school for college students reading as low as the 6th grade level. As a result of these studies, LTL has been approved for national dissemination by the U.S. Department of Education's Joint Dissemination Review Panel.

LTL has recently been adapted for use in junior and senior high schools.

History and Theory

Learning to Learn has a 20-year history of research and practice. Its genesis was in the work of a group of researchers at the University of Michigan in the 1960s. This group attempted to identify critical thinking skills common to successful learners by asking good students to talk aloud their thinking while they were engaged in a variety of academic tasks. The group found that successful learners could "program" their learning, breaking up large tasks and complex ideas into components; engage in a covert dialogue with author or lecturer, reading or listening for confirmation; devise informal means of obtaining ongoing feedback in their learning progress; and focus on instructional objectives, directing their learning toward those objectives.

The group theorized that variations of these skills are fundamental to all learning, both academic and non-academic. For example, the act of crossing a street involves aspects of these skills: one looks for feedback, engages in a covert dialogue about the possibilities of crossing against the light, breaks up the task into parts, and has a goal—getting across the street. These skills, however, are generally not explicitly developed, or the transfer demonstrated, when children come to school. Emphasis on memorizing facts and answering the teacher's, rather than their own, questions reinforces students' sense that "book learning" is somehow fundamentally different from other kinds of learning. Learning to Learn bridges the gap between students' out-of-school learning skills and those needed for school. The developers of the system believe that it is effective because it teaches students to harness skills they have long been using in informal learning situations.

LTL vs. Study Skills

Since LTL applies a set of strategies directly to academic work, it has a superficial relation to traditional "study skills," such as outlining or time management. However, when students stop actively using most study skills, they stop benefiting from them. In contrast, after students master LTL, they can stop overtly using the skills and still perform well academically; the process of learning how to learn becomes externalized. All of the LTL skills are taught in relation to each other, and to the four basic learning principles mentioned above. Students become more active learners because they continually generate questions about their work—increasingly more complex questions that reflect the field under study. Learning becomes a kind of game in which students "play" with the material, devising their own strategies for learning material from different academic disciplines.

Objectives

LTL is initially presented to students as separate but interrelated skills related to identifiable objectives. As students use the system, LTL becomes less a set of discrete "techniques" than variations on means of question generating and talking aloud the thinking process.

LTL is taught in three stages—input, organization, and output—and includes both general and subject-specific skill areas. Students who fully implement the system achieve the following objectives:

Input Stage

1. *Generating questions from lecture notes.* Using notes taken in class or discussion groups, students create questions that are increasingly like the ones the instructor will include on examinations.

2. *Reading to answer questions I: Nontechnical textbooks.* Students learn to read to answer their own questions, break up chapters into learning units, and assess their mastery of chapter content.

3. *Reading to answer questions II: Reading without headings and subheadings.* Students learn to adjust the comprehensiveness of their questions relative to each course and its instructional objectives.

4. *Reading as problem solving.* Students learn to direct their reading toward finding solutions to mathematically based problems, to discriminate textual information that facilitates problem solving, and to assess their short- and long-term mastery of the material.

5. *Reading graphs, tables, and diagrams.* Students generate questions about illustrations, translate the illustrations into a series of statements, and use imaginary data to draw variations of the illustrations.

6. *Reading for examples.* Students learn to identify examples of general principles and ideas in their textbooks and use their own examples to construct definitions of these terms.

7. *Developing editing checklists.* Students learn to edit their own grammatical writing errors rather than completing textbook exercises. Students build and use their own error checklists. A similar exercise helps students find idiosyncratic math errors.

Organization Stage

1. *Flowcharting.* Given complex assignments, such as research papers or biology laboratory reports, students construct flowcharts to sequence their work activities.

2. *Question charts.* Given two or more items that can be compared and contrasted, students construct question charts. They compare items with respect to questions generated from notes and readings, and insert key words (indicating answers to questions) in the charts.

3. *Scheduling.* Students perform weekly homework analysis. Using an LTL Task Checklist, they convert assignments into a series of small tasks.

Output Stage

1. *Writing to answer questions.* Students learn to write papers as a series of answers to student-generated questions, rather than following rigid outline formats.

2. *Systematic problem solving.* Given math-based problems, students use step-by-step procedures for working through the problems. They solve problems by answering a series of questions.

3. *Analyzing exams.* Students examine and categorize the types of questions asked on their midterms; they modify their questions accordingly for the remainder of the term.

4. *Writing mock exams.* Students generate and take mock exams prior to the official, in-class exams. Given short-answer or essay questions, students write brief, keyword diagrams, outlining their answers.

As students work, they learn to recognize two basic skills: generating questions and breaking down complex ideas and tasks into manageable elements. Their learning becomes more goal-directed, and they are able to assess their own progress. They come to see the skills as tools that become automatic and are integral to learning. In addition, they begin to see the relationships between the kinds of learning that occur in school and out of school.

Instructional Settings

Learning to Learn is incorporated directly into content-area classrooms of junior and senior high schools. For example, a 9th grade social studies teacher might give a brief lecture on the main points of a chapter in the textbook, and ask students to take notes and then generate questions from those notes. The questions might then form the basis of discussions or more complex question building, or provide direction for students in reading the chapter itself. In chemistry class, students might work in pairs, using systematic problem-solving methods on assigned problems; in English, students might use individually derived checklists to edit their grammatical errors in writing.

On the senior high school level, Learning to Learn instruction is reinforced through a year-long course in which students apply the skills to all their content area courses. LTL is generally offered for credit in psychology and includes related readings on the psychology of learning. Students taking the course come to understand the skills in terms of the learning principles they derive from, and they become

Learning to Learn

Developers:	Marcia Heiman and Joshua Slomianko
Goals:	To improve students' academic performance in content areas across the curriculum; and to improve students' skills in reasoning, reading, writing, and listening.
Sample Skills:	Generating questions from notes, books, handouts; constructing information maps and flowcharts; reading for examples; reading to solve problems; using an editing checklist for math problem solving and written composition; systematic problem solving.
Assumptions:	All successful learning has the following elements. The learner is: • Generating questions, raising and testing hypotheses. • Breaking down complex tasks and ideas into manageable components. • Devising informal feedback mechanisms to assess progress toward goals. • Directed toward achieving specific goals.
Intended audience:	Junior and senior high school students.
Process:	In junior and senior high school, content area teachers incorporate LTL activities into classroom and homework assignments. In senior high, students take a year-long course in which they adapt the LTL skills to all their content area courses, learn the principles underlying LTL, and devise LTL exercises based on these principles.
Time:	No extra time when LTL is part of classroom instruction since the method helps students master the content material in an efficient way. A year-long course at senior high level.
Available from:	Learning to Learn, Inc., 28 Penniman Rd., Allston, MA 02134

more independent learners, able to readily adjust the LTL skills to their future content courses.

Anticipated Results

Schools fully adopting the Learning to Learn system can anticipate several positive effects. These include:

• Improved student motivation, reflected by higher student attendance and retention in school through graduation.
• Improved student performance in academic courses.
• Higher scores on basic skills test in the areas of reading, writing, and listening.
• Increased rates of student admission to post-secondary institutions.

14

Creative Problem Solving

Sidney J. Parnes

It appears that some people have experiences that develop their facility in intellectual processes associated with creativity and intelligence. Research seems to demonstrate that we can design educational programs for many of these experiences, rather than merely waiting and hoping for them to happen.

—Sidney J. Parnes

Perceptual, emotional, and cultural blocks to creative thinking are demonstrated and discussed in Creative Problem Solving (CPS). Perceptual blocks include matters such as difficulty in isolating problems, difficulty in narrowing problems, inability to define or isolate attributes, and failure to use all the senses in observing. Cultural and emotional blocks are evidenced by conformity; overemphasis on competition or cooperation; excessive faith in reason or logic; fear of mistakes, failure, or looking foolish; self-satisfaction; perfectionism; negative outlooks; and reliance on authority.

Early in the course, students are taught the deferred-judgment principle (artificially separating imaginative from judicial thinking in each of the steps) as applied to individual thinking and group brainstorming. Deferred judgment allows students more freedom to apply other techniques that are introduced. Students are taught to use their imagination first and judge afterwards.

Within the freewheeling atmosphere that the principle of deferred judgment provides, students learn to look at issues from a variety of viewpoints. When considering other uses for a piece of paper, for example, students are taught to look at each attribute of paper—its whiteness, its four corners, its straight edges, and so on. Each of these attributes then suggests a number of possible uses.

Checklist procedures are encouraged, such as Osborn's checklist of idea-spurring questions. In this procedure stu-

dents are taught to analyze problems by asking questions, such as: How might we simplify? What combinations might be used? What adaptations might be made?

Forced relationship techniques are also applied in the course. For example, students produce a list of tentative solutions to a problem. Each of these ideas is then related to each of the other ideas on the list in order to force new combinations. Sometimes a somewhat ridiculous idea is used as a starting point. By associating the idea with the problem, a series of associations is produced that often leads to a solution for the problem.

The course emphasizes the importance of taking notes (recording ideas at all times, rather than just when trying to solve problems), setting deadlines and quotas for producing ideas, and allotting time for deliberate idea production.

Informal procedures are also used throughout the course. Students are placed in small groups to provide practice in collaboration, and are given opportunities to lead these groups.

Problem-Solving Practice

Students are provided many opportunities to practice solving problems, with emphasis given to problems from their personal lives and studies. They are taught to sense problems, challenges, and opportunities, and to effectively define them for creative attack.

During problem analysis, students are taught to list every fact that could conceivably relate to the problem. They then apply their judgments to select the most important data. Next, students list the longest possible group of questions and sources of additional data that might help solve the problem; they then return to the process of selecting the most important questions and sources of data. This alternating procedure continues throughout the final stages of evaluating and presenting ideas.

Creative Problem Solving (CPS)

Developer:	Sidney J. Parnes (based on the work of Alex F. Osborn)
Goals:	Develop abilities and attitudes necessary for creative learning, problem sensing, and problem solving.
Sample skills:	Setting goals and objectives; sensing problems, challenges, and opportunities; searching out data; defining and analyzing problems; generating ideas; discerning criteria for effective evaluating; developing and implementing solutions; developing feedback systems; planning and gaining acceptance; anticipating new challenges from actions taken.
Assumptions:	• Creativity involves the *application* of knowledge, imagination, and judgment to learning, problem sensing, and problem solving. • Everyone has the capacity, at his or her own mental level, for using creative approaches to learning, problem sensing, and problem solving. • Continued practice in using these approaches leads to ever-increasing proficiency, whether the person is mentally retarded, average, or gifted. • CPS processes should be taught deliberately, both as general thinking skills and as applications to learning within all subject matter areas.
Intended audience:	Middle (especially for the gifted) and secondary levels (all). (Lower level materials based on CPS available from D.O.K. Publishers, Buffalo, N.Y.)
Process:	Students use activities sheets for practice exercises to strengthen CPS processes under direction of the teacher using an instructor's guidebook. This guidebook offers additional exercises, readings, films, and bibliographic sources. Alternatively, students do independent self- or group-study and practice with specially designed text. Transfer of learning is emphasized in all materials.
Time:	Flexible time patterns are suggested in the teacher's guide. Material is programmed for instructional blocks of approximately one hour. Programs are based on extensive research and field testing.
Available from:	Creative Education Foundation, 1050 Union Road, Buffalo, NY 14224.

Objectives

The major objectives of the Creative Problem Solving program are to assist students in developing:

1. Awareness of the importance of creative efforts—in learning, the professions, scientific and artistic pursuits, and personal living.

2. Motivation to use their creative potential.

3. Self-confidence in their creative abilities.

4. Heightened sensitivity to the problems that surround them—an attitude of "constructive discontent."

5. An open mind toward the ideas of others.

6. Greater curiosity—an awareness of the many challenges and opportunities in life.

7. Improved abilities associated with creativity, enabling them to:

• Sense problems, challenges, and opportunities.

• Observe, discover, and analyze relevant facts.

• See problems from different viewpoints and redefine them productively.

• Defer judgment and break away from habit-bound thinking.

• Discover new relationships.

• Use checklists to discover new ideas.

• Refine unusual ideas into useful ones.

• Evaluate the consequences of one's proposed actions—taking into account all relevant criteria.

• Develop and present ideas for maximum acceptability.

• Develop action plans and implement ideas and solutions.

• Check the effectiveness of actions and take corrective measures when advisable.

The teacher of any subject may wish to emphasize a particular mental ability or attitude, using sessions specially designed for the specific objectives listed above. The program covers all of the objectives while teaching a methodical yet creative approach to problem solving. It has been scientifically evaluated in numerous research investigations.

In one literature review, 20 of 22 research studies of the specific Osborn-Parnes CPS program showed consistent positive effects (Torrance 1972). Rose and Lin (1984) used a new statistical technique, meta-analysis, on the creativity research literature. This procedure compiles data from a wide range of studies. The study concluded, "The substantial impact of Osborn and Parnes' CPS on verbal creativity, combined with the conclusions from both Torrance's and Parnes and Brunelle's reviews, provide strong evidence to support the effectiveness of this program."

REFERENCES

Osborn, A. F. (1963). *Applied Imagination.* New York, N.Y.: Scribners.

Parnes, S.J.(1981). *The Magic of Your Mind.* Buffalo, N.Y.: Bearly Limited Publishers.

Torrance, E.P. (1972). "Can We Teach Children to Think Creatively?" *Journal of Creative Behavior* 6,2.

Rose, L.M., and Lin, M.T. (1984). "A Meta-Analysis of Long-Term Creativity Training Programs." *Journal of Creative Behavior* 18, 1.

15

The Junior Great Books Program of Interpretive Reading and Discussion

Howard Will

To say that all human thinking is essentially of two kinds—reasoning on the one hand, and narrative, descriptive, contemplative on the other—is to say only what every reader's experience will corroborate.

—William James

Since 1962, the Junior Great Books program of interpretive reading and discussion has given elementary and secondary school students the opportunity to discuss high-quality works of literature under the guidance of teachers and parents trained by the Great Books Foundation. The aim of the program is to provide all students with the experience of reading a text closely and purposefully in search of its meaning. In Junior Great Books, students read for full comprehension of a story—for ideas and content, not merely for plot. Such highly motivated reading is made possible through the *shared inquiry* method of preparation and discussion.

The Great Books Discussion Method

At the start of shared inquiry discussion, the leader poses an interpretive question, that is, an open-ended question about the meaning of the work the group has read. This opening question is one for which the leader does not yet have a satisfactory answer—a question that he or she is genuinely interested in exploring with the group.

As students begin to respond, the leader follows up by asking how their comments relate to the initial interpretive question, to other ideas put forward by the group, and to the text. Throughout shared inquiry, the leader provides guidance only by careful questioning, intended to broaden students' understanding of a subtle and complex piece of literature. Because the leader does not provide answers, participants are challenged to think for themselves. By trying out ideas and exchanging opinions, they build their own answers to the interpretive question under discussion, and develop their own ways of understanding the work.

Only serious literature can sustain the kind of thoughtful analysis practiced in shared inquiry discussion. A Junior Great Books selection is challenging not because of unusual vocabulary or advanced sentence structure, but because its texture of ideas and depth of characterization demand interpretation. Students must build upon their initial thoughts and reactions to piece together a coherent understanding of the whole work.

In addition to improving their reading comprehension, students in Junior Great Books gain repeated exposure to a sustained, orderly process of rational inquiry. As they work together to build their answers to the leader's questions, they develop self-respect, a heightened sense of responsibility for their own ideas, and an increasing openness to the ideas of others. Over time, students gain confidence in approaching original and challenging works of literature, and acquire the habits of independent reading and reflective thinking.

The Junior Great Books Curriculum

Although Junior Great Books focuses on higher-level reading and thinking skills, it is not a program exclusively for the gifted. The Great Books Foundation has developed new curriculum materials that will make the Junior Great Books program easier to carry out with students of varying reading ability.

The new Junior Great Books curriculum materials provide a schedule of activities that is followed, in its fundamentals, at every grade level of the program. Each unit of activities—approximately a week of language arts work—focuses on a single story in the Junior Great Books series. Work on a unit is built around two readings of the story, and discussion; for younger participants, the first reading is done orally by the teacher. Other activities are designed to prepare students to connect with the ideas and situations they are about to encounter in their reading; to help them become more aware of their reactions as they read, organize their ideas, and take useful notes; to lead students through the analysis of meaningful words and dense passages; and to guide them in synthesizing and exploring new ideas about the story through post-discussion writing.

Each activity in the new program is "story specific"—that is, designed in response to the interpretive problems and issues presented by a particular story. By maintaining an emphasis on interpretation and discussion, these activities preserve the unique, open-ended quality of the Junior Great Books experience.

The Junior Great Books Read-Aloud Program

In fall 1990, the Great Books Foundation will introduce the first of its Read-Aloud series for kindergarten through 2nd grade. This program will serve as a bridge to the Junior program by providing young children with an opportunity to share their thoughts about high-quality stories and poems. Like the Junior Great Books curriculum, the Read-Aloud program will offer children a variety of interpretive activities, including dictating their own questions and original stories in response to the selections, and holding discussions based on their own questions, dramatizations, and artwork. A distinctive feature of the Read-Aloud program is the role parents will play in complementing classroom work at home. Parents will do one of the readings of a selection, and guide their child through a simple, interpretive activity.

The Readings

Selections in all Great Books Foundation reading series have been carefully chosen for their ability to support in-depth preparation and discussion that will sustain student, as well as teacher, interest. Providing selections that have as much meaning for adults as for children helps ensure that discussion will be a collaborative effort in which all parties are genuinely involved in reaching a fuller understanding of a work. The Read-Aloud series and the Junior Great Books series for grades two through nine are collections of outstanding traditional and modern literature, including children's classics, folk and fairy tales, and modern short stories from cultures around the world. Introduction to Great Books (recommended for high school and junior college) includes short selections from great works of philosophy, political science, psychology, and economics, as well as classical drama and modern fiction.

Training for Teachers

In shared inquiry discussion, the experience and ability of the teacher is central to success. Leadership is not a passive role in which the teacher merely acts as "monitor" or "facilitator." The leader helps students explore, support, and develop insights that originate with them, and serves as a model of a person whose mind has been stimulated by an intellectual problem.

To help prepare teachers and school volunteers to be effective discussion leaders, the Foundation provides an intensive two-day, inservice training course. The Basic Leading Training Course is required for all leaders of Read-Aloud, Junior, and Introduction to Great Books groups. The Great Books Foundation conducts Basic Leader Training Courses in any district or school that has decided to adopt its programs. Foundation instructors train more than 20,000 leaders a year in more than 700 courses conducted coast-to-coast.

For additional information, please contact:
The Great Books Foundation
40 E. Huron Street
Chicago, Illinois 60611-2782
Telephone: 1-800-222-5870
In Illinois: 312-332-5870

Established in 1947, the Great Books Foundation is an independent, nonprofit, educational corporation.

16
Building Thinking Skills®

John D. Baker

The Midwest Publications Analytic and Critical Thinking Program offers a sequential plan for instruction in analysis skills at the elementary and secondary levels and critical thinking skills at the middle and high school levels. The analysis skills developed in the Building Thinking Skills® series prepares learners for the formal and informal logic concepts in the Critical Thinking series (see Figure 1). These supplementary activities are approached through use of the overhead projector and involvement of the students in cooperative and open learning exchanges.

Building Thinking Skills

This series provides supplementary activities for cognitive skill development and analytical reasoning instruction in a carefully sequenced instructional plan. A variety of thinking skills required for better academic performance have been organized into four basic types: similarity and difference, sequence, classification, and analogy.

Each skill is developed in figural and verbal form. Figural Similarities and differences take the form of visual discrimination, similarity, congruence, extrapolation (enlarging or reducing), and symmetry. Verbal similarities and differences include synonyms, antonyms, denotation, and connotation.

Figural sequences include arranging by size, color, marking, or shape. More elaborate versions include paths, rotations, folding, and reflection. Verbal sequences include degree of meaning, comprehending the meaning of transitive or negative statements, following sequential directions, putting statements in order of occurrence, recognizing cause and effect, and comprehending implicational statements.

Classification involves grouping by common characteristics. Figural classification allows the learner to practice observation and categorization skills regardless of vocabulary development. The learner uses graphics (Venn diagrams, branching diagrams, and matrices) to organize figural forms and later to organize words and ideas for clear comprehension. Verbal classification is primarily useful in learning and remembering new words and perceiving correct word relationships and inferences. A more complex form involves classifying concepts and abstract ideas, a form of classification commonly used in science and social studies curriculums.

Analogy involves relational thinking and drawing proper comparisons. Figural analogies give the learner concrete practice in relational and proportional reasoning. Verbal analogies involve the correct interpretation of word relationships. Analogies promote vocabulary development and test-taking skills. Analogous reasoning forms the basis for using and interpreting figurative language (simile, metaphor, and personification).

The *Primary Book* uses concrete manipulatives for hands-on figural activities and group discussion of analytic thinking strategies. These are followed by the use of paper/pencil/crayon drawings for visual verification of appropriate responses and teacher evaluation. It is recommended for primary grades or for older students who need to begin with concrete exercises.

Book 1 uses a vocabulary level of the first thousand words of functional reading and is recommended for middle elementary or secondary students with limited vocabularies.

Book 2 employs vocabulary not exceeding the second thousand words and is recommended for middle school or secondary students in need of vocabulary and concept development.

Book 3 Figural features complex figural and spatial perception exercises and is recommended for advanced middle school or high school students.

Book 3 Verbal uses vocabulary appropriate for junior high and high school students. It prepares students for formal logical thinking by introducing inferential statements using

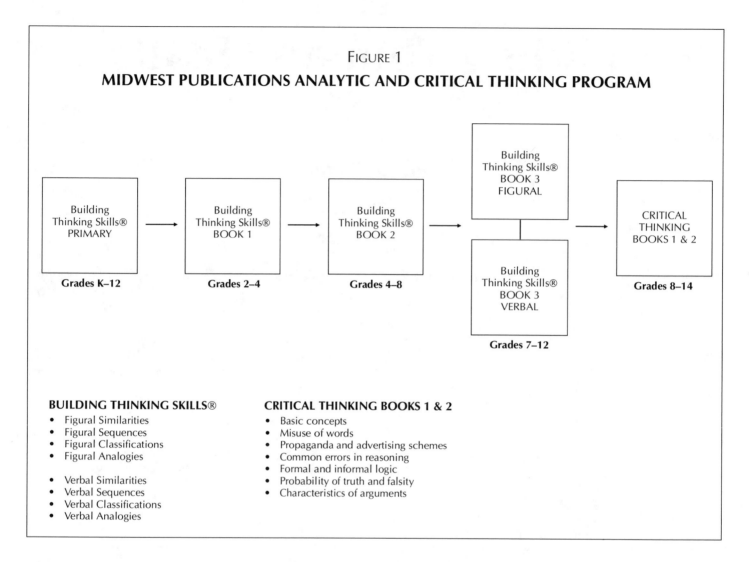

FIGURE 1
MIDWEST PUBLICATIONS ANALYTIC AND CRITICAL THINKING PROGRAM

Building Thinking Skills® PRIMARY — Grades K–12

Building Thinking Skills® BOOK 1 — Grades 2–4

Building Thinking Skills® BOOK 2 — Grades 4–8

Building Thinking Skills® BOOK 3 FIGURAL

Building Thinking Skills® BOOK 3 VERBAL — Grades 7–12

CRITICAL THINKING BOOKS 1 & 2 — Grades 8–14

BUILDING THINKING SKILLS®
- Figural Similarities
- Figural Sequences
- Figural Classifications
- Figural Analogies

- Verbal Similarities
- Verbal Sequences
- Verbal Classifications
- Verbal Analogies

CRITICAL THINKING BOOKS 1 & 2
- Basic concepts
- Misuse of words
- Propaganda and advertising schemes
- Common errors in reasoning
- Formal and informal logic
- Probability of truth and falsity
- Characteristics of arguments

the logic connectives "and," "or," "not," and "if . . . then." Since complex thinking skills activities are presented at a relatively low vocabulary level, the items are more difficult than the vocabulary level suggests.

The books contain paper-and-pencil exercises on thinking skills basic to content objectives. These exercises are followed by class discussions during which the thinking process is examined, clarified, and refined. Follow-up exercises provide practice and reinforcement.

Accompanying each book is a teacher's lesson plan manual that provides the rationale for teaching a skill, instruction dialogue for introducing and modeling the lesson, suggestions for group discussion, and detailed answers. Examples of skill application to many content areas and life experiences are also given.

Objective tests used to evaluate the Building Thinking Skills series include:
- Cognitive Abilities Test (Riverside Publishing)

- Developing Cognitive Abilities Test (American Testronics)
- Ross Test of Higher Cognitive Processes (for use with *Book 3 Verbal* only, Academic Therapy Publications).

Critical Thinking Series

This series (grades 8–14) is a course in formal and informal logic, written at the 5th grade reading level. The objectives are discernment in reading and listening and clarity in speaking and writing. Students consider a variety of situations by performing exercises that draw on newspaper articles, letters to editors, advice columns, commentaries, newscasts, advertisements, political speeches, everyday conversations, and government regulations. The material is relevant and appealing to young adults because the fundamental teaching approach is class discussion. The books make a good mini-course or semester course and can be taught in one or more disciplines. The texts explain:

- Basic concepts in critical thinking—discussions, disagreements, and arguments; general statements and counterexamples;
- Misuses of words—connotation and denotation, implications and inferences, and ambiguity;
- Inconsistent, contradictory, and misleading statements;
- Propaganda and advertising schemes;
- Logical reasoning fallacies;
- Formal logic with and without quantified statements;
- Probability of truth and falsity;
- Characteristics of arguments;
- Applied logic—debate and problem solving.

For the past 12 years, the Critical Thinking series has been used widely in junior high school gifted programs or as a supplement to high school or junior college English, social studies, and mathematics. The Watson-Glaser Test of Critical Thinking (published by the Psychological Corporation) or the Cornell Test of Critical Thinking (Midwest Publications) can be used to evaluate the series.

The Building Thinking Skills series has proven effective when used with students from all socioeconomic and ability levels. Teachers are impressed with the increase in thinking ability and content test scores and the visually apparent changes in their students' approaches to problem solving. Teachers also appreciate the fact that the series can be used without extensive teacher training. The lessons can be explored and extended on many levels of difficulty according to individual group needs and teacher time and ability. All activities are nongrade identifiable. Use of these materials has also served as an effective tool for mainstreaming non-English-speaking students and identifying gifted minority students.

Specific Test Results

Maria DeArmas, Dade County Schools, Room 534, 1450 N.E. 2nd Ave., Miami, FL 33132. Telephone: 305-376-1993.

Building Thinking Skills series—Results from the Dade County Office of Educational Accountability with underachieving, average-ability minority students in five-year "Team Project"; 26 schools participating (one classroom per school funded by district); Midwest activities sole extra treat-

ment; after two years, 26 percent of the students were selected for gifted programs.

- Stanford Achievement Test; grades 2–3, 800+ students; pre- and post-test results showed improvement significant to the .0001 level.
- Peabody Picture Vocabulary Test; grades 2–3, 800+ students; pre- and post-test results showed improvement significant to the .0001 level.

(Copies of the official Dade County detailed test results may be obtained by telephoning Midwest Publications, 800-458-4849.)

Sylvia Autry, Principal, Poplar Springs Elementary, 4101 27th Ave., Meridian, MS 39305. Telephone: 601-482-0123.

Building Thinking Skills series—Results of the pilot program were so impressive (95 percent of all students tested at or above grade level) that the series has been instituted as part of the regular curriculum at all grade levels except kindergarten.

- Stanford Achievement Test; grade 2, all students (90), 78 percent in top quartile, 18 percent in second quartile, 0 percent in bottom quartile (Complete Bat Total); grade 4, all students (112), 64 percent in top quartile, 31 percent in second quartile, 0 percent in bottom quartile (Basic Bat Total).

Additional Thinking Skills Materials

Additional help for teachers and administrators can be found in the following books, which are available through Midwest Publications/Critical Thinking Press, P.O. Box 448, Pacific Grove, CA 93950 (Telephone: 800-458-4849):

- The Practitioners' Guide to Teaching Thinking Series (three books):
  - *Teaching Thinking: Issues and Approaches* by Robert Swartz and D. N. Perkins
  - *Evaluating Critical Thinking* by Stephen Norris and Robert Ennis
  - *Techniques for Teaching Thinking* by Arthur Costa and Lawrence Lowery
  - *Thinking and Learning: Matching Developmental Stages with Curriculum and Instruction* by Lawrence Lowery
- *Organizing Thinking (Graphic Organizers)* by Howard and Sandra Black

17

HOTS

Stanley Pogrow

The Higher-Order Thinking Skills (HOTS) program was designed specifically for at-risk students in Chapter 1 and Learning Disabilities (LD) programs in grades 4–7. The thinking activities replace all the supplemental remedial education for these students. For the fall of 1990, more than 800 schools in over 35 states adopted HOTS as either their Chapter 1 or LD program. HOTS has also started to be used with gifted students in grades K–1 and as a tool for early identification of minority gifted students in grades 1–2. HOTS is one of the few thinking skills programs that has been validated by the National Diffusion Network.

Results

The thinking activities in HOTS have been designed to produce gains in standardized test scores without supplemental remediation or content instruction. Indeed, HOTS students improve in reading and math at twice the rate of Chapter 1 students nationally. As the program has been refined, test scores have improved even more. Some sites are now reporting reading gains of more than five years' growth in the first year.

HOTS is a tremendously robust program. It can function within the real-world limitations of most schools with a high percentage of disadvantaged students. The program has been validated on a large scale, with populations as diverse as children of migrant workers, low-income rural families, and white-collar professionals. It has worked in school settings ranging from Barrio schools in Arizona and largely African-American urban schools in Detroit, to one-school rural districts and affluent suburbs. In the fall of 1990 HOTS has been adopted in 35 urban districts.

HOTS meets the new mandates of Chapter 1 to provide advanced skills and provides greater standardized test score gains. HOTS has demonstrated that a higher-order thinking approach can develop basic skills even while enhancing thinking skills. In addition, the same thinking activities can simultaneously produce large gains in both reading and math, eliminating the need for separate programs.

HOTS also turns students into sophisticated learners. In several schools, some Chapter 1 students were moved to gifted programs after one year in HOTS. Other HOTS sites have reported that Chapter 1 students outperformed gifted students. At one site, 36 of the Chapter 1 students made the honor roll. Another indicator of the growth of cognitive ability—as well as self-confidence—is the growth in the amount and sophistication of students' articulation.

Why is HOTS Successful?

Remedial students often have trouble retaining content after the 3rd grade. This is a symptom of a much larger problem—their inability to understand "understanding." They are unable to construct the types of relationships needed to retain content—or even to know that they are supposed to. They do not know how to work with the simplest ideas or to construct meaning around any of the more integrated content presented after the 3rd grade. Reteaching content makes this problem worse. The lack of content knowledge is not the problem—rather, it is students' lack of understanding of how to work with ideas.

This problem derives from a lack of adult conversation, either in the home or school, which models basic thinking processes. Indeed, in most cases, it appears that the students have never had an adult give them the opportunity to construct their own meaning about an idea, and then converse with an adult about their conclusions. Instead of helping students learn how to make inferences, many teachers assume that students already have internalized such skills and focus on judging their ideas.

HOTS is effective as a Chapter 1 program because it provides the type of conversations that model key thinking

Higher-Order Thinking Skills (HOTS)

Developer:	Stanley Pogrow (based on cognitive psychology theories of organization of information in the brain)
Goal:	Develop higher-order thinking skills to improve basic skill achievement, problem-solving ability, and social confidence.
Sample skills:	• Developing and testing strategies for the solution of problems. • Interpreting computer-generated feedback to determine quality of problem-solving strategy. • Integrating and synthesizing information from a variety of sources for the solutions to problems. • Generalizing information across content areas and computer environments.
Assumptions:	• Most compensatory students are really quite bright and should be challenged intellectually. • Compensatory students are unable to construct the types of relationships needed to retain content because they do not understand "understanding." • The key to improving problem-solving ability is to get students to internalize general thinking strategies.
Intended audience:	Chapter 1 and learning-disabled students in grades 4–7; gifted and near-gifted students in grades K–1.
Process:	The program uses computers, together with specially designed curricular materials and Socratic teaching strategies. A Socratic environment is developed by training teachers to probe student answers and act as coaches who guide students to construct and test their own understanding in solving problems posed by the teacher. The computers provide a continuous flow of information for the students to process as they develop strategies.
Time:	The program requires 35 minutes per day, four days a week, for two years. Gifted students may require less time.
Available from:	Stanley Pogrow, Room 109, College of Education, University of Arizona, Tucson, Arizona 85721. Telephone: 602-621-1305.

processes in a sufficiently intensive way to help students internalize an understanding of how to work with ideas. Students then spontaneously apply these processes to the learning of all content—the first time it is taught.

A Socratic General-Thinking Approach

Chapter 1 students' lack of understanding of how to work with ideas is so profound that it is impractical to try to solve it with thinking-in-content activities. (For example, in the HOTS program, it is usually four months before students understand the difference between guessing and using strategies, six months before they put reasons in their answers, and 8–11 months before they can articulate a change of strategy and the reasons for the change.) Putting such students who do not understand "understanding" into a thinking-in-content approach will ensure that they neither learn the content nor learn how to think. Instead, HOTS uses a general thinking approach to develop the concept of "understanding," with only occasional linkage to content.

The HOTS program requires 35 minutes per day, four days a week, for two years. The program uses computers, together with specially designed curricular materials and Socratic teaching strategies. A Socratic environment is developed by training teachers to probe student answers and act as coaches who guide students to construct and test their own understandings. (The training takes a week and is provided in small group settings around the country in the summer.)

The thinking conversations are specified in a detailed curriculum. The activities are designed to develop the thinking skills of (a) metacognition, (b) inference from context, (c) decontextualization, and (d) information synthesis. These thinking skills are critical to the learning of all content.

The Socratic conversations are conducted around computer-use activities. Computers are used because of their ability to enhance motivation and respond immediately to student's ideas. The feedback generated by the computer provides a continuous flow of information for the student to process, which leads to improvements in comprehension and problem solving.

A new approach to using computers, specifically designed for at-risk students and called "Learning Dramas," was developed for the HOTS program (see Pogrow 1991 and Pogrow 1990 a, b, c). Learning drama techniques are the opposite of computer-assisted instruction. Instead of using the software to teach concepts, learning dramas use the computer to allow students to test their ideas and strategies. The actual learning results from the conversation between student and teacher—not from the computer. The more sophisticated the conversation and the more skillful the teachers' probing and reactions to student answers, the greater the cognitive growth.

The thinking skills and strategies are not taught. They are discovered by the students and internalized as a result of using them consistently in interesting social settings. The students learn to think much as they learned to talk—by imitation and having adults react to their initial attempts.

HOTS curricular and pedagogical techniques can coexist with any classroom curriculum. The techniques develop the problem-solving skills students need to integrate and retain new content the first time it is taught. There are also occasional linkages to classroom content, wherein students enter questions and answers about content into the computer and generate quizzes and puzzles to be shared with the whole class.

Future Directions

Future plans are to continue to expand the use of HOTS with Chapter 1 students—particularly at the middle school level—and to extend general thinking techniques to middle school math. A follow-up "thinking in mathematics" course for middle school students is currently being developed. This two-year course will cover math objectives for grades 6–8. The course, however, will present mathematics in an innovative way. Students will infer most of the rules and will then apply them to problem-solving situations. The emphasis will be on a language-comprehension, problem-solving ap-

proach to mathematics. Research will be conducted to demonstrate (a) that students who are first provided with general thinking activities, such as those in HOTS, do better in sophisticated thinking-in-content curriculums and (b) that it is possible to design thinking skills approaches that increase the learning of specific content objectives.

REFERENCES

Pogrow, S. (1991). "Learning Dramas: An Alternative Curricular Approach to Using Computers with At-Risk Students." In *Developing Minds: Programs for Teaching Thinking*, edited by A.L. Costa.

Pogrow, S. (January 1990a). "Challenging At-Risk Students: Findings from the HOTS Program." *Phi Delta Kappan* 71, 5: 389–397.

Pogrow, S. (February 1990b). "A Socratic Approach to Using Computers With At-Risk Students." *Educational Leadership* 47, 5: 61–66.

Pogrow, S. (1990c). *HOTS: A Validated Thinking Skills Approach to Using Computers with At-Risk Students*. New York: Scholastic, Inc.

18

Tactics for Thinking: A Program for Initiating the Teaching of Thinking

Robert J. Marzano

The advantage of a bad memory is that one enjoys several times the same good things for the first time.
—Friedrich Nietzsche

Tactics for Thinking (Marzano and Arredondo 1986; Marzano and Paynter 1989) is a program that includes strategies for increasing competency in 22 cognitive skills (see figure 1). The 22 strategies within the program are arranged into three broad categories: learning-to-learn strategies, content thinking strategies, and reasoning strategies.

Learning to Learn

The tactics within the learning-to-learn section of the program provide students with strategies for regulating their own learning and processing information in a way that is personally meaningful and easily accessible. The tactic of Attention Control makes students aware of their responsibility to pay attention (even in situations in which they do not find it easy) and provides them with specific techniques for doing so. Similarly, the tactic of Power Thinking makes students aware of the need to monitor and control their attitudes about completing specific classroom tasks and provides techniques for doing so. The tactics of Deep Processing and Memory Frameworks help students use various aspects of imagery (e.g., mental pictures, physical sensations, and emotions) to integrate information into their existing knowledge base in such a way that it is easily retrieved and used.

Content Thinking

The content thinking tactics are designed to help students comprehend and more deeply process information presented by the teacher or the textbook. Tactics in this category deal with both declarative and procedural information. Declarative information can be characterized as a knowledge of what—concepts, principles, and various types of schema within a given content area. The tactics of Concept Attainment and Concept Development help students initially acquire and then ultimately make fine distinctions about important concepts. The Pattern Recognition tactic helps students organize and process principles as well as information that conforms to such organizational schemata as time sequences and causal networks.

Procedural information is more process oriented—it can be characterized as knowledge of how to. The tactic of Proceduralizing is designed to help students identify and articulate the important steps in content-related processes. In addition, it helps students set up a practice schedule so that they can develop the process under study until it becomes automatic to them.

Reasoning

The reasoning tactics are designed to help students use information in ways that expand and restructure their understanding of the content. For example, the Extrapolation tactic helps students understand how the abstractions underlying one piece of information also underlie another piece of information. The Evaluation of Evidence tactic helps students

---

FIGURE 1
Tactics for Thinking

Learning-to-Learn Strategies

Attention Control—Strengthens concentration and lengthens attention span.
Deep Processing—Raises memory potential and depth of information processing.
Memory Frameworks—Helps students recall key information.
Power Thinking—Cultivates better student attitudes toward their own capabilities.
Goal Setting—Helps students create a vision for their own success.
The Responsibility Frame—Boosts students' ability to learn independently.

Content Thinking Strategies

Concept Attainment—Introduces a method for understanding new concepts.
Concept Development—Provides a way to study new concepts in depth.
Pattern Recognition—Improves ability to organize and comprehend spoken or written information.
Macro-Pattern Recognition—Expands comprehension of large bodies of information.
Synthesizing—Teaches a method for integrating large amounts of new knowledge.
Proceduralizing—Shows students how to learn new skills.

Reasoning Strategies

Analogical Reasoning—Prepares students for aptitude tests and helps them see relationships.
Extrapolation—Helps students see relationships between information at an abstract level.
Evaluation of Evidence—Develops ability to analyze information for accuracy and relevance.
Examination of Value—Shows how to objectively analyze differing views on a controversial topic.
Decision Making—Helps students select from among alternatives.
Non-Linguistic Patterns—Identifies numeric, spatial, and recursive patterns.
Elaboration—Demonstrates how to infer from reading.
Solving Everyday Problems—Provides a framework for analytical problem solving.
Solving Academic Problems—Equips students with tactics for solving school-related problems.
Invention—Stimulates creative thinking and development of unique but meaningful products.

---

analyze information for its validity and relevancy. The Invention tactic helps students use information to create unique but meaningful products.

Implementation

The Tactics program is not meant to be used as a "pull-out" program. That is, the strategies are not designed to be taught in a separate course isolated from content. They should be taught and then used in a regular classroom situation to enhance students' learning of important content. At first the strategies must be cued by the teacher; once students become familiar with them, however, they are used as needed to enhance learning. For example, initially a teacher might begin a class by reminding students of the Attention Control tactic and guiding them through its use to increase their instructional focus. The teacher might then present a new concept using the Concept Attainment or Concept Development tactics. Finally, the teacher might help students see how the new concept relates to other concepts by guiding students through the Extrapolation tactic. When students have internalized the tactics, however, they then can use them without aid or cueing from the teacher. For example, a student might notice that she is not focused on the lesson and then use the Attention Control tactic to enhance her readiness for learning. As the teacher presents the lesson, the student might decide to use aspects of the Concept Development tactic to help her understand an important concept that has been presented. Finally, she might decide to use aspects of the Extrapolation tactic to make connections not explicit in the lesson with other information she has learned.

Ultimately, the Tactics program is a way for individual teachers, schools, or districts to begin exploring the teaching of thinking. In effect, it is not meant to be implemented as a complete program, since individual teachers, schools, or districts select those tactics that they find most useful for their particular content area or classrooms. Additionally, teachers are encouraged to adapt the strategies to meet their specific needs. For example, teachers who use the program commonly collapse aspects of the Concept Attainment tactic and the Concept Development tactic into a single strategy that guides students through the initial introduction of a concept to its mature development.

At a more formal level, some schools and districts embed selected tactics into their curriculum objectives. That is, they select specific tactics from the list of 22 to be taught at specific grade levels or in specific content areas. For example, Figure 2 shows eight tactics selected by a school: Attention Control, Deep Processing, Power Thinking, Concept Attainment, Pattern Recognition, Extrapolation, Evaluation of Evidence, and Everyday Problem Solving. The school has determined that Attention Control will be taught at the 2nd grade level as an aspect of classroom rules and procedures. Deep Processing will be taught at the 3rd grade level as part of language arts, and so on. In this way, various tactics are systematically introduced into the curriculum without burdening teachers or students.

The list in Figure 2 doesn't mean that tactics can't be taught prior to their designated times. For example, a 3rd grade teacher might decide to introduce Pattern Recognition as part of her reading class even though that tactic is not slated to be taught until the 4th grade. Specifying where selected tactics should be taught in the curriculum simply ensures that students will be introduced to them sometime in their school experience. Thus, teachers can safely know which tactics students have been exposed to and not waste valuable class time introducing those tactics. For example, knowing that Extrapolation has been taught at the 5th grade level as part of social studies instruction, the 6th grade science teacher can use the tactic without having to teach it. Of course, some review and reteaching might be necessary; however, with very little review the tactic can probably be used to help students better understand science content.

History and Program Evaluation

The Tactics program was developed at the Mid-continent Regional Educational Laboratory in Aurora, Colorado.

	FIGURE 2
Placement of Selected Tactics in Curriculum	
Tactic	**Grade Level/Content Area in which Tactic is Introduced**
Attention Control	2nd grade: classroom rules and procedures
Deep Processing	3rd grade: language arts
Power Thinking	3rd grade: classroom rules and procedures
Concept Attainment	3rd grade: science
Pattern Recognition	4th grade: reading
Extrapolation	5th grade: social studies
Evaluation of Evidence	6th grade: social studies
Everyday Problem Solving	7th grade: health

To construct a theoretical base for the program, the literature in cognitive psychology, philosophy, and self-efficacy was reviewed. From that review a theoretical framework was developed and reported in *Teaching Thinking: A Conceptual Framework* (Marzano and Hutchins 1985). Strategies were then developed (where none existed) or adapted from existing programs for the various areas of cognition important to learning suggested by the theoretical framework. These strategies were field-tested for their feasibility by over 100 classroom teachers. As a result of this "first-level testing," a number of strategies were dropped from the model because of their apparent lack of classroom utility. Other strategies were changed to reflect the formative evaluations by classroom teachers.

The strategies that remained were then field-tested a second time in four major sites, involving 77 teachers and more than 1,900 students. Data were gathered on the effects of the strategies on student performance, as perceived by both students and teachers. The results of that phase of field testing were published in *An Evaluation of the McREL Thinking Skills Program* (Marzano 1986). Since that time, a series of more rigorous experimental/control studies have been conducted on each of the strategies. Additionally, studies were conducted on the effects of the tactics strategies on standardized tests. The results of these studies were reported in the *Summary Report of Evaluations of the Tactics for Thinking Program* (Marzano 1989). Briefly, in this latter set

Tactics for Thinking

Developers:	R. J. Marzano, D. E. Arredondo, D. E. Paynter
Goal:	Infusing specific learning strategies into content area instruction.
Skills:	Learning-to-Learn Skills provide students with strategies to take responsibility for their own learning and communicate the need to do so. Content Thinking Skills provide students with strategies for understanding and processing content area information. Reasoning Skills provide students with strategies for processing information in more critical and creative ways.
Assumptions:	• The teaching of thinking should be overt, teacher-directed, and part of regular classroom instruction. • To a large extent, successful students have acquired the essential cognitive skills outside of regular classroom instruction. • The direct teaching of thinking within formal education will necessitate a change in or restructuring of curriculum, instruction, and assessment techniques.
Intended audience:	K–12.
Process:	Students are taught cognitive strategies selected by the teacher as appropriate for the content and students. The strategies are then used to learn classroom content more effectively and efficiently.
Time:	Each skill takes from 30 to 60 minutes to teach. Once taught, skills are used by teachers and students as necessary to enhance learning.
Available from:	Association for Supervision and Curriculum Development, 1250 N. Pitt Street, Alexandria, Virginia 22314-1403. Telephone: 703-549-9110.

of studies it was found that: (1) students perform better in the tactics when they receive explicit instruction in the tactics, and (2) instruction in the tactics has the greatest effect on the standardized test scores of students who are not performing well academically.

The first finding is not surprising, given that explicit attention to the various components of any new cognitive process being learned will generally increase proficiency in the process. The second finding is also not surprising if we assume that the students who are doing well academically probably are already proficient in the strategies within the Tactics program. In fact, they are probably using cognitive strategies of their own design (albeit similar to those in the Tactics program) that aid them in learning and using academic content. Low-achieving students usually have not developed their own learning strategies, so direct instruction in the Tactics gives them strategies similar to those that high-achieving students are already employing to learn and use content.

* * *

Tactics for Thinking is ultimately a place to start. It is simply a set of cognitive strategies to be taught by teachers and used by students to enhance their control over and facility with the learning process. Once a few selected tactics have been introduced by the teacher and internalized by students, teachers and students both move on to more complex, and more self-initiated, learning strategies.

REFERENCES

Marzano, R. J. (1986). *An Evaluation of the McREL Thinking Skills Program* (Technical Report). Aurora, Col.: Mid-continent Regional Educational Laboratory. ERIC Document Reproduction Service No. ED267907.

Marzano, R. J. (1989). *Summary Report of Evaluations of the Tactics for Thinking Program* (Technical Report). Alexandria, Va.: Association for Supervision and Curriculum Development.

Marzano, R. J., and D. E. Arredondo. (1986). *Tactics for Thinking: Teacher's Manual.* Alexandria, Va.: Association for Supervision and Curriculum Development.

Marzano, R. J., and C. L. Hutchins. (1985). *Thinking Skills: A Conceptual Framework.* Aurora, Col.: Mid-continent Regional Educational Laboratory.

Marzano, R. J., and D. E. Paynter. (1989). *Tactics for Thinking: Classroom Blackline Masters.* Alexandria, Va.: Association for Supervision and Curriculum Development.

19

Connections

Shari Tishman

Good thinking is a matter of making connections—and knowing what kinds of connections to try to make.
—David Perkins

Connections is a program that helps teachers infuse the teaching of thinking into the subjects and topics they regularly teach. The leading idea behind Connections is that teaching thinking need not be an "add-on" to an already overcrowded curriculum. There are already plenty of opportunities for higher-order thinking in existing school subjects. Connections provides a systematic way for teachers to restructure instruction so that students develop their critical and creative thinking abilities *while* deepening their understanding of content.

The Connections Approach

Connections takes a "natural problem type" approach to teaching thinking. This means that higher-order thinking is taught in the context of real problem situations in standard school subjects. Solving problems, making decisions, and gaining deep understanding are all examples of natural problem types. They are higher-order thinking "tasks" that naturally occur in a variety of contexts, in and out of school.

Connections reflects the belief that the challenge of natural problem types is best met by the use of thinking strategies. A thinking strategy is a constellation of thinking skills organized in a goal-directed way. In its present version, Connections teaches three thinking strategies to deal with three natural problem types: Decision Making, Deep Understanding, and Inventive Thinking.

The Connections materials do two important things. First, they help teachers identify thinking opportunities in the curriculum. Second, they help students learn the strategies in the context of topics teachers already teach.

How Do Connections Strategies Fit into the Curriculum?

There are many opportunities for strategic thinking in most school subjects. Consider understanding. Gaining deep understanding is a thinking task that students encounter in virtually all subjects. How to understand fractions? How to understand different types of governments? The structure of a poem? How a microscope works? The rules of grammar? While the information relevant to the understanding task varies from topic to topic, the basic structure of the problem remains the same—*how* to achieve deep understanding. The Connections Understanding Strategy teaches students a step-by-step way of looking at all sides of the object of understanding in order to "unpack" its deeper meanings.

Or consider decision making. Students encounter many decision points both in and out of school. In their day-to-day lives they must decide how to spend their time, what to believe, what to buy. In history, they are exposed to decisions historical figures have made; in reading, they encounter the decisions of fictional characters. The Connections Decision Making Strategy helps students think through decision points such as these systematically, critically, and creatively.

These are just a sample of the many opportunities to use Connections strategies. Because the strategies are designed to address broad thinking *goals*, they can be used on a variety of topics, and can be infused into virtually any curriculum.

How Do the Strategies Work?

Connections strategies consist of several steps, organized somewhat like a sandwich. The inner steps, or "filling" of the strategies, consist of what are called "powerful questions." Each strategy has a different set of powerful questions. For example, the three powerful questions at the core of the Decision Making Strategy tell students exactly what to do in order to make a careful decision. The powerful questions in the Understanding Strategy ask students to examine the purposes and the features of something, in order to understand how, and how well, it works.

The outer steps of the strategies are the first step and the final two steps. These come before, and after, the powerful questions, and they are the same for every strategy, regardless of its goal. The reason they are always the same is that they are *mental management (metacognitive)* steps, and the skills involved in good mental management remain the same no matter which strategy is being used. These steps help students put themselves in the best frame of mind for thinking strategically, and help them integrate and summarize what they have learned. Figure 1 shows in more detail how the inner and outer steps work.

The Powerful Questions

These are at the core of each strategy. They lead students along an effective, creative, and thorough path toward the thinking goal in question. For example, the three powerful questions of the Decision Making Strategy are:

1. What are the options?

2. What are the complete reasons, pro and con, for the most promising options?

3. What is your careful choice?

The three powerful questions of the Understanding Strategy are:

1. What are the purposes of the object of understanding?

2. What are its features and the reasons connecting the features to the purposes?

3. How well does it work?

Each powerful question is accompanied by *standards* to help guide students' thinking. The standards are based on findings in current research that indicate where the typical shortcomings in thinking at each strategy step are likely to occur. For instance, research shows that when faced with a decision point, people tend to see it as an either/or choice and tend not to look beyond the obvious choices for creative or unusual options. Accordingly, the standards for the first powerful question in the Decision Making Strategy direct students to look for many options and press them to look beyond the obvious options for *creative, unusual,* and *hidden* options.

The point of the standards is to help students learn to take responsibility for their own thinking. The standards teach students to monitor and assess their own thinking as they proceed through each step of a strategy. In this way, students not only learn *which* thinking skills to use, they learn *how* to use them as well.

FIGURE 1

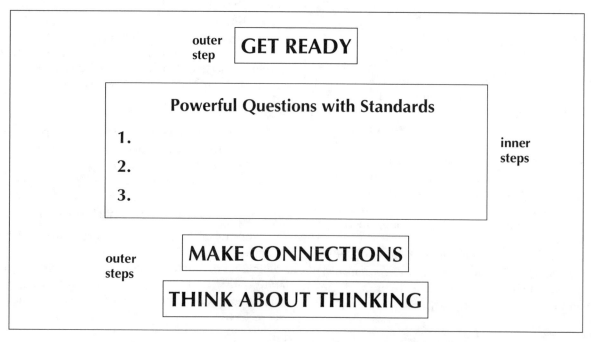

Connections Strategy Design

outer step **GET READY**

Powerful Questions with Standards

1.

2.

3.

inner steps

outer steps **MAKE CONNECTIONS**

THINK ABOUT THINKING

Connections

Developers:	David N. Perkins, Shari Tishman, and Jill Mirman Owen, with support from The Regional Laboratory for Educational Improvement of the Northeast and Islands
Goal:	To infuse the teaching of higher-order thinking strategies into the regular curriculum.
Sample skills:	Decision making, deep understanding, inventive thinking, and metacognition.
Assumptions:	The challenge of teaching higher-order thinking is effectively met by teaching thinking strategies to deal with "natural problem types" in the existing curriculum.
Intended audience:	Connections materials are written for grades 3-6. However, the strategies themselves are appropriate for any grade level.
Process:	Each strategy is presented in a 10-lesson module. Teachers infuse the strategies into their regular curriculum and students practice them in the context of regular subject matters.
Time:	Varies. Each lesson takes between 15 and 45 minutes. At least two Connections lessons should be taught each week. It takes about two months to complete a module.
Available from:	Jill Mirman, The Regional Lab, 290 S. Main Street, Andover, MA 01810. Telephone: 508-470-1080

The Mental Management Steps

No matter what its goal, effective strategic thinking has three important "generic" elements. These three elements correspond to the first step and last two steps of the Connections strategies.

The first step of every strategy is called Get Ready. It asks students to prepare themselves to do their best thinking by putting themselves in the appropriate frame of mind. Get Ready asks students to do three specific things. First, it asks them to *pause* and take a moment to focus their thoughts. This means taking a moment of quiet time to pull their "thinking energies" together. Second, it asks them to *remember* the difficulties they had last time they used the strategy and the improvements they might make in their use of it this time. For example, if last time they used the Decision Making Strategy they had difficulty finding lots of creative options, this time around they might remind themselves to use more brainstorming tricks. Third, Get Ready asks students to *imagine* the topic of the strategy in action. For example, if the decision making strategy is being used on a historical decision point, students try to visualize that moment in history—who is there, what the landscape looks like, and so on. Once they've done Get Ready, students plunge into the powerful questions.

The last two steps of all Connections strategies are: Make Connections and Think About Thinking. These steps come after students have finished answering the powerful questions. Make Connections is the "transfer" step. It asks students to connect the thinking they've done while using the strategy to other topics. The point of Make Connections is to help students integrate the new understanding they've gained during a particular strategy application into their general "web of knowledge." Make Connections guides them in generalizing about the new ideas they've had and helps them see how the topic they've worked on relates to other topics in the curriculum.

The Think About Thinking step concludes all Connections strategies. It is a metacognitive step that asks students to review their thinking process to see how well they've done. It helps them to identify what parts of their thinking went well, what parts were difficult, and how they can improve their use of the strategy next time. Think About Thinking is incorporated into the Get Ready step the next time around; when Get Ready asks students to remember improvements from last time, they recall the improvements they devised during the previous Think About Thinking step.

The overall message of the three "generic" strategy steps is that thinking is something one can control. By observing and evaluating their own thinking processes, students learn how to shape, direct, and chart their own course of intellectual progress.

Connections Materials

Connections currently consists of three modules: Decision Making, Understanding, and Inventive Thinking. Additional modules are in draft. Each module takes about two months to complete, presuming one to two lessons are taught per week. The modules consist of approximately ten lessons. In the first lesson, the basic strategy is introduced to students. The remainder of the lessons take anywhere from 15 to 45 minutes. The lesson formats are varied: students work on paper, in small groups, and as a whole class. When considering lesson times it is important to remember that Connections lessons do not really take time away from the curriculum because they're used on topics *that students are already studying.*

The bulk of Connections materials are mainly for teachers. A strategy poster is provided for students; the rest of the materials help teachers identify opportunities to infuse the strategy in their regular lessons and guide them through the infusion process. Included in the teacher materials are:

1. Straightforward explanations of each strategy,
2. Plenty of concrete examples of how the strategies work in the classroom,
3. Classroom lesson guides,
4. Guides for assessing student performance, and
5. Troubleshooting guides for trouble spots.

20

Talents Unlimited

Deborah E. Hobbs and Carol L. Schlichter

Far out thinking is a means to an end—To him whose elastic and vigorous thought keeps pace with the sun, the day is a perpetual morning.

—Henry David Thoreau

Picture this . . . 25 first graders cluster excitedly around their teacher as she prepares to launch a balloon with a message attached. This launching ceremony is the product of an instructional activity in which children use planning skills to apply concepts they have learned in a science unit on air.

The final step of their launch plan calls for the identification of problems that could inhibit the success of their project. One problem cited by this group of six-year-olds is that their balloon might not lift off because the message might be too heavy.

The balloon is launched and 25 children and their teacher watch it bobble across the ground. Instead of being dejected, one child looks up at her teacher and says, "Well, we were right. Now we'll have to use our productive thinking talent and think of ways to solve this problem." The teacher smiles at her TALENTS kids as she guides them in using their productive thinking talent to generate many, varied, and unusual strategies to solve the problem of the "unlaunchable" balloon.

This bright-eyed six-year-old and her classmates are TALENTS kids in Mobile, Alabama. They have been instructed in a thinking skills model called TALENTS UN-LIMITED (TU), which was originally researched and developed in the Mobile County Public School System from 1971–1974 under the Elementary and Secondary Education Act of 1965 Title III grant. This model, which has been disseminated throughout the world since 1974 as an exemplary educational program of the National Diffusion Net-

work, attributes its great popularity to the fact that TALENTS UNLIMITED is a thinking skills model that works.

Theoretical Base

Based on Calvin Taylor's (1967) theory of a multiple talent approach to teaching, TALENTS UNLIMITED aims at helping teachers give students six ways to express their smarts: productive thinking, communication, forecasting, decision making, planning, and the traditional academic talent. It is Taylor's belief that if children in a heterogeneously mixed classroom are given six ways to be smart, 9 out of 10 children will experience success in at least one way (Taylor 1968).

Underlying the multiple talent approach is the belief that people have abilities or talents in a variety of areas not measured by traditional school tests. Research on multiple intelligences attests to the power of training for enhancing, and fostering, positive feelings about self.

TALENTS UNLIMITED Project Objectives

In the original research project, the research team developed a three-faceted multiple talent model that included the following components: (1) training teachers to recognize and nurture students' multiple abilities; (2) developing materials to support the integration of the talent processes into regular classroom instruction; and (3) evaluating student performance.

In the dissemination of the model, two additional objectives have been added: providing technical assistance for implementation and providing training for trainers. Through the dissemination process, the project staff has discovered that the real growth in the teaching of the TALENTS UN-LIMITED model occurs when a teacher first begins working with children; the initial inservice workshop for teachers is only their academic beginning.

From its inception, the TU project was intended to focus on teacher training, since the teacher was perceived to be the key person in developing student talent. In the TU inservice model, teachers develop skills in writing and critiquing talent activities, in implementing and evaluating talent instruction with students, and in evaluating student response to instructional activities. Teachers receive structured observational feedback and use both peer feedback and self-evaluation techniques.

The TALENTS UNLIMITED inservice model was originally designed as a competency-based training program for the development of the knowledge, skills, and attitudes necessary to implement the multiple talent approach to teaching. A hierarchy of skills was identified to guide the implementation and evaluation of training activities. Four major categories of activities and strategies are employed in the training: (1) input sessions on multiple talent theory and talent skills definitions; (2) modeling and demonstration; (3) classroom practice sessions; and (4) one-to-one and small-group planning sessions. These four categories of training activities demonstrate the emphasis on coaching teachers in the use of new concepts and strategies in talent development (Schlichter 1986a).

Initial Research

In 1971 four experimental and four control schools, matched for socioeconomic level and racial composition and representative of the highly diverse population of Mobile County, were used in the experimental research design. Thirty-seven classroom teachers from grades 1 through 6, representing a cross-section of the teaching population of Mobile County, were trained and then participated as "talents" teachers for the entire three years of the research project. The students in both the experimental and control schools represented a wide range of intellectual ability and achievement. Each was pre- and post-tested in the following: (1) Torrance Tests of Creative Thinking, (2) Coopersmith Self-Esteem Inventory, (3) the Stanford Achievement Test, and (4) TALENTS UNLIMITED Criterion Referenced Tests (CRT). The CRT (1974) battery of 10 measures was developed by the project staff and a university research team to assess changes exhibited by students in each of the talent areas. These tests formed the basis for comparing students who participated in the TALENTS UNLIMITED program (experimentals) with students who did not participate (controls) in the project research and in many adoptions of TALENTS UNLIMITED (Chissom and McLean 1980).

In a technical report on the research findings of the TALENTS UNLIMITED program, Chissom and McLean (1980) discussed the impact of the use of the multiple talent model on student performance during the second and third years of the project. Measures of creativity and self-esteem were reported for the second year only.

Analyses comparing the experimental and control groups over the four dimensions of the Torrance tests (i.e., fluency, flexibility, originality, and elaboration) showed significant differences ($p < .05$), favoring the experimental group for all measures. Of the three grade levels (3–5) assessed on the Coopersmith Self-Esteem Inventory, experimental groups in grades 4 and 5 performed significantly better ($p < .05$) than the control groups; results at grade 3 were nonsignificant.

Notable differences between experimental and control groups occurred between the second and third years on measures of academic achievement and talent development. At the end of the second year (after approximately 14 months of talent training), results on the Stanford Achievement Test for grades 2 through 5 indicated great variation within the battery of subtests, as well as among the grade levels, for both experimental and control groups; no definite pattern in achievement was suggested by the data. At the end of the third year (after approximately 22 months of talent training), the results revealed significant achievement ($p < .05$) in favor of the talent group. Results on 14 of 35 subtests indicated significant improvement on only 3 of the subtests. Results from 18 subtests were not significant.

On the 10 measures of talent development (CRT) administered to grades 2 through 5, student performance at the end of the second year of the talent program revealed significant differences ($p < .05$) in gain scores in favor of the experimental group. Results on 18 of 40 measures favored the talent group, while only 1 measure of 40 favored the control group. Twenty-one of the measures were nonsignificant. CRT results at the end of the third year indicated that experimental students continued to exhibit significant gains over the control group.

Taylor (1968) postulated that 90 percent of the children in school can be identified as above average in at least one of the six talent areas, provided these talents have an opportunity to develop through the total instructional program. This hypothesis was tested in the TALENTS UNLIMITED research, and the findings on the CRT showed that approximately 85 percent of the students at each grade level (grades 1–6) achieved "above average" scores in at least one talent area (Chissom and McLean 1980), although the academic talent area was not one of these areas.

Validation and Diffusion

The success of the TALENTS UNLIMITED program in identifying and developing individual student talents resulted in national validation of the project by the Joint Dissemination Review Panel (JDRP) and its membership in the National Diffusion Network (NDN) as a developer-demonstrator project. This and other innovative programs are described in *Education in Action, 50 Ideas that Work* (Park 1978) and *Education Programs that Work* (1978), both published by the United States Office of Education.

In the past 15 years, TALENTS UNLIMITED has been adopted in 49 states, the U.S. Virgin Islands, Puerto Rico, and 15 foreign countries. In an impact study of this project, McLean and Chissom (1980) summarized experimental results from a sample of the adoption sites. The results support the validity of the TALENTS UNLIMITED program. All results favored the use of the multiple talent model, and most achieved statistical significance (p .05). Data were included from all talent areas, grades 1 through 6, and from all areas of the continental United States and Alaska. In the most recent reporting year, 1987–1988, TU had 1,364 adoptions (a school site implementing the model)—more than any NDN program that year.

The TALENTS UNLIMITED Model

In the TALENTS UNLIMITED Model, there are six talents—the academic or the base talent plus productive thinking, communication, forecasting, decision making, and planning. The academic talent is viewed as the traditional talent that children use to acquire information. This talent might be called the status quo talent because it focuses on acquisition of knowledge in its present state without manipulation. Memorization of information and rote practice of skills are typical behaviors associated with the academic talent, and the "one right answer" is characteristic of the instructional outcome.

Although one right answer might yield a good score on a school test, success in the real world of work demands a variety of abilities, including skills in generating numerous solutions to a problem, analyzing and evaluating alternatives, organizing and implementing plans of action, predicting causes and effects, and communicating ideas and feelings. Maintaining the status quo is incongruous in a world in which new information and technology are escalating at mind-boggling rates.

The TU model is designed to enhance the acquisition of basic knowledge and skills by training students to use their knowledge to create new solutions to problems. As students learn to use a variety of creative and critical thinking skills to help them accomplish the academic objectives in science,

math, language, social studies, and so on, they are also practicing the kinds of thinking that are highly related to success in the career world.

For example, a group of 4th graders is becoming familiar with the way interdependent members of the food chain cycle materials and energy through the ecosystem. The teacher asks how many of the students have heard of the artificial turf used on sports fields and in commercial landscapes. After briefly discussing their experiences with artificial turf and examining a sample, students are asked this question: *What if people were so pleased with the fact that this type of grass is always green, doesn't die, and doesn't have to be watered and mowed, that all grass in our neighborhood were replaced by artificial turf? Predict the many, varied effects of such a situation.*

The responses students offer reflect some scientific connection making; for example, they predict that cows and other animals would have to find something else that's green to eat and that erosion would be a major problem because artificial turf provides no roots to hold soil. In addition, some students make connections of another order by suggesting that people wouldn't enjoy going barefoot and that there wouldn't be the odor of freshly mown grass anymore. It is apparent from the responses of these 4th graders that TU teaching enhances the academic program.

As Figure 1 indicates, each talent has designated behaviors targeted for the teaching of certain thinking abilities. The productive thinking talent is the mind-stretching talent. Based on Torrance's definition of creative thinking (fluency, flexibility, originality, and elaboration), productive thinking asks students to think of many, varied, and unusual solutions to a problem and add to their ideas to make them better. There are many activities that encourage students to do this. For example, in a 2nd grade class lesson on the study of geometric shapes, each child is given a green triangle to transform; the children's ideas reveal that these seven-year-olds see where geometric shapes have a place in their world. In a 7th grade social studies class, midway in the study of the Revolutionary War, students are asked for many, varied, and unusual strategies that the patriots could have used to show their dislike of "taxation without representation"—other than tossing tea into Boston's harbor.

Decision making is defined by four observable student behaviors: (1) identification of many different alternatives to solving a problem; (2) the use of criteria to evaluate each alternative; (3) the selection of the best alternative; and (4) the formulation and statement of many different reasons for the final choice. The sequence of skills in this definition is notable, since it differs from the standard textbook order of skills in which the generation of solutions (alternatives) comes after the development of criteria. In TU, ideation is

FIGURE 1
The TALENTS UNLIMITED Model

Talent Areas	Definition	Sample Activity
Productive Thinking	To generate many, varied, and unusual ideas or solutions and to add detail to the ideas to improve them or make them more interesting.	Students working in a math unit on surveying and graphing are asked to think of a variety of unusual topics for a survey they will conduct and graph.
Decision Making	To outline, weigh, make final judgments, and defend a decision on the many alternatives to a problem.	Students who are preparing to order materials through the Scholastic Books campaign make final selections by considering such criteria as cost, interest, and reading level.
Planning	To design a means for implementing an idea by describing what is to be done, identifying the resources needed, outlining a sequence of steps to take, and pinpointing possible problems in the plan.	Students who are studying the unusual characteristics of slime mold are asked to design experiments to answer questions they have generated about the behavior of the mold.
Forecasting	To make a variety of predictions about the possible causes and/or effects of various phenomena.	Students who are conducting a parent poll on their school's dress code are encouraged to generate predictions about the possible causes for low returns on the survey.
Communication	To use and interpret both verbal and nonverbal forms of communication to express ideas, feelings, and needs to others.	In an attempt to describe the emotions of different groups of colonists, 5th graders studying the American Revolution role-play both Loyalists and Rebels as they hear a reading of the Declaration of Independence.
Academic	To develop a base of knowledge and/or skill about a topic or issue through acquisition of information and concepts.	Students read from a variety of resources to gain information about the impressionist period and then share the information in a discussion of a painting by Monet.

placed before evaluation.

For example, in a 3rd grade class students may decide on the best project for a culminating activity in their study of dinosaurs. Some of the questions they might ask themselves about the decision are: Do I have enough time? Is this something that I'm really interested in? Are the resources/materials available? Is this transportable?

The decision-making talent empowers children and teaches them that they *are* decision makers, but that with that right comes the responsibility of being accountable for their decisions and the consequences of those decisions.

The major goal of the planning talent is organizing for the implementation of a project or the solution of a problem. For example, a 1st grade class may plan their first field trip; a 6th grader may plan the presentation of a vocabulary word for a language arts class so that the class will never forget its meaning; or an 11th grader may plan the production of a model rocket for a class in aerospace studies. In each of these plans, the students must (1) state their objective; (2) identify the resources needed for implementation; (3) state and organize the steps or procedures for implementation; and (4) consider potential problems that might inhibit the implementation of the plan.

Forecasting is defined by the TALENTS UNLIMITED model as having one basic goal: the generation of many, varied predictions about a situation or event. The term "forecast" suggests looking ahead, imaging the future, and many questions that call for forecasting are stated in the future mode (e.g., What might happen if all plants were eliminated from earth? What could happen next in this story?). Cast in these ways, forecasting deals with the prediction of consequences, effects, or outcomes. But in spite of the future orientation of the talent name, the forecasting talent has been defined to include many, varied predictions about the causes of some event or situation (e.g., What caused the extinction of the dinosaur? Why was George Washington willing to become the leader of the Continental Army?). Forecasting, then, as defined by TALENTS UNLIMITED, includes prediction of both causes and effects.

Finally, in the communication talent students are taught to romance their language—the world's greatest discriminator. The goal of the communication talent is to increase students' facility in using verbal and nonverbal language to share their thoughts, ideas, and feelings; specifically, the objective is to increase the richness of expression and move students away from cliche-ridden expression. The

TALENTS UNLIMITED

Developer:	Carol L. Schlichter (based on the work of Calvin W. Taylor)
Goal:	To identify and nurture a broad range of student talent.
Sample skills:	Productive thinking (ideating); decision making (evaluating); planning (organizing); forecasting (predicting); communication (writing, speaking, acting)
Assumptions:	• People have abilities or talents in a variety of areas. • Training in the use of these thinking processes can enhance potential in various areas of talent and at the same time foster positive feelings about self. • Training in particular talent processes can be integrated with knowledge or content in any subject area. • The multiple talents are linked to success in the world of work.
Intended audience:	K–12, all ability levels.
Process:	Students are taught systematically the skills of the talent clusters: productive thinking, decision making, forecasting, planning, and communication; and talents instruction is integrated into general curriculum and into all subject areas by teachers who are trained in specific instructional strategies.
Time:	There should be at least two talents activities a week integrated into the content over a period of at least two years.
Available from:	TALENTS UNLIMITED, Dr. Deborah E. Hobbs, Director, Mobile County Public Schools, 1107 Arlington St., Mobile, AL 36605. Telephone: 205-690-8060.

specific definition of the communication talent includes six skills (see Figure 1). According to the operational definition developed by the TU project staff, each skill may function independently (i.e., each may be the focus of an entire activity) even though it is acknowledged that the skills are not mutually exclusive in general practice. For example, the describing words generated with the first skill may be used in the development of a descriptive paragraph as students focus on the fifth skill. On closer examination, the skills of communication suggest that there is an implied hierarchy of complexity, ranging from the generation of single words (skills one and two) to phrases (skill three) to a network of ideas (skills four, five, and six). The skills reflect the use of the cognitive and affective abilities, and skill six draws specifically on psychomotor ability.

An example of a skill functioning independently occurred in a TALENTS 3rd grade science class. The children were studying the butterfly, and upon examining a specimen the teacher had provided for the class, one of the students commented that the butterfly's wings were very fragile. So that children would have a better appreciation for the concept of "fragile," the teacher asked her students to think of other things in their world that are fragile like butterfly wings. One student said, "A butterfly's wings are fragile like my feelings."

The success of the TU model as a tool for teaching thinking is reflected in its attention to at least three factors that researchers associate with effective thinking skills instruction: (1) teaching students the procedural components of the thinking skills in the model; (2) integrating the teaching of thinking with all subject matter; and (3) providing regular guided practice of skills over a sustained period of time. Details on instructional strategies used at different grade levels and with students in regular classroom programs and special programs for the gifted are provided in other sources (Schlichter 1986b; Schlichter, Hobbs, and Crump 1988; Schlichter 1989).

Adoption and Implementation

In order for students to become "talents kids," an adoption of TALENTS UNLIMITED must occur. An adoption is the owning of the model through training and then implementation in the classroom, school site, or district. In order for a successful adoption of TALENTS UNLIMITED to occur, the following must be in place:

• A nucleus of teachers in the school must commit to a minimum of 12–18 hours of training and must have the attitude to work at implementing such an innovative program. These teachers should represent contiguous grades because successful implementation of TALENTS UNLIMITED is based on at least a two-year commitment to implementation.

• There must be commitment from the building instructional leader and the administration. This commitment means attending and participating in the teachers' inservice workshop or in one designed solely for administrators. In addition, the project's implementation should be monitored.

• There must be support in the central administrative office of the school district in which the adopting school resides.

• There must be enough financial support for the basic inservice workshop, follow-up to the workshop, technical assistance, and any materials or supplies that teachers need to aid implementation.

• There must be parental and community support.

The project staff has developed multiple strategies for assisting in the implementation and assuring longevity of the TALENTS UNLIMITED model at an adopting site.

* * *

TALENTS UNLIMITED is a process model for the teaching of critical and creative thinking. The activities are always tied to the curriculum, are enhancers to the academic program, and are highly motivational because students have an opportunity to shine and thereby feel good about themselves. Used with many diverse populations, TU serves as a model that enriches the learning experience for each population it serves—regular classroom, ESL, EMR, "learning differently" kids, and gifted students involved in independent research projects. Although the activities look like "just good teaching," they are essentially different from "just any interesting activity." In a TALENTS activity, the objective is the teaching of thinking. A TALENTS activity does more than offer learners the opportunity to perform; it challenges them to engage in and identify thinking tasks and to transfer their newfound knowledge to other areas. TALENTS UNLIMITED enhances the academic while teaching work and life-related skills. Thus, it prepares students for the basic of the future—thinking.

REFERENCES

Chissom, B. S., and McLean, J. E. (1980). *Talents Unlimited Program: Technical Report Summarizing Research Findings.* Mobile, Ala: Mobile County Public Schools. ERIC Document Reproduction Service No. ED 179 556

CRT. (1974). Criterion Referenced Tests of Talents. Mobile, Ala: Mobile County Public Schools.

Educational Programs That Work. (1978). 5th ed. Washington, D.C.: United States Office of Education.

McLean, J. E., and B. S. Chissom. (1980). *Talents Unlimited Program: Summary of Research Findings for 1979–1980.* Mobile, Ala.: Mobile County Public Schools. ERIC Document Reproduction Service No. ED 198 660

Park, J. S., ed. (1978). *Education in Action: 50 Ideas That Work.* Washington, D.C.: United States Department of Health, Education, and Welfare.

Schlichter, C. L. (1986a). "Talents Unlimited: An Inservice Education Model for Teaching Thinking Skills." *Gifted Child Quarterly* 30, 3: 119–123.

Schlichter, C. L. (1986b). "Talents Unlimited: Applying the Multiple Talent Approach in Mainstream and Gifted Programs. In *Systems and Models for Developing Programs for the Gifted and Talented,* edited by J. S. Renzulli. Mansfield Center, Conn.: Creative Learning Press, Inc.

Schlichter, C. L., D. Hobbs, and W. D. Crump. (April 1988). "Extending Talents Unlimited to Secondary Schools." *Educational Leadership* 45, 7: 36–40.

Schlichter, C. L. (April 1989). "More than a Passing Thought." *Teaching K–8* 19, 7: 55–57.

Taylor, C. W. (1967). "Questioning and Creating: A Model for Curriculum Reform. *Journal of Creative Behavior* 1, 1: 22–23.

Taylor, C. W. (December 1968). "Be Talent Developers as Well as Knowledge Dispensers." *Today's Education* 14, 8: 67–69.

21

Intelligence Applied: A Triarchic Program for Training Intellectual Skills

Robert J. Sternberg

The whole of science is nothing more than a refinement of everyday thinking.

—Albert Einstein

The triarchic program contains two basic elements for developing the intellectual skills of secondary and college-level students: a student's text, which contains narrative material and exercises for students to complete, and a teacher's guide, which contains material teachers can use to maximize the effectiveness of the program.

The Student's Text

At the heart of the triarchic program is the student's text, *Intelligence Applied: Understanding and Increasing Your Intellectual Skills*. The text is suitable for a semester or year-long course at the secondary or college level and is divided into five parts.

Part I: Background

Part I contains two chapters that provide a brief, but not cursory, introduction to the nature of intelligence and of attempts to train it.

Chapter 1: Views of Intelligence. The first chapter describes, at an elementary level, the major approaches to understanding intelligence: the definitional approach, the learning-theory approach, the psychometric approach, the Piagetian approach, and the cognitive approach. It also dis-

cusses other attempts at increasing intelligence. The goal of the chapter is to set the historical and theoretical stage for the introduction of the triarchic theory of intelligence, which underlies and motivates the training program. The text emphasizes that the conventional approaches to understanding intelligence are largely complementary, emphasizing as they do different aspects of intelligent thought and behavior. A comprehensive theory, and a training program built on this theory, would join the best elements of these theories, regardless of the particular experimental paradigms or methods that gave rise to the theories, and add to them the ingredients that are needed to construct a systematic and comprehensive theory that does justice to the full range of thought and behavior that constitutes intelligence. The triarchic theory will later be presented as a step in this direction.

In order to understand and appreciate the background of a program for training intellectual skills, we must understand not only early conceptions of how intelligence can be taught, but also contemporary examples. Three exemplary programs are described here—Feuerstein's Instrumental Enrichment, Lipman's Philosophy for Children, and Jones' Chicago Mastery Learning Program—in order to show the main features of existing programs and discuss how these programs are similar to and different from each other.

Chapter 2: The Triarchic Theory of Human Intelligence. This chapter introduces the triarchic theory of intelligence as an approach to understanding intelligence in terms of (a) the internal world of the individual (i.e., the cognitive mechanisms underlying intelligent performance), (b) the external world of the individual (i.e., the environmental contexts on which intelligence operates), and (c) the experience of the individual in the world (i.e., the interface between the internal and external worlds of the individual).

The first, componential part of the triarchic theory specifies three basic kinds of information-processing components:

• *metacomponents*, which are executive processes used to plan, monitor, and evaluate one's strategy for solving problems;

FIGURE 1

Main Elements of Triarchic Program for Training Intellectual Skills

TRAINING PROGRAM

Part I.   *Background*

    Chapter 1:   Views of Intelligence
    Chapter 2:   The Triarchic Theory of Human Intelligence

Part II.   *The Internal World of the Individual Components of Human Intelligence*

    Chapter 3:   Metacomponents (executive processes used to plan, monitor, and evaluate problem-solving performance).
    Chapter 4:   Performance Components (nonexecutive processes used to carry out the instructions of metacomponents).
    Chapter 5:   Knowledge-Acquisition Components (nonexecutive processes used to learn how to solve the problems controlled by metacomponents and solved by performance components).

Part III. *The Experience of the Individual: Facets of Human Intelligence*

    Chapter 6:   Coping with Novelty
    Chapter 7:   Automatizing Information Processing

Part IV. *The External World of the Individual: Functions of Human Intelligence*

    Chapter 8:   Practical Intelligence
        • Adaptation to environmental contexts
        • Shaping of environmental contexts
        • Selection of environmental contexts

Part V.   *Personality, Motivation, and Intelligence*

    Chapter 9:   Why Intelligent People Fail (Too Often)

TEACHER'S GUIDE

    1. Purpose of Chapter
    2. Chapter Outline
    3. Main Ideas
    4. Questions for Class Discussion
    5. Suggested Paper Topics
    6. Supplementary Activities
    7. Suggested Readings
    8. Suggested Time Allocation

• *performance components*, which are nonexecutive processes used to carry out the instructions of the metacomponents for solving problems; and

• *knowledge-acquisition components*, which are nonexecutive processes used to learn how to solve the problems in the first place.

The contextual part of the triarchic theory specifies the functions to which components are applied in coping with the external world. These functions are:

• adapting to existing environments, which involves changing yourself to better fit into these environments;

• shaping existing environments, which involves changing the environments in order to better fit these environments to yourself; and

• selection of new environments, which involves replacing one or more current environments with one or more new ones that seem to have more favorable characteristics.

The experiential aspect of the triarchic theory specifies the regions in the continuum of experience—from the totally unfamiliar to the thoroughly familiar—that most directly tap the components as they function "intelligently." There are two of these regions: (1) relative novelty and (2) automatization of information processing. Relative novelty refers to the region of experience in which a task or situation is fairly, but not totally, new. Adapting to the mores of a foreign country that you are visiting for the first time would be an example of relative novelty; you have some relevant experience to bring to bear on the situation, but not a great deal. Automatization of information processing refers to the transition between conscious, controlled information processing and subconscious, automatic information processing. Examples are learning to read or learning to drive. Initially, reading and driving are very deliberate, purposeful, and resource consuming. Eventually, though, reading and driving become essentially automatic, so that you scarcely think about *how* you do them while you do them; in fact, you can perform these "actions" without even consciously realizing that you are doing so.

The triarchic theory does not contradict most previous theories of intelligence; instead, it integrates some of their most critical aspects, while dispensing with aspects that are idiosyncratic or simply wrong. Its intent is to highlight what is right, not reveal what is wrong. The theory seeks to represent the best of previous theories, while incorporating new elements, including new elements of integration among the aspects of intelligence.

Part II: The Internal World of the Individual: Components of Human Intelligence

Part II consists of three chapters, one on each of the three kinds of information-processing components of intelligence: metacomponents, performance components, and knowledge-acquisition components.

Chapter 3: Metacomponents. This chapter specifies the metacomponents of intelligence and contains material that helps students develop skill in using these metacomponents. Each metacomponent section opens with some real-world examples of the metacomponent in action or inaction, and the consequences of this action or inaction. The introductory section illuminates the material that follows and shows how the metacomponents are important in everyday life, as well as in "academic" life.

The next section provides several tips on how to use the metacomponents more effectively. These tips provide concrete suggestions for improvement, rather than leaving the learner to figure out just what changes in thought or behavior might produce more effective intellectual functioning. A set of problems follows, each of which requires use of the metacomponential skill under consideration. Students are generally asked first to try to solve each problem on their own. They are then given the answer and shown how the metacomponent applies to the solution of the problem.

The metacomponents addressed are:

- defining the nature of a problem,
- selecting the components or steps needed to solve a problem,
- selecting a strategy for ordering the components of problem solving
- selecting a mental representation for information,
- allocating mental resources, and
- monitoring solutions.

The section on defining the nature of a problem is typical of the approach to each metacomponent. It opens with concrete examples of inadequate definitions of problems. Three suggestions are given for improving your definition of problems. The first is to reread or reconsider the question; often, a problem seems unsolvable simply because it has been misconstrued. The second suggestion is to redefine your goals; if an initial problem is not solvable, a more modest attempt to solve a series of subproblems can often lead to the whole solution or to at least a part of this solution. The third suggestion is to ask whether the defined goal is the true goal. In some instances, an alternative goal can be found, perhaps through a different method of attack on a different problem, that will yield results that are satisfactory, even though they are different from those originally sought.

Finally, three problems that involve the metacomponent of defining the problem are presented.

Chapter 4: Performance Components. The performance components of intelligence implement the plans that the metacomponents formulate. The number of performance components in an individual's repertoire is very large. Fortunately, for both theoretical and practical purposes, the number of performance components that is critical for intellectual performance is relatively small. The reason for this is that a few performance components crop up again and again in intellectual tasks. These general performance components are those that are of greatest interest from both a theoretical and a practical point of view.

Some of the most important performance components are:

- inferring relations between stimuli,
- applying previously inferred relations to new stimuli,
- mapping higher-order relations between relations, and
- comparing attributes of stimuli.

These are four of the six or so performance components that form the core of inductive reasoning tasks, such as analogies, series extrapolations, and classifications. Chapter 4 shows how to apply these and other performance components to a variety of different kinds of problems, from the academic to the practical.

The section opens with a practical example of an inference. The first major subsection details the kinds of verbal inferences most frequently encountered. Next, students are shown how inferences can serve either constructive or destructive purposes. Inferences are destructive when they reflect inferential fallacies. Nineteen kinds of inferential fallacies are described. Later problems build on the information contained in the inference section. After other components are introduced, problems that require exercise of the inference performance component are presented (e.g., verbal and nonverbal analogies, classifications, and series extrapolations). Later, more complex problems that require inference in more ecologically relevant settings are presented. For example, in one type of problem, students must infer which of two legal principles is relevant to solving a particular case. In a second type of problem, students must infer which of two principles for interpreting Rorschach Ink Blot protocols is relevant for making a diagnosis in a particular case. (Of course, imaginary principles are used in both the legal and clinical inference items, and students are informed of this fact.)

The goal in these problems, as in all the problems, is for students to use the various performance components in a wide variety of problems and to recognize when the various kinds of components need to be used, regardless of surface-structural differences between problem types that may mask the deep-structural similarities in the performance components of solution.

Chapter 5: Knowledge-Acquisition Components. This chapter deals with the topic of knowledge acquisition, in general, and of vocabulary acquisition, in particular. The training material is based on a theory of verbal comprehension which postulates that there are three basic ingredients involved in learning vocabulary from context:

• the processes used to figure out meanings of words from context;

• the kinds of information—or cues—to which these processes are applied; and

• textual variables that mediate how well the processes can be applied to the cues.

The three processes are those mentioned earlier: selective encoding, selective combination, and selective comparison. Selective encoding is used to decide what information in a passage is relevant for figuring out the meaning of an unknown word. Selective combination is used to put these informational cues together into a unified definition. Selective comparison is used to relate the new word and its definition to information you already have, both about words in particular and the world in general.

It is not enough, however, just to be able to draw upon these three processes. We have to apply them to the particular content of a given passage. We do this through the use of contextual cues of different kinds. For example, *setting cues* specify the time, place, or situation in which a given concept appears. *Class membership cues* specify a class of which the unknown concept is a member. *Value/affect cues* describe evaluative connotations associated with the concept. *Active-property cues* specify actions performed by or to the concept. These and other cues serve as "objects" for the knowledge-acquisition processes: They are the stuff to which the processes are applied so that the meanings of new words can be inferred.

It is not always equally easy to apply the processes of knowledge-acquisition to the contextual cues. The passages contain mediating variables that make application of the processes either easier or harder. For example, the distance of the cue from the unknown word is one such mediating variable. It is easier to apply the processes to the cues if the cues are in close proximity to the unknown word. A second mediating variable is the number of different contexts in which the word to be learned appears. It is easier to learn the meaning of the word if it appears in a few contexts. More than one context is needed to get a fix on the word's meaning, but too many contexts can be confusing and can actually impede learning the word's meaning.

Students are trained in all three aspects of the theory and are given concrete examples of each of the aspects of the

theory as they go along. The training is incremental: rather than learning the theory all at once, students learn bits at a time, and are asked to apply what they learn as they learn it.

Part III: The Experience of the Individual: Facets of Human Intelligence

The triarchic training program deals with both facets of intellectual experience that are proposed (by the triarchic theory) to relate the experience of the individual to the individual's intelligence: coping with novelty and the automatization of information processing.

Chapter 6: Coping with Novelty. This chapter extends the theory of the processes of knowledge acquisition to learning in unfamiliar domains. The chapter opens with an overview of alternative views of insight. It then quickly proceeds to the triarchic view of insight, according to which insights can involve one or more of the three processes of selective encoding, selective combination, and selective comparison. Selective encoding insights involve discerning between relevant and irrelevant information in unusual ways. Selective combination is important when someone has to put together clues. Selective comparison involves seeing analogies. As the processes are explained to the students, examples of insights involving these processes are given in order to concrete the processes, and in order to motivate the students to use the three processes of insight in their own thinking. Students are then given tips about how to use the insights in their own thinking.

Finally, several kinds of problems that challenge students to apply these three forms of insightful thinking are presented. They include:

• arithmetical/logical word problems,

• information-evaluation problems,

• mystery problems,

• conceptual projection problems (using limited information to predict future states of the world),

• novel analogies (like ordinary analogies, except that students must sometimes consider an altered state of the world), and

• scientific insight problems (practical and theoretical).

Chapter 7: Automatizing Information Processing. This chapter opens with a description of the difference between controlled and automatic information processing and discusses examples of each, as well as the relation between the two kinds of information processing. The chapter then proceeds to an explication of ten principles for expediting the automatization of processing. For example, one principle is that it helps to learn the task you wish to automatize under moderate speed stress. Another principle is that automatization is likely to be more rapid if you are able to devote your full attentional resources to the task at hand. Students are encouraged to apply these principles to their own information processing to facilitate its automatization.

Students are then presented with several relatively simple information processing tasks in which they can use the principle to speed automatization of their functioning. The first task, Letter Comparison, involves comparing pairs of letters and indicating whether they have the same name. The second task, Visual Search, involves determining whether a target letter appears in a subsequent string of letters. The third task, Digit-Symbol, is similar to a task that appears on many intelligence tests. Students are presented with an initial pairing of digits and symbols—for example, "∧, 1, (, 2, + 3, % 4." Students are then presented with a set of 120 symbols and must match digits to them as rapidly as possible. The fourth and last task is Complex Letter Scanning. This task is a more complex version of the Visual Search task. Students are initially presented with one to four target letters. They must indicate, for each problem, whether any of those letters appears in a two-dimensional array of letters. The two-dimensional array is unsystematic, so that students must scan their entire visual field in order to find the letters.

Part IV: The External World of the Individual: Functions of Human Intelligence

Part IV of the training program contains contains just a single chapter on practical intelligence. The chapter includes several kinds of material for the development of practical intellectual skills.

Chapter 8: Practical Intelligence. The chapter opens with four motivating vignettes and continues with a definition of practical intelligence: intelligence that operates on real-world contexts through efforts to achieve adaptation to, shaping of, and selection of real-world environments. It then proceeds to a discussion of alternative means that have been used to assess practical intelligence. There are then several kinds of exercises to develop practical aspects of intelligence. The first kind involves a behavioral checklist. Students rate on a scale of 1 to 9 the extent to which each of a set of behaviors characterizes their own behavior. The checklist contains a set of behaviors that can be used to measure three factors that laypersons and experts alike agree are central to intelligence: practical problem-solving ability, verbal ability, and social competence.

A second and quite different type of exercise involves decoding nonverbal cues. Students are shown two kinds of photographs: pictures of couples ostensibly involved in romantic relationships and pictures of pairs of workers, one of whom is the other's supervisor. For the first kind of photograph, the students' task is to guess which pictures represent genuine couples and which represent pairs of

individuals posing as though they were romantically involved. For the second kind of photograph, the students' task is to guess which of the two individuals is the other's supervisor. In each case, students are invited to try the task either with or without reading about the nonverbal cues that facilitate these decisions.

A third task involves reading a vignette of an everyday situation and selecting a course of action to pursue in that situation. One course of action stresses adapting to the environment, one stresses shaping the environment, and one stresses selecting another environment. Students are encouraged to ask themselves certain questions to help decide which course of action is most appropriate.

A fourth kind of exercise involves the display of tacit knowledge. Students are asked to put themselves in the roles of two individuals, a business manager and a professor of psychology. Their task is to answer a series of questions the way a successful executive or psychologist would. The questions assess a person's knowledge of what it takes to get ahead in a particular life course. The answer key provides the responses made by experts.

The last kind of exercise involves a series of situations calling for resolution of conflicts. Some of these situations involve interpersonal conflicts, some involve organizational conflicts, and some involve international conflicts. The students' task is to read each conflict and then rate the suitability of each of a series of possible modes of conflict resolution for its appropriateness for resolving each of the given conflicts.

The chapter closes with a description of the Janis-Mann balance sheet technique, which is a decision-making aid that is useful for people who need to make difficult decisions. The balance sheet takes into account favorable and unfavorable potential outcomes of a decision for both the person making the decision and others and weighs these outcomes in terms of their positivity or negativity, as well as in terms of their importance.

Part V: Personality, Motivation, and Intelligence

Chapter 9: Why Intelligent People Fail (Too Often). This final chapter discusses 20 impediments to the full realization of intelligence. Although these impediments are not, strictly speaking, intellectual, they interfere with the use of intelligence, and hence are quite relevant to a course for training intellectual skills. Each impediment is defined and discussed, and examples of each are given.

Teacher's Guide

The Teacher's Guide helps the teacher implement the triarchic program for training intellectual skills. It contains

Intelligence Applied

Developer:	Robert J. Sternberg
Goal:	To develop the intellectual skills of secondary and college-level students.
Sample skills:	• Using the metacomponents of intelligence (e.g.,defining nature of a problem, selecting steps needed to solve the problem, monitoring solutions).
	• Using the performance components of intelligence (e.g., inferring relations between stimuli, applying previously inferred relations to new stimuli, comparing attributes of stimuli).
	• Using the knowledge-acquisition components of intelligence (e.g., deciding what information in a passage is relevant for figuring out the meaning of a new word; putting cues together to form a definition).
Assumptions:	Intelligence can be understood in terms of (a) the internal world of the individual, (b) the external world of the individual, and (c) the experience of the individual in the world).
Intended audience:	Secondary and college-level students.
Process:	Combines class discussion, written exercises, papers, projects, quizzes, group work.
Time:	Two or three 40-minute periods per week for one school year.
Available from:	Harcourt Brace Jovanovich, College Division, 1250 Sixth Ave., San Diego, CA 92101. Telephone: 619-699-6238.

chapters that correspond to those in the student text and each chapter is divided into the following eight sections:

• *Purpose of Chapter*. This section simply describes what the chapter seeks to accomplish.

• *Chapter Outline*. This section outlines the chapter, using two levels of headings.

• *Main Ideas*. This section summarizes the main ideas of the chapter and varies widely in length, according to the subject and function of the particular chapter.

• *Questions for Class Discussion*. These questions are intended to help students better understand the material, primarily by helping them apply the material in formulating and evaluating answers to the questions themselves.

• *Suggested Paper Topics*. This section presents topics for papers. It is strongly recommended that teachers require at least several short papers during the term in order to stimulate thinking about the skills taught in the program.

• *Supplementary Activities*. These are projects that stu-

dents can undertake in order to improve their understanding and use of the content of the course.

• *Suggested Readings*. This annotated bibliography suggests readings relevant to the topic of each chapter. These readings are appropriate for both students and teachers. The readings are important; a comprehensive course will go beyond the main text to other related readings that reinforce and elaborate on points made in the main text.

• *Suggested Time Allocation*. This section suggests the amount of time that should be allocated to each chapter for both a year-long course and a semester course.

* * *

Intelligence Applied: Understanding and Increasing Your Intellectual Skills provides a new and, I hope, exciting option for the development of intellectual skills in secondary and college-level programs.

22

The Touchstones Project: Discussion Classes for Students of All Abilities

Geoffrey J. Comber, Nicholas Maistrellis, and Howard Zeiderman

Communication is a process of sharing experience till it becomes a common possession. It modifies the disposition of both parties who partake in it.

—John Dewey

Touchstones discussion classes are implemented as a required weekly class. The class lasts 30–45 minutes and is for students of all ability and skill levels from grades 6–12. The skills of listening, cooperating, questioning, and thinking for oneself, which emerge in the Touchstones discussion format, transfer readily to regular classes. In addition, motivated students become more reflective, and passive students become motivated. Touchstones discussion groups always use a selection from one of the four Touchstones volumes. The selections are short and readable and require no preparation. If preparation were required, those students not in the habit of preparing would be blocked from participation. Yet a central purpose of the project is to change such behavior.

Participants sit in a circle, the teacher among them. The teacher is the discussion leader but not the source of information or the authority on content. All participants must take responsibility for the success of the activity. The text is read aloud and silently, so that both readers and nonreaders can participate.

The discussion begins with a question from the teacher. The question opens discussion but is not necessarily the theme of the discussion. The discussion lasts until the bell rings. There is no closure, summary, or conclusion; discus-sion is open-ended, and students often continue it in corridors and in the cafeteria. Although the text remains central, students may offer personal experiences when these illuminate some aspect of the text. In this way, students learn to take texts seriously because they recognize the continuity between their work in school and their outside experiences. They also develop the ability to make matters that are private and personal available and useful to others.

The project is implemented in urban, rural, and suburban areas throughout the country, and more than 80,000 students are now involved. They range from the highly gifted to special-education and at-risk students. Class sizes are 25–30 students, though in some areas the project has been used in classes of 38 students. Private and parochial schools as well as public schools use the project.

The major change for middle and high school students who regularly participate in discussions occurs in their disposition to learn. Students become less passive and begin to take responsibility for their own learning, often rethinking their perceptions of their academic strengths and weaknesses. In particular, students' fears about all subject areas, including mathematics and science, often diminish. Perhaps most important, the diversity of students' abilities, skills, and talents, which often leads to a rigid hierarchy within the student population, leads instead to respect for differences.

The ways in which different student groups jointly participate in Touchstones discussions can be appreciated by examining the two crucial elements of such classes: the text and the teacher-leader.

The Discussion Texts

A number of the texts are selections from classic works, but the project does not seek traditional forms of intellectual enrichment, such as accumulated facts. Rather, the discussions develop particular skills that will enable all students to work more effectively in their regular classes—the ability, for example, to teach oneself, to cooperate with others of different backgrounds and abilities, and to feel comfortable and be able to think in situations of great uncertainty.

For the first year of the project, the texts are short (1 to 1½ pages), do not require preparation, and are characterized by a blend of familiarity and strangeness. These stipulations downplay the role of intellectual mastery, which is both the virtue and the vice of the higher-functioning student, and make it possible for all students to begin the discussion on an equal footing.

Whether the text is Homer's *Iliad*, Bacon's essay "About Revenge," or Newton's *Principia*, all the works in Volume I defy the familiar classifications that stronger students so easily grasp and so often use to advantage. The use of Euclid's definitions of geometry illustrates how the text can set the stage for true discussion. This selection is recognizably mathematical; thus, it invites participation from the more able mathematical students. Yet it is radically different from textbook mathematics; thus, it affords room for the less-skilled students to join the discussion.

As the group begins its work, the text itself plays a subordinate role; it is used to evoke student responses. The classics contain concepts and structures that are embedded in many of our own experiences today, and their use in Touchstones discussions enables lower-functioning students to realize that their realm of expertise—their own experience—is appropriate in an academic setting. Higher-performing students need encouragement and practice in situations where definite answers are not available and where candor, rather than subtlety of interpretation, is required. But should the text be given too much prominence in the beginning, the higher-performing students will dominate the class as usual, and the discussion group will not achieve its purpose.

This opportunity for students to present their own experiences should not be viewed as just an opportunity: it must be seen as a *necessity* in the first year or so of the project, which is when students learn how to cooperate with one another and depend less on the teacher as an authority. In Touchstones classes, the emerging independence of young people becomes a strength rather than a weakness.

In order to reconnect lower-performing students with academic enterprises later, their experiences must be depersonalized and shared with others who will comment on and analyze the presuppositions involved. For example, in Volume I there is an excerpt from Francis Bacon's essay "About Revenge." Students usually have no lack of experience with revenge and generally, the less-skilled students are much more forthcoming about their thoughts, feelings, experiences, and attitudes on this subject than the academically oriented students. Bacon's essay, while touching on an attitude familiar to our culture, does so with quite unusual forms of reasoning, partially because it is noncontemporary. It is this aspect of the work—the blend of the

---

The Touchstones Project

Developers:	G. Comber, H. Zeiderman, and N. Maistrellis
Goals:	To create dispositions to learn in students and a willingness to take responsibility for their own education.
Sample skills:	Teaching oneself, active listening, intellectual cooperation, thinking in contexts where models and paradigms are inapplicable, questioning, inferring, evaluating evidence, verbal skills.
Assumptions:	• All students have strengths and weaknesses that a discussion format can engage. • A properly conceived discussion format enables students to use the strengths of others first to compensate for and then to modify their own weaknesses. • Skills developed in the discussion format translate readily to improvements in regularly taught classes.
Intended audience:	Students of all abilities and levels of skills, grades 6–12.
Process:	A specially prepared, noncontemporary text from one of the Touchstones volumes is read aloud at the start of class. Students first work in groups of four to five students to devise questions and approaches to the reading. The groups are then brought together into a large discussion circle where either a teacher or student initiates discussion by asking a question. The teacher is the discussion leader and not a source of information.
Time:	One 30- to 45-minute session per week.
Available from:	The Touchstones Project, 6 N. Cherry Grove Ave., Annapolis, MD 21401. Telephone: 301-263-2121.

familiar and the strange—that invites the participation of the more skilled students, who push the discussion more toward the text.

In Touchstones discussions, high-performing students learn to be more reflective and less dependent on teacher approval. For these students, the result of discussing texts is an increased thoughtfulness about, and understanding of, what they have previously taken for granted. Less-skilled students, by experiencing the recognition of their classmates and teachers, gain confidence in their ability to contribute to and learn from academic activities.

The strengths of each group—the experiential and the intellectual—are equally necessary for true discussion, and the skills of one group enable the other to overcome its characteristic weakness and lack of skill. But for this to occur, the texts must eventually be employed as texts. If they are used as examples of problems, as cultural enrichment, or merely as ways to explore a concept or a theme, then, although certain gains will be made, they will not be the skills that are most desirable in a discussion format.

The Teacher-Leader

In Touchstones discussions, the teacher is neither a source of information nor a source of clarification. On the other hand, the teacher never becomes merely a passive observer. Teacher-leaders must constantly make decisions about whether to intervene, whether to move the discussion closer to or further away from the text, how to encourage silent students to speak, and how to get talkative students to listen. Teachers can learn these skills by participating in a training workshop, watching a video training tape, and using and reading the *Guide for Teaching Discussions Using Touchstones Volume 1.*

Ultimately, as students become more skilled, they will assume most of these tasks themselves. In fact, the long-range goals of the project are to motivate students to take responsibility for their education and to encourage them to cooperate with others during learning.

The main barriers to achieving these goals are the habits and expectations that have been continually built up in school: that teachers are the only source of knowledge and that students are passive recipients. Students respond in one of two ways to this traditional incidental training. They either accept it and become "good" students whose learning is mediated by, and dependent on, the teacher, or they reject it and become "unmotivated" students or "behavioral problems." In Touchstones classes, students are able to modify these role extremes, but they find they need one another's strengths to do so.

In the first few weeks of implementation, "good" students often encounter difficulty. They may speak and listen well to teachers but have little skill in speaking and listening to other students. And they may be uncomfortable because they are not receiving approval for their comments from the traditional authority.

For poor students, once they realize that the teacher's role has changed, quite the opposite occurs. Some of their defects as students—their inability or unwillingness to depend on the teacher—now become strengths. They often feel comfortable addressing remarks to other students and listening to them; in fact, their speaking and listening skills are frequently remarkable. Indeed, the class usually begins to become a discussion group because the "problem" students possess discussion skills.

The content of their comments, however, is usually bereft of application to subject matter. This is not to say that they talk about trivial issues; in fact, much of what they talk about is thoughtful and serious. Rather, they concentrate on the concerns of the streets and playgrounds—power, honor, friendship, love, desire.

Once the discussion group begins to take form, the task of the teacher-leader is to reengage the generally high-performing students in the discussion. One way to do this is to deliberately move away from the reports of direct experience and back toward the text. Better students tend to respect what is written in texts. At this stage, a teacher can reengage them with references to the text, questions about meaning, or remarks suggesting a connection between a student's experience and something in the text that everyone has read.

This action is a strategic move to widen participation in the discussion group. In making this move toward the text, the teacher must not allow the better students to direct their remarks to the teacher or to dominate the discussion. Once these students are reengaged, other goals will give the group the latitude to depart from the text again.

Toward a Community of Learners

As all the students in class begin to listen to and speak with one another, the distinction between textual and non-textual discussions starts to atrophy. Discussions center on matters of real concern to all students, yet these discussions are increasingly mediated by a text. For low-performing students, this means that a text and a formal classroom activity become less alien to their interests. The barrier between in-school and outside-of-school begins to break down, and frequently their experiences in the Touchstones classes act as a bridge for their reentry into their regular classes as more motivated members. For the high-performing students, participation in Touchstones discussions often leads to greater thoughtfulness about what they are learning and less reticence about acknowledging mistakes and confusion. Both groups of students become less adversarial toward teachers and each other; they also ask more relevant questions in regular classes. In addition, and perhaps most important, all students learn how to become active listeners, more sensitive to the spoken and written word.

For all students in Touchstones classes, the gains are both intellectual and social. And these outcomes are increasingly important in a society where the scars of racial and sexual discrimination may be replaced by the equally insidious wounds of discrimination based on educational achievement.

23

Creative Learning and Problem Solving

Scott G. Isaksen and Donald J. Treffinger

Everyday life at school, home or on any job presents many opportunities for problem solving. Too often, people—adults as well as youngsters—think of a "problem" only as something that's wrong, an unpleasant or difficult concern or a troublesome situation that needs "fixing up." Our definition is much broader and more inclusive: A problem is any situation in which you need and want new ideas and a plan to put those ideas into action. Creative Learning and Problem Solving is an approach that students, teachers, and administrators can learn and apply in dealing with any of these problems. It uses a set of "tools" or strategies that can be applied deliberately, using creative thinking or imagination as well as critical thinking or judgment in better harmony for greater success.

Becoming a Better Problem Solver

To increase creative productivity, we follow a three-level approach (Treffinger 1988). Level One involves learning many "tools" or techniques for creative thinking (generating many ideas) and critical thinking (analyzing, refining, and evaluating). Level Two involves learning how to incorporate those "tools" into a systematic Creative Problem Solving (CPS) process, which we based on more than three decades of research and development (Isaksen and Treffinger 1985). Level Three provides opportunities to apply CPS to real problems and challenges. These three levels are illustrated in Figure 1.

CPS has been studied carefully in a number of experimental investigations by educational and psychological researchers, and its effectiveness has been evaluated in practice by many organizations. From these studies, we know that people *can* become better problem solvers (Treffinger 1986;

Isaksen 1987). CPS methods and techniques can be used in the classroom, as elsewhere, to increase the effectiveness with which students use their creativity to generate many varied and unusual ideas, and their critical thinking to make better choices and decisions.

The Creative Learning Model provides a conceptual framework for organizing our approach to instruction in thinking skills and problem solving. Two fundamental principles, along with the CPS model, Figure 2, provide the dispositions and structure supporting the specific problem-solving techniques and strategies.

Two Fundamental Principles

Two important principles serve as the foundation for creative learning and problem solving:

• *Deferred Judgment.* When students attempt to use their creative imagination to generate many ideas, it is important that they, and their teacher, defer or suspend judgment or evaluation of their ideas in order to give themselves permission to let flow as many ideas as possible. Evaluation in the form of praise or criticism can inhibit or stifle productivity during the idea generation process. Criticism of ideas can lead to defensiveness, giving up, or "shutting down" the production of new possibilities. Even praise can have a negative effect by leading to premature closure ("We like that idea, so why think of any more?") or unnecessarily narrowing or limiting the search for ideas. Whenever students are in a "brainstorming" mode in which the goal is to produce many varied or unusual ideas, they need to let all ideas flow freely, to stretch their thoughts to produce some novel or unusual ideas, and to be alert for opportunities to combine ideas or make new connections.

FIGURE 1

Creative Learning Model

Level One:
Learn and Use Basic Thinking "Tools"

Begin with direct instruction in thinking "tools," then incorporate those thinking skills into existing course content.

Examples of Level I Skills: Brainstorming, Attribute Listing, Idea Checklists, "What if..." or "Just suppose" Questions, Forced Relationships, Morphological Analysis, Analogies, Judging Relevant Data, Making Inferences, Comparing/Contrasting, Evaluating Statements or Conclusions... ... [and many more]

Students need to learn the tools; direct instruction is both appropriate and necessary at Level One!

Level Two:
Learn and Practice A Systematic P/S Process

Continue by providing opportunities for students to learn and practice systematic steps or processes for effective problem solving.

Level Two uses and extends the usefulness of the "tools" from Level One, providing a structure or system for their application in solving problems/ Examples: Case Studies, Simulations, Role Playing or Socio-drama, Future Study Scenarios, Group Work on (contrived) Practice Problems...

Increased competence and commitment of students calls for varied use of appropriate Leadership Styles.

Level Three:
Working With Real Problems

The goals of instruction or training in thinking skills lead towards effectiveness in dealing with real problems and challenges, not just doing "exercises" and "activities."

In a "Real" problem, we need and want new ideas. They are characterized by strong "ownership" or investment. Examples include: personal or group concerns; community needs or issues; new products, programs, or actions; individual/organizational needs or opportunities; special projects...

In working with others at this stage, you need to be able to serve as a Facilitator.

© 1988, Center for Creative Learning

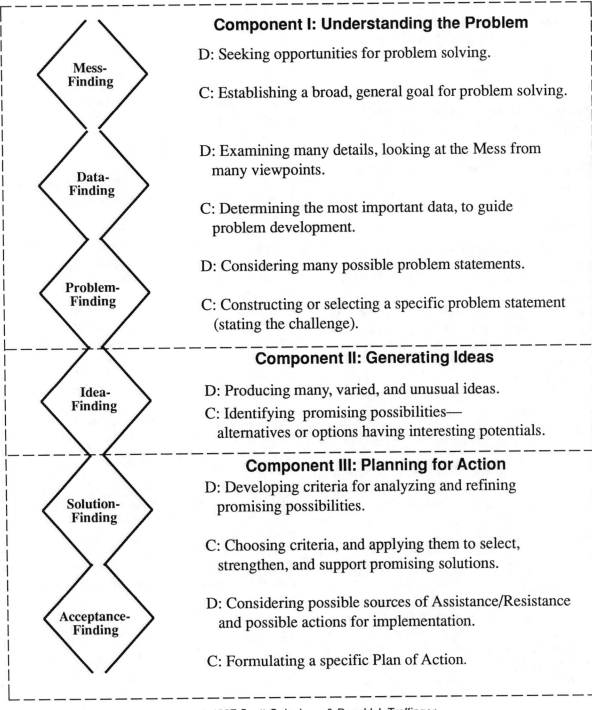

FIGURE 2

Creative Problem Solving
Three Main Components and Six Specific Stages

Component I: Understanding the Problem

Mess-Finding

D: Seeking opportunities for problem solving.

C: Establishing a broad, general goal for problem solving.

Data-Finding

D: Examining many details, looking at the Mess from many viewpoints.

C: Determining the most important data, to guide problem development.

Problem-Finding

D: Considering many possible problem statements.

C: Constructing or selecting a specific problem statement (stating the challenge).

Component II: Generating Ideas

Idea-Finding

D: Producing many, varied, and unusual ideas.
C: Identifying promising possibilities—alternatives or options having interesting potentials.

Component III: Planning for Action

Solution-Finding

D: Developing criteria for analyzing and refining promising possibilities.

C: Choosing criteria, and applying them to select, strengthen, and support promising solutions.

Acceptance-Finding

D: Considering possible sources of Assistance/Resistance and possible actions for implementation.

C: Formulating a specific Plan of Action.

© 1987 Scott G. Isaksen & Donald J. Treffinger

• *Affirmative Judgment.* Once students have generated many ideas, they must be able to analyze them carefully and refine them. Examining ideas critically is not just a matter of criticizing them or finding out what's wrong with each one. Effective idea development and decision making comes from being able to examine possibilities thoroughly but constructively. Students need to deliberately consider the advantages, limitations, and potentials of new ideas, and use specific methods to analyze their ideas from several perspectives. They need to look for ways to get the most out of ideas, rather than searching only for "the one perfect idea."

CPS: Methods and Techniques for Deliberate Problem Solving

The Creative Problem Solving model includes three components: Getting the Problem Ready, Generating Ideas, and Planning for Action.

Getting the Problem Ready

Most people are in such a hurry to solve a problem that they frequently overlook the importance of asking the right questions to begin with. As a result, it is not uncommon for a group to invest a great deal of time and energy in trying to solve a problem, only to discover that they haven't succeeded because they have been working on the wrong question! It doesn't do much good to brainstorm 50 or 100 possibilities if they are all concerned with a question that no one really wanted to ask. We need to keep in mind that, as Albert Einstein once said, "a problem well-stated is more than half solved." Thus, the first component of CPS (which involves three of the six specific "stages" in the CPS process) serves the major goal of helping to carefully define the real problem to be solved.

The three CPS "stages" that help students define and focus a problem are:

• *Mess-Finding.* Problem solving does not usually begin with a well-defined, carefully prepared statement of the problem. Instead, most of us usually start by struggling with a very broad, ill-defined challenge or concern, which we call a "Mess." During the Mess-Finding stage, the problem solver searches for or tries to recognize many possible broad opportunities, needs, or concerns that might become the primary focus or goals of the CPS effort and then determines which of those "Messes" warrants immediate attention. Mess statements have three general characteristics: they are broad, brief, and beneficial. That is, they are expressed in general terms (e.g., "We want to reach more new customers," or "I'd like to earn better grades"). They are worded concisely, in a "headline" format, and focus on positive results or goals.

• *Data-Finding.* Any "Messy" situation may present many possible problem-solving opportunities, not just one. If you're a student, for example, "earning better grades" might involve changing your study habits, convincing your teachers that your attitude has improved, attending class more often, finding a quiet place to study each day, cutting back on your social life, or many other specific issues. Data-Finding provides students with methods for looking more closely at a Mess, to understand better what aspects of that Mess are really the major challenges or directions to investigate. Data-Finding helps students determine what parts of the Mess represent the principal areas of opportunity, or to locate specific obstacles or concerns, by considering key questions about the Mess (for instance, Who? What? When? Where? Why? and How?) and by investigating not only the "facts" about the situation, but the students' feelings, impressions, attitudes, and questions as well. The major purpose of Data-Finding is to establish a clearer, sharper, or more refined focus for developing a specific problem statement from the Mess.

• *Problem-Finding.* During this stage, students seek a specific question to use in guiding and directing their problem-solving efforts. Too often people express problems in negative, depressing ways. ("The problem is . . . I have too many chores and not enough time to study.") It is more effective to state the problem in ways that invite the development of ideas. To do so, students might begin their problem statements with an "invitational stem," such as "In what ways might I . . . ?" or "How might we . . . ?" A good problem statement is also concise, expressing the major focus of the Mess, and free of any criteria that might inhibit the flow of ideas.

Beginning with the Mess of "earning better grades," for example, a student might discover in Data-Finding a major area of concern: that her time is divided among too many activities and, as a result, her study time is limited. Her Problem-Finding efforts might include such specific problem statements as, "How might I schedule my time better?" or "How might I expand my study time?" or even "How might I work more study time into my busy schedule?"

When students have progressed from a broad, general Mess to a focused, invitingly worded problem statement, they will be ready to move along to the second major component of CPS.

Generating Ideas

This component involves using the final problem statement that was selected (or constructed) at the close of Problem-Finding as the starting point for searching for new ideas and possibilities. The specific CPS stage in this component is

Creative Learning and Problem Solving

Developer:	Scott G. Isaksen and Donald J. Treffinger (based on the work of Osborn, Parnes, Noller, and others)
Goal:	Development of effective strategies for problem solving, integrating both creative and critical thinking.
Sample skills :	• Three levels (learning basic "tools," learning and practicing a systematic problem-solving process, and dealing with real problems and challenges). • Three components in problem solving: understanding the problem, generating ideas, and planning for action. • Six specific stages within these components (Mess-Finding, Data-Finding, Problem-Finding, Idea-Finding, Solution-Finding, and Acceptance-Finding).
Assumptions:	Creative productivity is natural for all people and important to personal and vocational success. All learners are capable of using creative and critical thinking to solve problems productively. All people can improve their creative productivity through deliberate means.
Intended audience:	Young children through adults.
Process:	Students are taught guidelines and thinking "tools" or techniques for generating and analyzing ideas. Next, these tools are applied as part of a systematic process for dealing with open-ended or ill-structured challenges, and the students are guided in applying that process in many structured situations. Finally, students work autonomously (independently or in groups) to identify and deal effectively with real problems and challenges.
Time:	Varies. Extensive research supports the effectiveness of the program from several hours of training through extended training of a year or more.
Sources:	Buffalo State College, Center for Studies in Creativity, Chase Hall, 1300 Elmwood, Buffalo NY 14222. Telephone: 716-878-6223. FAX: 716-878-4040. Center for Creative Learning, 4152 Independence Court, Suite C-7, Sarasota, FL 34234. Telephone: 813-351-8862. FAX: 813-351-9061.

Idea-Finding. Idea-Finding invites students to generate ideas that might become parts of an effective solution. Some of the ideas they generate may be *adaptive*—that is, extensions, modifications, or enhancements of existing ideas or practices, taking what they're already doing and building on it to make it more effective. Other ideas may be more *innovative*, representing new possibilities, a way of doing something differently than it's been done before. Both types of ideas can lead to effective solutions; neither should be overlooked. The more possibilities students can find, the more likely that at least some of them will be useful. Problem solvers should be flexible enough to think about new "angles" or directions and to try to generate some ideas that are unique or unusual.

Planning for Action

Students often believe that problem solving is finished when they have generated some new and interesting ideas. Unfortunately, they may discover that there is quite a difference between a good idea and a useful idea. The third component of CPS, Planning for Action, is concerned with how to give good ideas the best possible chance to become useful solutions for the problem. In this component, there are two specific CPS stages.

• *Solution-Finding.* During this stage, students try to analyze and refine the ideas that seemed most promising during the Idea-Finding stage. With specific criteria in mind,

they focus on taking interesting or intriguing possibilities and improving them, shaping them into solutions for the Mess. This might involve screening the ideas, setting priorities among them, selecting the ideas that are most appealing, and strengthening attractive possibilities to maximize the likelihood of success.

• *Acceptance-Finding.* No matter how good a possible solution might be, the chances are that successful implementation will depend on the cooperation and support (or perhaps the lack of opposition) of other people. A successful solution also requires attention to many other concerns: timing or scheduling, materials, and places. In Acceptance-Finding, the student's task is to consider many possible "assisters," and how they can best be used to implement the solution, as well as many possible "resisters," and how they might be avoided or overcome. Finally, students need to develop a specific Plan of Action for carrying out the solution.

REFERENCES

Isaksen, S. G. (1987). *Frontiers of Creativity Research.* Buffalo, N.Y.: Bearly Limited.

Isaksen, S. G., and D. J. Treffinger. (1985). *Creative Problem Solving: The Basic Course.* Buffalo, N.Y.: Bearly Limited.

Treffinger, D. J. (1986). "Research on Creativity." *Gifted Child Quarterly* 30: 15–19.

Treffinger, D. J. (May-June 1988). "A Model for Creative Learning: 1988 Update." *Creative Learning Today* 2, 3: 4–6.

24
Thinking, Reading, and Writing

Sydney Billig Tyler

Everyone can think. This attribute, common to all human beings but distinct and unique within each, means that all children come to school ready to invent, explore, create, imagine, and work innovatively across all learning areas. For this reason, the learning environment that our students experience upon arrival and from then on should mirror and support this readiness. Thinking should be encouraged and taught in order to enrich students' writing, innovative expression, and oral language abilities.

Children may not walk through the door able to print their names, but they can tell you a story and watch you write it down. For example, the concept of pronouns may be murky at best, but the design of a snow-clearing machine can capture the interest of a nonreading 7-year-old, and seeing her explanations printed on paper, as in Figure 1, will encourage far more interest in words than all the pre-primers ever printed.

FIGURE 1

Design a machine to clear away snow.

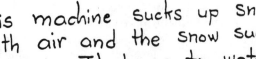

This machine sucks up snow with air and the snow sucks right in. It turns to water and rolls out the back of the machine. This machine drives on wheels.

Kindergarten/Grade One
Teacher: Mrs. Lee H.T. Argabrite. Ithaca, New York.

Source: Stretch Think® Program One
Copyright © Sydney Billig Tyler

To go a bit further, arriving ready to learn and being given the opportunity to learn can be two quite different experiences, but such disparities do not need to be perpetuated. By the simple expedient, for example, of teaching primary numeral recognition, formation, and amount equivalencies as whole-group writing and thinking lessons, with color recognition as an added bonus, you can turn tiresome practice sheets into fun, time-saving, action lessons. Here are two examples:

Hand each child a piece of writing paper and a box of crayons. Ask the class to listen as you write in green chalk, "4 ○○○○ Four green circles." Count the circles and read the words together. Then ask the class to copy it, using a green crayon, while you walk around the room. Help each child work to the best of his or her ability. Presto! Your students have learned the concepts of "green," "4/four," and "circles," and practiced reading and forming letters—all in less than ten minutes with no comprehension problems. Do this with appropriate variations for 20 minutes a day until colors, numerals, and so on are mastered. Figure 2 shows another example of this kind of activity.

Use a thinking program and give each child an active, participatory opportunity to hunt for, identify, and count topic areas, which couple these skills with language development.

What about reading? How we go about teaching reading can be one of our problems. Young children naturally create, invent, play with pencils and crayons, and try to form pictures and words to express their ideas. Instead of teaching reading by helping students develop rich variations in their own thoughts, observations, and life experiences, which means supporting and assisting them in the cohesive development of these creative images and initial practices--a method that not so incidentally removes comprehension problems--we force children into artificial schemes and the stilted ideas of others. When you invent or create and then explain something, irrespective of the particular language in which ideas are expressed, you by definition understand. If you did not, you would not have drawn or created it in the first place. All people, including children, start from what they know.

Content expansion and process skills (factor consideration, decision making, etc.) need attention too, however. A descriptive "this is my house" activity done once or twice is fine, but without additional detail it loses something as a content base for developing language and thinking abilities. Instead, tell students something like "Today I would like you to show me how you would put a giraffe into a helicopter, so you can take it to the zoo" (Tyler 1982). Figure 3 shows one student's response to this activity. And Figure 4 shows a similar activity.

Drawing, writing, discussing, and imaginative invention are brought together in a thinking lesson. The whole class has an opportunity to talk about and push around an interesting idea and then participate in an interactive drawing session, all the while having a marvelous time.

A discussion of the old food in grocery stores (Tyler 1983), during which the alternatives, possibilities, and choices (process skills) would be explored before a decision (process skill) is made, would follow a similar pattern. Once the issue has been explored with the whole class, students would be asked to write, with help as required, a short description of how they would deal with the old food, followed by the design of a system for transporting food to hungry people.

What is it that everyone is enjoying? First, each child's thinking forms the base for a picture and story or explanation. Experientially, this makes a powerful, positive statement about the value of ideas, work efforts, and abilities. Second, even very young children have the importance of thinking impressed upon them:

FIGURE 2

Put a purple circle and a puppy into one picture.
Explain or tell a story about your picture.

The purple circle is the ring around the sun.

The puppy is growling at the cat. It is a warm day.

Cabrillo, USD, California
Kindergarten

Source: Young Think™ Program Two
Copyright © Sydney Billig Tyler

Copyright © 1990 by Sydney Billig Tyler.

FIGURE 3

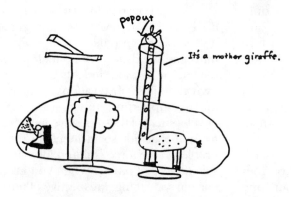

Draw a picture to show how you would put a giraffe into a helicopter, so you can take it to the zoo.

popout

It's a mother giraffe.

The giraffe is standing up in the helicopter. There is a tube in the roof of the helicopter and the giraffe puts his head through it. There is a small bush in the helicopter for him to eat off. The tube is made out of plastic so the giraffe can see out of it.

Zoo

Source: Just Think® Program Five
Copyright © Sydney Billig Tyler

"Your work's a bit messy. Did you stop to *think* about what you were doing?"

"You should *think* about what might happen before you say mean things to your friend."

Thinking is seen, in consequence, as an important and grown-up activity. Third, and finally, in this context all students can participate, whether they read grade-level basal texts or excel on the spelling team. This tells children that everyone's thinking is valued by the teacher.

Experiential learning also far outweighs other activity modes in developmental terms. This means, as amply proven by medical research, that what is learned in this mode speeds up the acquisition of skill and knowledge. Children who learn experientially learn more in less time than children plodding through basal readers and the companion seatwork assignments. Why, at the simplest level, use less efficient methods and modes when happier, more exciting, more interesting, and more efficient ones lie close at hand?

Creating your own books, writing your own stories, explaining your ideas, and discussing your thoughts about an issue, problem, or situation are experiential learning activities. Movies, workbooks, basal texts, and television are not. Experiential means that you do something and that you learn as a result of the action. *Hot* is not hot until you experience it.

Finally, much has been made of the work and time required for the teaching of writing and, by extension, thinking. No one trumpets the fun, the joy, the excitement, the

FIGURE 4

Put a wolf, soap, and wave into one picture. Explain or tell a story about your picture. Be sure that all three dissimilar elements are related to each other in some kind of logical way, however imaginary.

Mr. Wolf slipped and fell into a mud hole. All his fur stuck together. He took his bar of soap to the beach and washed off the mud in the waves.

Source: Just Think® Program Five
Copyright © Sydney Billig Tyler

FIGURE 5

Design a factory to clean coconuts, package the coconut meat, and put the coconut milk into cartons or jars. Label/explain each part.

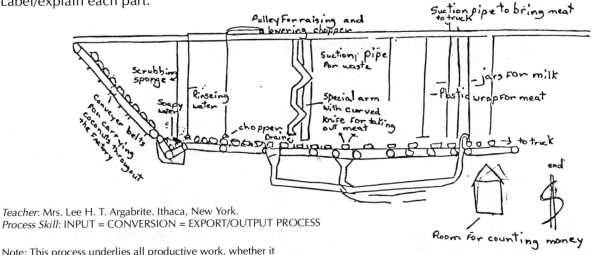

Teacher: Mrs. Lee H. T. Argabrite. Ithaca, New York.
Process Skill: INPUT = CONVERSION = EXPORT/OUTPUT PROCESS

Note: This process underlies all productive work, whether it be a think tank and ideas or a production factory, as shown here. Each program includes lessons specifically designed to teach students this process.

Source: Just Think® Program Five
Copyright © Sydney Billig Tyler

Young Think™, Just Think®, and Stretch Think® Programs

Developer:	Sydney Billing Tyler
Goal:	Teaching thinking, Pre-school through Grade 8.
Sample skills:	Process skills, problem and issue analysis, synthesis, oral and written language development.
Intended audience:	Teachers and parents.
Process:	Curriculum to teach thinking. Each program is a reusable, year-long curriculum, which includes everything the teacher needs for implementation.
Time:	30 to 90 minutes per week.
Source:	Thomas Geale Publications, Inc., P.O. Box 370540, Montara, CA 94037. Telephone: 415-728-5219

beauty, and the professional rewards inherent to this way of working. The Gesell Institute talks about the internal development pace of each person, which differs from age to age and from child to child. If you listen to, watch for, and work with this natural clock, you maximize each student's learning rate. Force-feeding runs counter to every natural growth and learning principle. This is no different in a classroom than in a nursery, and it means that learning programs that are convergent with the natural pace of childhood will enjoy far greater success rates.

Think about it! Ways to maximize learning and create a luminous learning environment do exist. Figure 5 shows the results of one teacher's creativity. All you need is paper, writing implements, a minimal lesson outline, and your own instructional talents.

REFERENCES

Tyler, S. B. (1984). *Stretch Think® Program Two*. Montara, Calif.: Thomas Geale Publications.
Tyler, S. B. (1983). *Just Think® Program Five*. Montara, Calif.: Thomas Geale Publications.
Tyler, S. B. (1982). *Just Think® Program Three*. Montara, Calif.: Thomas Geale Publications.

25

The Thinking to Learn™ Series

Educational Testing Service

At ETS, the focus will be on new assessments that promote the improvement of learning and of educational opportunities. These changes are not dreams. They are initiatives already begun that will yield significant results in the 1990s.

—Gregory R. Anrig, President,
Educational Testing Service, March 1, 1990

The results of a variety of educational assessments in the past decade indicate that students in the United States possess limited skills in thinking and reasoning. This condition restricts their ability as individuals to make informed decisions and take full advantage of their opportunities in a free nation. It also threatens the position of the United States in the world politically, economically, and technologically.

The *Thinking to Learn*™ series of products and services from Educational Testing Service is intended to help educators address this problem. The series has a dual focus: staff development for educators and instructional materials which incorporate thinking skills with instruction in a specific subject area.

Part I: Staff Development

Strategies for Teaching Critical Thinking Across the Curriculum is a two-phase staff development program that aims to provide secondary-level teachers (grades 7–12) with a variety of methods for integrating the teaching of thinking skills into subject area instruction. It is available both at ETS offices and as an inservice program.

Copyright © 1990 by Educational Testing Service. Thinking to Learn™ and Inside Story™ are trademarks of Educational Testing Service.

Strategies was developed under the following assumptions:

- Thinking skills are basic.
- Thinking skills are best taught in the context of regular content instruction.
- Professional development should be locally controlled.
- Learning is experiential.

The belief that students will learn thinking skills by virtue of regular content instruction has led to two misconceptions: that not all students are capable of good thinking and that thinking skills do not lend themselves to instruction. Neither is true. All students are capable of careful, sound thinking, and thinking skills do lend themselves to instruction.

Strategies is designed for students of all ability levels and in all disciplines. It is intended to enable participants to incorporate the teaching of thinking skills into any curriculum and to pass their new expertise on to their colleagues in their own schools and districts. As a part of the program, participants reflect on their own thinking processes and engage in intensive activities involving the very thinking skills to be taught to their students.

Strategies consists of two courses. "The Thinking Framework" teaches thinking skills and methods for integrating these skills into regular classroom instruction. Participants return to their classrooms at the conclusion of the course with the newly learned concepts and redesigned lesson plans. Six to nine months later, these same people return for the second phase of the program, in which they acquire the knowledge and skills to effectively teach "The Thinking Framework" to their colleagues and to provide ongoing support and follow-up as needed. If participants do not have teaching responsibilities, it is recommended that they "borrow" a class after the first course to gain firsthand experience with student responses to the thinking skills before returning for the second course.

"The Thinking Framework" is composed of eight three-hour modules on six major clusters of thinking skills, which were chosen for applicability to school curriculums:

- Introduction to Thinking Skills
- Organizing Information: Classification
- Concept Formation
- Representing Related Concepts
- Finding Patterns, Making Inferences
- Formulating and Testing Hypotheses
- Understanding and Constructing Meaning
- Presentations and Summary

This design enables school districts to offer the course in a variety of configurations to fit its particular needs. For example, the course might be taught one evening a week for eight weeks or one day a week for four weeks (two modules per day). It might also be offered as part of a summer institute or a continuing education program, perhaps even for university credit.

Participants receive background material, selected readings, and sample lessons that illustrate different thinking skills. Each module cuts across three major concerns—curriculum, instruction, and assessment—and is divided into four parts:

- An extended activity that illustrates the skill, challenges the thinking of participants as adults, and shows the range and power of the skill.
- Group collaboration to meet the challenges posed by the activity and discussion of the developmental, environmental, and instructional aspects of the skill.
- Individual reflection by way of participant journals on the activity and ways of integrating the skill into their classroom teaching.
- Transfer to content teaching in which participants work with others from their discipline to redesign their lesson plans to integrate instruction of thinking skills with their subject area curriculum.

Throughout the course, participants identify the elements of a thinking classroom and use various instructional models involving questioning and discussion and the connection between thinking and writing. By matching specific thinking skills with specific subjects, they learn to help their students master subject area content as well as new skills for thinking. They also develop an array of techniques for assessing student learning of thinking skills and improving the quality of student thinking. And by adopting the role of students, participants rediscover the importance of a supportive environment in encouraging risk taking, the free exchange of ideas, and learning in general.

Phase two, which is designed to equip participants to teach "The Thinking Framework" to their colleagues, consists of the following aspects:

- *Detailed examination of each module.* Participants review the overall structure and core activity of each module, discuss misunderstandings experienced by teachers, and examine new ways of presenting the ideas.

- *Presentation skills.* Participants learn how to present information and lead discussions effectively, and to incorporate a variety of approaches in engaging participants in the thinking skills included in the course.

- *Workshop and staff development design.* Participants learn how to structure a staff development program and how to best fit "The Thinking Framework" into the needs of their particular school or district.

- *Institutionalization of change.* Participants learn how to implement a successful, long-term staff development program and provide effective follow-up, support, and peer coaching.

Part II: Instructional Units

ETS has several research and development projects underway whose focus is student learning. To varying degrees, these projects incorporate thinking skills, computer technology, and assessments of student progress with instructional relevance. Among these projects is *Inside Story: Dateline Brazil*, which is a three-week instructional unit for 6th and 7th graders that incorporates thinking skills with the language arts.

With *Inside Story: Dateline Brazil*, students learn to model strategies important to critical thinkers by adopting the role of investigative reporter. They engage in interactive computerized activities, as well as supplemental classroom activities, to develop critical thinking skills, knowledge of a particular genre of literature—mythology—and skills in reading, writing, and oral communication. Teachers gain assessment information to guide further instruction of their students as needed.

Inside Story: Dateline Brazil is based on an African-Brazilian myth that explains fertility brought to a barren land through seasonal floods. The events of the myth are mysterious and dramatic; they call for interpretation, and the myth does not include information that would explain the motivation for the actions of the characters. The myth thus provides a rich context for exploring the value of evidence in investigating events and characters, the limits of available evidence, the questions that the myth leaves unanswered, and the use of evidence in creating an interpretation of events and characters.

The language arts objectives of *Inside Story: Dateline Brazil* are:

• To develop students' expertise in assimilating information and understanding text, developing a personal understanding, and monitoring their own reading and writing process;

• To develop students' ability to analyze such literary elements as character, conflict, theme, plot, and genre;

• To teach students about myths from various cultures around the world.

The critical thinking objectives will enable students to

• Find and support answers to questions;

• Formulate and substantiate or refute hypotheses;

• Effectively communicate their interpretations and evidence to others;

• Monitor, control, and reflect upon their thought processes;

• Take responsibility for their own thinking.

The unit fulfills these objectives by posing a significant question or problem for the students to resolve in the context of the myth they have just read.

In the process of engaging with *Inside Story: Dateline Brazil*, students learn to generate meaning by developing a number of cognitive skills:

• Formulating predictions and hypotheses about what will happen;

• Evaluating the plausibility of hypotheses;

• Analyzing alternative interpretations of the myths;

• Evaluating the accuracy of evidence and information;

• Relating their own experiences to the myths.

They later modify hypotheses, interpret events, gather evidence to support or refute an interpretation, and identify the need for more information. Such reflection processes as summarizing, drawing conclusions, connecting one text to another, and applying resulting concepts to new settings all contribute to the student's integration of new learning.

Students work in pairs on the computer; noncomputer classroom activities engage students individually and in small groups. Consequently, there are affective and social, as well as cognitive, aspects to these units. By considering others' views and sharing their own, students enlarge their perspectives and test their theories. *Inside Story: Dateline Brazil* creates an environment that encourages cooperative learning, risk taking, collaboration, consensus building, a tolerance for multiple questions and points of view, and an open exchange of ideas. The interactive nature of the activities gives students a sense of self-determination and empowerment in their own learning.

During administration of *Inside Story: Dateline Brazil*, teachers lead classroom activities that complement the computer activities, facilitate discussion, monitor students' progress, and provide enrichment activities and guidance as needed. Instructions for taking advantage of the specific opportunities for assessment integrated within the instruction are provided. In addition, student notebooks serve to document and aid students' learning and foster their own self-assessments. Although the materials contain many suggestions for teaching, teachers are urged to adapt them to fit their own teaching styles and students. The materials for *Inside Story: Dateline Brazil* include a teacher's manual, student notebook, and software—along with instructions for using the software.

Thinking To Learn™

Developer:	Educational Testing Service	
Assumptions:	• Thinking skills are basic. • Thinking skills are best taught in the context of regular content instruction. • Instruction should drive assessment, and assessment should be linked to instruction. • Professional development should be locally controlled (*Strategies*). • Learning is experiential (*Strategies*). • Technology can be a useful tool for students to monitor their own thought processes (*Inside Story*).	

	Strategies staff development program	Inside Story™ instructional unit
Goals:	To help teachers in grades 7–12 integrate thinking skills with subject area instruction; to give districts in-house expertise for staff development	To integrate thinking skills with instruction in the language arts for students in grades 6 and 7
Cognitive Skills Addressed:	• Classify • Develop concepts • Visually represent concepts • Identify patterns and relationships • Formulate and test hypotheses • Construct meaning	• Monitor one's own reading and writing processes • Find and support answers to questions • Formulate, substantiate, or refute hypotheses • Communicate interpretations and evidence to others • Monitor, control, and reflect on one's own thought process • Take responsibility for one's own thinking and learning
Audience:	Trainers at the school or district level as instructors; teachers in grades 7–12 for first phase	Students in grades 6 and 7 at all levels of ability
Process:	Two-phase "training for trainers" model	Computerized and teacher-led classroom activities
Time:	7 days	17 days
Source:	Diane Wah, Project Director, Thinking to Learn™ Series, Educational Testing Service, Rosedale Road, Princeton, NJ 08541. Telephone: 609-921-9000, ext. 5244.	

26

Developing Thinking Skills

Margarita A. de Sánchez

The Developing Thinking Skills (DTS) program, initiated at the Instituto Technológico y de Estudios Superiores de Monterrey (ITESM) [Monterrey Institute of Technology and Higher Studies], aims to develop the intellectual abilities of high school students so that, upon entering college, they can demonstrate excellence in problem solving and decision making and success in the institutional academic environment. It is composed of five levels of courses that are incorporated into the regular senior high school curriculum.

ITESM is a nonprofit, private institution dedicated to fostering science, technology, and national culture; protecting traditional Mexican values; and developing professionals with a high level of preparation and a clear sense of personal dignity and social responsibility. ITESM involves 28 university campuses in 15 cities throughout Mexico, with 3,000 teachers and 40,000 students.

In 1983, ITESM invited me to begin the DTS program at its main campus in Monterrey, Nuevo Leon, Mexico. I had been the director of a program begun by Venezuela's Ministry for the Development of Human Intelligence, which was created in 1979 to develop students' thinking skills. In my work with the Venezuelan program, I sought the participation and support of Harvard and Yale universities and the cooperation of such well-known investigators as Edward de Bono, Reuven Feuerstein, Robert Sternberg, Ray Nickerson, David Perkins, and Richard Herrnstein, who assisted in developing, executing, and evaluating the various thinking skills programs that were implemented in Venezuela's schools.

Purpose of the DTS Program

DTS is intended to develop in students the cognitive structures and functions needed to improve their interactions with the environment, both in nonschool and academic situations. The program pursues the following objectives:

1. To teach the courses "Developing Thinking Skills I–V" in all high schools in the system (see Figure 1).

2. To progressively incorporate the application of thinking processes into subject area teaching.

3. To train teachers in the use of DTS so as to foster transference and infuse DTS processes into the teaching of curriculum subjects.

4. To promote activities that stimulate critical and creative thinking.

5. To advance teachers' cognitive development.

Program Rationale

A high percentage of students entering college have deficiencies in reasoning and critical and creative thinking that have been shown to cause a progressive decline in academic performance (Arons 1979; de Sánchez 1983, 1987; Whimbey and Lochhead 1986). These deficiencies are due to a lack of properly based cognitive structures for performing mental processes at the formal operation level (Gardner 1985).

Cognitive psychology has established the differences between the use of short-term and long-term memories. Short-term memory produces limited-time retention and is of little use in permanent learning. Long-term memory is an active system for the organization and deep processing of information, which enables human beings to establish relations, make generalizations, and achieve long-term and meaningful learning. The development of these cognitive structures does not constitute a spontaneous learning process; it must be stimulated through formal training in courses properly incorporated into the school curriculum. The timely use of long-term, active memory is only possible

FIGURE 1
DTS COURSE CONTENT

DTS I: Basic Processes of Thinking
1. Introduction: Definitions and Intelligence Development
2. Observation and Classification
3. Ordering
4. Hierarchical Classification
5. Analogies
6. Analysis and Synthesis
7. Spatial Reasoning

DTS II: Problem Solving
1. Linear Representations
2. Table Representations
3. Simulation Representation and Enactment
4. Systematic Trial
5. Clearing Up What is Understood

Verbal Reasoning
1. Assertions
2. Arguments

DTS III: Creativity
1. Introduction to Creativity
2. Expansion and Contraction of Ideas
3. Lateral Thinking
4. Inventive Thinking: Concrete and Abstract Designs

DTS IV: Metacomponents, Performance and Knowledge Acquisition Components
1. Introduction to The Triarchic Theory of Intelligence
2. Metacomponents
3. Performance Components for the Processing of Information
4. Knowledge Acquisition Components

DTS V: Novelty, Automatization, and Practical Intelligence
1. Dealing with Novel Situations
2. Automatization of the Processing of Information
3. Practical Intelligence
4. Intelligent Behaviors and Development of Thinking Skills

if people develop the cognitive structures that act as organizing and processing functions of information (Calfee 1981).

ITESM wanted to design instructional alternatives to the traditional teaching-learning process, to include courses that would develop students' thinking skills, and to transfer cognitive processes into the teaching of the disciplines at all levels (Reif 1981).

Definition of the DTS Program

The DTS program combines the principles of Project Intelligence, Sternberg's Triarchic Theory of Intelligence, and the Paradigm of Processes (*Proyecto Inteligencia* 1983; Sternberg 1986a; de Sánchez 1986a–1986e, 1987).

The Paradigm of Processes explains conceptual and methodological aspects of an approach to thinking that is based in the operationalization of the mental act of thinking and in the separation, at a conceptual level, of the two elements of thinking: (1) the processes, or cognitive functions, and (2) the contents of information or knowledge being handled. Knowledge is defined as "information about conceptual and theoretical facts, concepts, rules, and outlines that make up a discipline or a field of study" or, in the scope of everyday life, "incidental information about the facts or events of the world around the subject."

A process can be made up of one or more mental operations. It is a thinking operation capable of acting over concrete stimuli or over mental representations to produce new mental representations or motor actions.

Concepts are the cognitive entities over which processes act to generate new products. Every process, to be applied,

is transformed into a strategy or procedure. Practice of the procedure, under controlled conditions, generates thinking skills.

Process exists in itself, independent from the person who performs it, while ability is a skill within the person. Ability requires development through systematic and deliberate learning.

Teaching Based on Processes and Developing Thinking Skills

Teaching is the application of the process approach in order to stimulate thinking skills development and subject matter learning. Teaching exercises students' minds to improve their information-processing methods and techniques, which in turn stimulates their ability to apply critical and creative thinking to solving problems and making decisions. Such teaching involves two learning steps:

1. *Engaging in a series of stages that mark the evolution of cognitive development in relation to the application of the thinking processes*:

• The systematic, gradual, guided, deliberate, intentional, conscious, and willing practice of the procedures that form a given thinking process;

• The development of cognitive structures to allow identification of discrepancies between what is wanted and what is obtained and the necessary feedback processes to eliminate these discrepancies;

• The definition of criteria to allow the verification of achieved progress and to determine what is required to obtain the expected performance level.

The basic foundations of this process model are:
• Intentionality of the mental act and of the activity through which the individual's intellectual ability is aimed, focused, and optimized;
• Awareness of the mental act involved in the process;
• Internalization or achievement of the habit of applying the processes naturally and spontaneously;
• Transcendence of the achieved knowledge (metacognition);
• The use of the systems approach as a thinking tool and as the basis of the process methodology;
• Active participation of the learner to verify his or her thinking progress;
• The teacher as a mediator of the teaching-learning process (by monitoring the processes).

2. *Providing an appropriate psychological atmosphere.* Such an atmosphere requires the teacher's ability to:
• Stimulate the student's intellect;
• Provide corrective feedback;
• Develop student metacognition;
• Organize instruction according to mental acts of input, process, and output;
• Engage active participation;
• Create a safe, warm climate of free expression.

DTS Courses

The DTS program consists of 168 lessons that are grouped into 5 levels of courses, which are taught in the first five semesters of high school (see Figure 1):

DTS I: Basic Thinking Processes develops skills in logical reasoning and critical thinking, which are essential for improving students' abstract reasoning (de Sánchez 1986a–1986e).

DTS II: Problem Solving and Verbal Reasoning fosters the development of deductive reasoning skills. The course allows students to apply the basic processes of DTS I through the consolidation of new thinking styles and the application of language skills and verbal reasoning to problem solving and communicating.

DTS III: Creativity fosters the use of new thinking styles through mind activation, creativity, and inventiveness. Lateral thinking and divergent and convergent thinking, which are studied in the two previous courses, are developed and integrated here. Students' intellectual and experiential ranges are broadened, enabling them to generate creative products and to grasp, interpret, and improve the surrounding reality.

DTS IV: Metacomponents, Performance and Knowledge Components encourages metacognition—the awareness of one's own knowledge of the task and strategy, as well as of the processes that regulate and optimize intellectual development and performance. The course begins with a set of directive processes to manage information, such as planning, monitoring and evaluating. It provides a set of performance processes to guide mental activity toward the achievement of expected results, and it culminates with the application of an information processing model that facilitates knowledge acquisition and improves students' ability to learn from books, from the information received in classes, and from the environment.

DTS V: Novelty, Automatization, and Práctical Intelligence deals with three aspects of human behavior that contribute to managing experience and interacting with the environment. The first refers to the development of skills to deal with novel situations and to automatize information processing. The second refers to managing the environment and develops the ability to produce a variety of diverse answers when facing everyday problems. The third develops positive attitudes of personal growth, self-realization, and excellence.

Instructional Materials

Instructional materials include a series of teacher and student books that emphasize thinking processes, use of knowledge, and previous experience as a starting point to achieve the expected skills. Lessons center on the dialogue between the students and the teacher and between the individual and the team.

The exercises are a means for students to practice processes. They include situations ranging from the familiar to the unfamiliar, from the concrete to the abstract, from the trivial to the controversial, and from the simple to the complex. The exercises aim to raise students' level of abstraction and to prepare them to solve problems, make decisions, and perform adequately in the environment.

Teaching-Learning Methodology

The DTS teaching-learning methodology focuses on monitoring the processes; students' active participation; the teacher's use of a variety of instructional strategies and transactions; the use of questioning techniques and interaction to simulate students' mental activity; the indirect participation of the teacher as a mediator of the teaching-learning process; the collaboration between teachers and students; the stimulation of students' ability to develop on their own the skills for defining, validating, and applying thinking processes; and the verification of achievements in the teaching-learning process.

Implementation Strategy

Curricular Development Plan

The program's curricular development plan comprises seven broad aspects:

1. Progressive implementation of five courses fostering systematic and deliberate development of students' skills to think in terms of processes.

2. Teacher training in teaching based in processes.

3. Design of materials for fostering interaction of contents and processes.

4. Development of an evaluation system based on processes.

5. Encouragement of extracurricular activities to simulate critical and creative thinking.

6. Application or transference of these processes of teaching throughout the school curriculums.

Currently, all ITSM high school students participate in the DTS program by taking one three-hour class every week.

The program was implemented in four phases:

1. *The formative evaluation phase* involved teaching DTS courses to two or three groups of students in the second semester of high school in eight schools in 1983–84. Each group had 25 to 30 students.

The evaluation involved weekly work sessions for professors and the director of the program to analyze the application of the methodology, the use of materials, the professors' progress, and the students' performance and participation. The information obtained was used to define criteria for subsequent revision of the materials in order to more adequately bring them in line with the course objectives and Mexican culture.

2. *The extension phase*, which took place between 1984 and 1985, involved teaching the methodology to all high school groups in eight campuses of the ITESM system. During this phase the project was validated in the new context, and the materials as well as the methodology were adjusted and generalized to a larger group of students in every campus of the system.

3. *The generalization phase* involved the teaching of the methodology to all groups in the first semester of high school in 23 of the 24 campuses of the system (one campus did not have a senior high school). The application of the methodology was fully tested. This phase took place between 1985 and 1986.

4. *The institutionalization phase* has continued since 1986. Its purposes are to establish the permanent function, evaluation, and feedback mechanisms that guarantee the automatic operation and adjustment of the program in the best of conditions to preserve fidelity in the application of the methodology. The norms of the program have been designed and procedural manuals and follow-up instruments have been elaborated. This last phase contributes to the strengthening of the program as a whole. Some of the most important activities include: the teacher training program; a process-based evaluation bank; the infusion or transference of the methodology to the teaching of biology, ethics, language, and mathematics; the creation of the DTS Bulletin; the creation of the CREATEC contest (a systemwide contest on creativity); a research project on the impact of the methodology and follow-up of the high school students once they entered college; and the editing of the final versions of the five teacher and student textbooks.

Teacher Training

Teacher training in the methodology for DTS courses is the key to the program's success. It guarantees the fidelity of the application of the methodology and, consequently, ensures the adequate development of students' thinking skills.

To obtain the program's goals, the teacher gains information on conceptual aspects of thinking development and receives training in the appropriate techniques and procedures for teaching thinking, with emphasis on monitoring the teaching-learning process and centering the class on the student's learning.

Process monitoring is the activity through which the teacher encourages students to exercise their mind to bring out their ideas. In this way the teacher can observe each student's progress, diagnose faults, give the required feedback and appropriate stimuli, and regulate the desired intellectual advancement.

The training encompasses four different aspects:

• Courses in sequence on the different DTS levels.

• Courses in depth on the processes methodology.

• Courses on transferring the processes to the teaching of other subjects.

• The formation of facilitator workshops.

The training consists of practical courses, each lasting approximately 80 hours and distributed over 10 working days. Each lesson is studied, analyzed, and practiced through simulation. One participant acts as a teacher, another as an observer, and a third as a lesson analyzer. The rest of the participants play the role of the students.

At the end of the simulation, the "teacher" participant makes comments about his or her thinking and receives performance feedback from the observer, who focuses on areas in need of improvement.

The analyzer listens, and then explains the content, the structure, and the class procedure, pointing out the internal consistency among the different lesson components.

The training at each DTS level culminates during the first semester, when the teacher uses the methodology to teach a classroom lesson.

Teachers who have become fluent in the methodology can act as training facilitators on their own campuses.

The Evaluation System

Evaluation is one of the most important activities in the teaching-learning process. Apart from being a diagnostic for determining what teaching objectives have been achieved, it orients search for effective feedback.

Evaluating the teaching of processes has two specific purposes: to determine the quality of the product achieved by the student, and to verify how the student combines the information given (using the required process or strategy) to obtain the expected result. This separation guides evaluation and the corresponding feedback process.

Evaluation Bank and Computer Data Base. Each lesson was analyzed in order to produce a description of the procedures for developing various skills and the conditions for teaching them. Due to the diversity of the five DTS courses and the great range of types of problems to be evaluated, there was a need to adequately classify the problems using a computer data base.

The data base program generates 50-minute final exams consisting of randomly chosen problems. The problems are organized according to their degree of difficulty. The bank also prints a set of answers to the problems and the evaluation and grading key.

Extracurricular Activities

Along with DTS classes, special activities are designed to stimulate practical application of the thinking skills in solving both everyday and academic problems. One of the most important is CREATEC, the creativity contest. The contest takes place in two stages: Each of the 23 campuses carries out a contest where all the students' projects are presented. The projects are classified and awards are given in the following six categories: saving resources, developing thinking, organizing, entertaining, giving comfort, informing and communicating, and programming. First-place projects then compete at the systemwide level. The purposes of CREATEC are:

1. To stimulate the creativity of students in the third level of DTS.

2. To give the winners from each campus the opportunity to participate in a systemwide contest.

3. To show the ITESM community and the public in general the usefulness of the DTS program in one of its advanced phases.

4. To encourage the sharing of interests among the students and professors of the different campuses and to strengthen relationships and identification with the ITESM.

Program Research and Follow-up

Along with the materials design and DTS implementation, the impact of the methodology on students' intellectual development has been studied extensively. The performance of college students coming from the high schools that offered DTS courses was compared with the performance of students from other high schools to determine if there were significant differences in intellectual performance both at the beginning of schooling and throughout their academic career. The ITESM students were subdivided into two groups, one of students who completed three DTS courses in high school, the other of students who completed five DTS courses.

The tests used were Cattel (testing culture-free, Scale 3, Form A) and Whimbey's Problem Solving. Hypotheses about the average differences between the groups for the different variables of the study and correlations among the grades in each group were verified. The percentage of students failing one or two subjects was always higher for the non-ITESM group. The percentage of students failing no subjects was higher for the ITESM group. Total dropout was 3.32 percent, with 2.33 percent being non-ITESM students and only 0.99 percent being ITESM students. The percentage of meaningful mean differences in favor of ITESM was 32.70 percent versus 1.12 percent for the non-ITESM group. And the percentage of favorable differences for the ITESM was 46.24 percent versus 19.94 percent favorable to the non-ITESM group. To summarize, the ITESM group obtained better grading and averages in 78.94 percent of the cases.

What Has Been Achieved

So far the following goals have been achieved:
- DTS was incorporated as a subject in the school curriculum. Five courses on developing thinking skills are offered at all campuses of the system.
- A yearly creativity contest, CREATEC, has been instituted with all the system's campuses participating.
- Three transference projects are being developed to ensure process-based teaching in biology, philosophy, and Spanish.
- There is a permanent program to train professors in the process methodology and in developing thinking skills.

The value of the program for both teachers and students is evident in fundamental changes in the teaching-learning process and in students' social behavior, although neither has been measured at scientific levels. Research confirms the favorable effect of DTS on the intellectual performance of the students once they enter college.

In addition, support programs for DTS foster extracurricular activities that stimulate creativity and new approaches to teaching subjects in the curriculum focused on reasoning rather than memorization.

Finally, it is expected that ITESM students and professors will do the following:

• Change their learning methods so that they are no longer centered in fact and information memorization but in transformation and creation of new products.

• Replace memorizing styles based in repetition with more dynamic and efficient methods supported by the new thinking structures.

• Be better able to learn by themselves and regulate their own intellectual development.

• Show social sensitivity and the ability to integrate knowledge, practical experiences, and intelligent behaviors into a meaningful whole that will lead to continued personal growth and improvement of the environment.

BIBLIOGRAPHY

Adams, M. J. (coordinator), (1986). *Odyssey: A Curriculum for Thinking*. Watertown, Mass.: Mastery Learning Corp.

Arons, A. B. (1979). "Some Thoughts in Reasoning Capacities Implicitly Expected of College Students." In *Cognitive Process Instruction*, edited by J. Lochhead and J. Clement. Philadelphia: The Franklin Institute Press.

de Sánchez, M. (In preparation). "The Paradigm of Processes and the Development of Thinking Skills."

de Sánchez, M. (1987). "Teaching Thinking Processes." In *Thinking: The Second International Conference*, edited by D. N. Perkins, J. Lochhead, and J. C. Bishop. Hillsdale, N.J.: Lawrence Erlbaum.

de Sánchez, M. (1986a). "Proyecto Desarrollo de Habilidades de Pensamiento: Procesos Básicos de Pensamiento." Impresos y Tesis, Instituto Technológico y de Estudios Superiores de Monterrey.

de Sánchez, M. (1986b). "Proyecto Desarrollo de Habilidades de Pensamiento: Resolución de Problemas." Impresos y Tesis, Instituto Technológico y de Estudios Superiores de Monterrey.

de Sánchez, M. (1986c). "Proyecto Desarrollo de Habilidades de Pensamiento: Creatividad." Impresos y Tesis, Instituto Technológico y de Estudios Superiores de Monterrey.

de Sánchez, M. (1986d). "Proyecto Desarrollo de Habilidades de Pensamiento: Metacomponentes, Componentes de Ejecucion y de Adquisición de Conocimiento." Impresos y Tesis, Instituto Technológico y de Estudios Superiores de Monterrey.

de Sánchez, M. (1986e). "Proyectos Desarrollo de Habilidades de Pensamiento: Novedad, Automatización e Inteligencia Práctica." Impresos y Tesis, Instituto Technológico y de Estudios Superiores de Monterrey.

de Sánchez, M. (1983). "Proyecto Aprender a Pensar. Estudio de Sus Efectos Sobre una Muestra de Estudiantes Venezolanos." Caracas: ME y MEDI.

Calfee, R. (1981). "Cognitive Psychology and Educational Practice." In *Review of Research in Education 9*. Washington, D.C.: American Educational Research Association Publishers.

Costa, A. L. (November 1984). "Mediating the Metacognitive." *Educational Leadership* 42, 3: 57–62.

Gardner, M. K. (1985). "Cognitive Psychological Approaches to Instructional Task Analysis." In *Review of Educational Research 12*. Washington, D.C.: American Educational Research Association Publishers

Herrnstein, R. J., R. S. Nickerson, M. de Sánchez, and J. A. Swets. (November 1986). "Teaching Thinking Skills." *Journal of the American Psychological Association* 41, 11: 1279–1289.

Final Report, Project Intelligence: The Development of Procedures to Enhance Thinking Skills. (1983). Cambridge, Mass.: Harvard University and Bolt Beranek and Newman.

Proyecto Inteligencia: Series (I–VI) de Lecciones para Desarrollar Habilidades de Pensamiento. (1983). Cambridge, Mass: Harvard University, Bolt Beranek and Newman y Ministerio de Educación de Venezuela.

Reif, F. (May 1981). "Teaching Problem Solving.: A Scientific Approach." *The Physics Teacher* 19, 5: 310–316.

Sternberg, R. J. (1986a). *A Triarchic Theory of Human Intelligence*. New York: Cambridge University Press.

Sternberg, R. J. (1986b). *Intelligence Applied: Understanding and Increasing Your Intellectual Skills*. New York: Harcourt Brace Jovanovich.

Whimbey, A., and J. Lochhead. (1986). *Problem Solving and Comprehension*. Hillsdale, N.J.: Lawrence Erlbaum.

27

Cognitive Curriculum for Young Children

H. Carl Haywood, Penelope Brooks, and Susan Burns

The Cognitive Curriculum for Young Children (CCYC) is a systematic, theory-based educational curriculum designed primarily for use with children from three to six years of age who are either handicapped or at high risk of learning failure in the primary grades (based chiefly on factors related to socioeconomic level). It was developed in a close collaboration between developmental psychologists and preschool educators for use in conjunction with a good content-focused curriculum. That is to say, its emphasis is on helping young children to acquire and elaborate systematic processes of perceiving, thinking, learning, and problem solving, rather than on teaching specific academic content. Begun in 1979, it is now used in hundreds of classes in the United States, Canada, Mexico, France, Belgium, Switzerland, and Israel, serving several thousand disadvantaged and/or handicapped children.

The goals of CCYC are:

1. To enhance and accelerate the development of basic cognitive functions, especially those necessary to acquire concrete operational thought;

2. To identify and remediate deficient cognitive functions;

3. To develop task-intrinsic motivation;

4. To develop representational thought;

5. To enhance learning effectiveness and readiness for school learning;

6. To prevent inappropriate special education placement.

CCYC rests on several theoretical bases dealing with the nature and development of ability, cognitive development, and cognitive modifiability: (a) Haywood's transactional view of the nature and development of human ability; (b) Vygotsky's concepts of social cognitive learning and the "zone of proximal development"; (c) Piaget's views of the cognitive nature of preschool children, the hierarchical and sequential nature of cognitive development; and (d) Feuerstein's concepts of structural cognitive modifiability.

Haywood considers intelligence to be multiply (basically genetically) determined, multifaceted, resistant to change, and essentially different from cognitive processes, which are acquired and highly modifiable. There is a necessary and powerful transactional relation between cognitive development and the development of intrinsic motivation.

Vygotsky's powerful idea that important cognitive acquisition occurs in social contexts contributed to the definition of the role of parents and of teachers in this curriculum. His concept of the "zone of proximal (next) development" as the difference between performance and potential helped to define the program of cognitive early education (reducing that discrepancy).

Piaget's notions of sequential and hierarchical cognitive development helped to identify and sequence the lessons. His emphasis on the prerequisites and functions of concrete operational thought as essential to content learning in the early grades defined part of the content of CCYC, while his emphasis on equilibration as the fuel of cognitive progress provided an important part of the teaching approach.

The heaviest single conceptual debt, liberally acknowledged, is to Feuerstein's "theory of structural cognitive modifiability" and to his concepts of mediated learning ex-

Copyright © 1990 by H. Carl Haywood, Penelope Brooks, and Susan Burns.

Cognitive Curriculum for Young Children (CCYC)

Developers:	H. Carl Haywood , Penelope Brooks, and Susan Burns
Goals:	To help young children acquire, generate, and elaborate systematic processes of perceiving, thinking, learning, and problem solving.
Sample skills:	Regulating behavior, comparing, classifying, problem solving, using quantitative relations, conservation, seriation, role taking, identification by salient features.
Assumption(s):	Mediated teaching can help students learn cognitive principles and strategies that they can later apply to unmediated experiences.
Intended audience:	Three- to six-year-olds who have handicaps (mental retardation, learning disabilities, cerebral palsy, speech and/or language delays, emotional disturbance, deafness) or are at high risk of learning failure.
Process:	Teaching and classroom activities stimulate children's thinking about their own thinking processes, and about generating, applying, and evaluating appropriate learning and problem-solving strategies. One cognitive function is addressed each day through these classroom events: (a) planning time, (b) a cognitive small-group lesson, (c) a content-oriented large-group lesson, (d) a directed free-choice activity, (e) summary time.
Time:	30–40 hours teacher training; weekly class time for students can range from 8 hours to 30 hours.
Available from:	Charlesbridge Publishing, 85 Main St., Watertown, MA 02172.

perience and the modifiability of specific cognitive functions. Feuerstein's theoretical contributions are discussed and elaborated extensively in a set of papers that accompanies the curriculum.

The curriculum has six principal components:

1. A strong theoretical base.
2. A "mediational" teaching style.
3. Cognitive "small-group" units, which are daily lessons focused on the acquisition of specific cognitive functions. These units in sequence are: Self-Regulation, Quantitative Relations, Comparison, Classification/Class Inclusion, Role Taking, Seriation, and Distinctive Features.
4. "Large-group" lessons, which focus on academic content (colors, numbers, shapes, nature, etc.) but emphasize the same cognitive functions that are learned in the small-group lessons.
5. A "cognitive-mediational" system of behavior management.
6. A parent participation program emphasizing classroom participation, parent organizations, and family/home activities coordinated with in-class cognitive lessons.

Essentially *metacognitive* in its orientation and emphasis, CCYC uses teaching and classroom activities designed to stimulate children's thinking about their own thinking processes, and about generating, applying, and evaluating appropriate learning and problem-solving strategies.

The typical CCYC day has a "cognitive function of the day" and the following classroom events:

1. Planning time
2. Cognitive small-group lesson
3. Content-oriented large-group lesson
4. Directed free-choice activity
5. Summary time

Helping children to understand the generalized meaning of their experiences, of new learning, of relationships is an important aspect of mediational teaching. The goal of generalizability means that mediational teachers are constantly looking for opportunities to demonstrate the broader applicability of principles and strategies that children might need in their later (unmediated) experience. Mediational teachers make a special effort to "bridge" cognitive concepts, principles, and strategies to familiar and diverse contexts. In doing this, teachers are trying to make children more effective at learning how to learn by getting the children to generalize the process they have used—beyond the immediate learning situations.

CCYC differs from traditional, content-oriented curriculums in the following ways:

1. The fundamental goal is stimulating the development of effective processes of thinking, perceiving, learning, and problem solving, rather than imparting information or training behavioral skill.
2. Teaching consists primarily of mediating the principles and strategies of formal thought, rather than communicating specific content knowledge or bits of information.

3. Successfully applied, CCYC improves students' processes of formal thought and their ability to develop new processes on their own, without further mediation.

Evaluative research in three quite different settings has yielded evidence of the following effects:

- Significant IQ gain (an average of 10 to 12 points over one academic year versus no gain for comparison groups);
- Changes in teachers' behavior, such as more questioning, more process-oriented questioning, more optimism about students' ability to learn;

- Changes in students' behavior, such as more enthusiasm for mental work, more process questions, less "confirmation seeking";
- Greater probability of placement in "regular" classes.

Evaluation continues at several sites.

The CCYC program is available in English, French, and Spanish. Teachers are trained in intensive (30–40 hours) workshops, which are offered in English and French in North America, and in English, French, German, and Dutch/Flemish in Europe.

28

A Problem-Solving Approach to Mathematics Instruction Using an Embedded Data Videodisc

Michael Young, James Van Haneghan, Linda Barron, Susan Williams, Nancy Vye, and John Bransford

During the past several years, members of Vanderbilt's Learning Technology Center have been experimenting with new ways to structure the learning experiences of students.[1] Our ultimate goal is to help students develop the confidence, skills, and knowledge necessary to solve problems and become independent thinkers and learners. We have come to believe that computer and videodisc technologies make it easier to achieve these objectives than has been true in the past. Projects that focus primarily on literacy, history, and social studies are described elsewhere (e.g., Bransford, Kinzer, Risko, Rowe, and Vye in press; Bransford, Sherwood, and Hasselbring 1988; Bransford, Sherwood, Hasselbring, Kinzer, and Williams 1988; Bransford, Vye, Kinzer, and Risko in press; Cognition and Technology Group at Vanderbilt in press). In this chapter we focus on attempts to improve mathematical thinking.

Instruction in problem solving, a key part of mathematical thinking, has long been a weakness of the mathematics curriculum and, most recently, attention has focused on the middle school mathematics curriculum (Lesh 1985; Thompson and Rathmell 1988; Kouba, Brown, Carpenter, Lindquist, Silver, and Swafford 1989). Paulos' (1988) claim

that the majority of Americans are "innumerate," unable to understand the most fundamental concepts of numbers, logic, and probability, highlights some of the most visible needs for an effort to improve the way middle school mathematics is taught. Porter (1989) suggests two reasons for the poor record of American schools: the small amount of time spent on problem solving instruction and the reliance on traditional word problems.

There is also a growing awareness that students need to experience the complexity of real-world problems and encounter problems "situated" in realistic settings (e.g., Bransford, Hasselbring, Barron, Kulewicz, Littlefield, and Goin 1987; Brown, Collins, and Duguid 1989; Lesh 1985; Simon 1980). Add to this the emphasis placed on learning to *apply* mathematics rather than just compute, and the consensus seems to be that students should learn not only *how* to convert from fractions to percents, for example, but also *when* percents are useful and *when* to convert from fractions to percents or decimals. Schools have traditionally done a good job teaching *how* to do these operations, but have failed to provide the context for *when* to apply such concepts (e.g., Simon 1980).

We believe that video technology can provide the rich context-based experiences needed for practicing the application of mathematics skills. With the goal of providing a

An earlier version of this chapter was published under the same title in *Technology and Learning* 3, 4 (1989): 1–4.

context for problem-solving exploration and application of middle school mathematics, our research group has developed a videodisc-based story, enriched with data and a central distance-rate-time problem that requires more than 15 steps to solve. The videodisc, *The Adventures of Jasper Woodbury: Episode One*[2] (Tom Sturdevant, writer/producer/director), has been designed and produced to provide a "macro-context" for teaching planning and problem identification. A macro-context is a problem-solving environment in which students must generate, as well as solve, several subproblems in order to solve the larger overall problem. In this video, the problem is intentionally complex, reflecting the nature of problems experienced in everyday settings and the need to provide students with the opportunity to practice working with such problems.

The video story centers around Jasper, who has bought an old cruiser and hopes to sail it home that day. But it's 2:30 p.m., the boat has no lights, and it took his little runabout more than 80 minutes to make the trip upriver. Jasper decides to leave, and students are challenged to consider the question "Did he make the right decision?"—a question similar to many questions in real life, such as "When should I leave for the airport?" or "What will I need to take along on vacation?" Such questions highlight metacomponents of problems, such as problem identification and planning, that are important components of any problem-solving process (Bransford and Stein 1984; Sternberg 1987). Even so, these metacomponents are rarely the focus of classroom instruction, where instead concepts are often abstracted from the context in which problems arise (Brown, Collins, and Duguid 1989; Porter 1989). Macro-contexts, like the *Jasper* video, allow problems to be situated in natural settings where the purposes of problem solving are apparent to students (Bransford et al. 1987). The *Jasper* video includes all the information required to solve the problems that are encountered. We call this design principle *embedded data design*.

Design Principles for the Jasper Video

1. *Embedded Data.* Jasper begins his adventure by driving his small boat up the river to where he can see the big boat he eventually buys. On the way, Jasper is shown viewing his river map, listening to the weather report on the radio, buying fuel, and paying for a minor repair to his boat. All these items eventually become important information when he decides to bring the big boat home later. Once students discover the need to consider the time of sunset (because of the big boat's broken lights) and the need for money for gas (because of the small temporary fuel tank on the big boat), they can search the disc for all the relevant pieces of information. Of course, there is also a great deal of irrelevant

information presented in the story, so students can practice identifying and recalling relevant information, and thereby develop the perceptual and cognitive skills they rarely have the opportunity to use in traditional instructional settings. Embedding in the video all the data necessary to solve problems is a unique feature of this instructional video series, and its use is facilitated by the random-access capability of the videodisc.

2. *Videodisc Format.* The videodisc enables students to retrieve the appropriate video segments quickly by using the random-access capability of the disc. Students are challenged to watch closely and to learn to notice important information, to look for problems, and to set up a framework for solving them. Teachers can use the search for embedded data to externalize search strategies for students (Vygotsky 1978). For example, the instructor can show several segments and ask students to determine which ones contain relevant information and why. In this way, the typically internal thought processes of individual students can be made public and discussed by the class. The search for relevant data is often aided by students who are infrequent contributors in traditional mathematics classrooms but who have observed an important piece of information that most of the class has missed. This helps those individuals gain confidence in their mathematical abilities. After students have defined the problems and searched out the required information, they use their computation skills, which they now see as useful and purposeful, to solve the problems.

3. *Realistic Goals.* Traditional word problems have historically been one of the few opportunities for students to practice applying their mathematics skills and their problem-solving strategies. Yet traditional word problems tend to have little meaning for children (Silver 1986; Van Haneghan and Baker 1989). Word problems often lack realistic goals beyond finding the answer. For instance, some addition problems ask how many of something two characters have "altogether." But in the real world, a question would be asked only if the characters had some mutual goal in mind; for example, they might want to put their money together to buy a present for a friend. The video contexts we are designing contain explicit goals for problem solving. Realistic goals enhance mathematical learning by providing retrieval cues for *when* mathematics and other problem-solving strategies can be used.

4. *Student-Generated Problems.* Traditional word problems are presented with the question already formulated. In the *Jasper* video, many of the problems are unstated and none of the problems is set up for the viewer. Students must discover and define these problems to solve the central problem posed. Once students discover the subproblems, they can apply their knowledge of middle school mathe-

matics to solve them, just as with traditional word problems. The unique challenge of the *Jasper* video is in defining problems, gathering information, and developing a plan for Jasper to get his new boat home. Requiring students to define the problems enhances their recall of the overall problem and its solution, a process known as the *generation effect* (Anderson, Goldberg, and Hidde 1971; Slamecka and Graf 1978). Recalling specific problems and their solutions is one key to the development of subject matter expertise (Chase and Simon 1973), and the ability to identify and define problems is a key attribute of building problem-solving expertise (Bransford and Stein 1984; Porter 1989). While conventional instruction often leads to knowledge that is available only to answer questions on a test—what Whitehead (1929) calls "inert" knowledge—instruction using a macro-context can make information useful and accessible for solving real-world problems (Sherwood, Kinzer, Hasselbring, and Bransford 1987; Bransford, Sherwood, Hasselbring, Kinzer, and Williams 1988).

Research Findings

The *Jasper* videodisc has been evaluated in studies of 5th and 6th graders working in groups in classroom settings, and in separate studies of individuals and pairs of students. Initial studies that challenged individual students to solve the main problem posed by the *Jasper* video, without assistance or mediation, showed that students were unprepared to handle the complexity and unstructured nature of the problem. Porter's (1989) report that the current elementary school mathematics curriculum emphasizes computational skills and not conceptual understanding reinforced our own expectation that students would initially have trouble with the complexity and unstructured nature of the *Jasper* videodisc problem. An intervention study was then conducted that compared an experimental class where students practiced their planning, problem finding, and problem organization skills with a control class where students rehearsed techniques for solving conventional word problems. An analysis of problem-solving protocols and pretest-posttest results indicated that students in the experimental class made significant and impressive gains in their ability to define problems and subproblems and to plan when faced with ill-defined problems when given an isomorphic video transfer problem containing all the elements of the *Jasper* video (Van Haneghan, Barron, Williams, Young, Vye, and Bransford in preparation).

Our research findings are encouraging, but it is important to note that our intervention included more than simply presenting the videodisc problem. We used the video as a tool to help students see the thinking processes involved in solving a complex problem. Students attempted to solve the problems with incomplete information, to identify problems and required information, and to estimate results. They were also given an opportunity to review the videodisc to find important information. In addition, students worked in small groups, which allowed their ideas to be refined through group discussion. Effective teaching coupled with the video context, rather than the video alone, has improved student performance. The videodisc can provide a rich source of data, a mutually shared experience, and a context for teacher-student interactions. But the videodisc cannot replace the teacher, and it cannot be considered a panacea that will teach students thinking skills without the guidance of a skilled teacher.

Next Steps

The Adventures of Jasper Woodbury: Episode One is the first in a series of videos that will use the embedded data design. In order for the demonstrated gains in students' planning and problem finding to transfer beyond boating contexts and even beyond mathematics problems, we expect that students will need to experience a number of these challenges across a broad range of topics and subject areas (e.g., history, geography, and science).

At the Learning Technology Center, we are planning a series of six to eight videos using the embedded data design to enhance mathematical and scientific thinking. The next video in the series involves the flight of an ultralight airplane and represents a transfer task for the distance-rate-time topics raised in the boating context of the initial Jasper story. Other videodiscs are planned that encourage the use of charts, tables, calculators, and special-purpose computer programs to automate the calculations required by the problem challenge. We also envision videodiscs that would conceptually precede the existing *Jasper* videodisc, and that would focus on planning for and discovering simpler problems.

Our plans for future development also include the use of technology to supplement the information embedded on individual videodiscs and to help integrate the problem-solving objectives of the *Jasper* series into existing middle school curriculums. Learning Technology Center staff members are designing and evaluating computer data bases that interact with the video and are designed to supplement the data embedded in the stories. We hope to encourage students and teachers to research and submit information to these data bases, and to share the information widely using telecommunications services such as Bitnet and the proposed Kidsnet.[3] Teachers are being given preservice and inservice training on the use of these materials and, with the help of expert teachers, model school programs are being developed.

NOTES

[1]This research has been supported in part by a grant from the James S. McDonnell Foundation.

[2]The research and development of the instructional videodisc series has been funded in part by the James S. McDonnell Foundation, St. Louis, Missouri, and Vanderbilt University, Nashville, Tenneseee.

[3]Bitnet is an electronic mail service available to colleges and school systems internationally. Discussion of the development of a national/international Kidsnet is currently underway. Bitnet members can participate in the discussion of the system by contacting KIDSNET@PITTVMS.BITNET.

REFERENCES

Anderson, R. C., S. R. Goldberg, and J. L. Hidde. (1971). "Meaningful Processing of Sentences." *Journal of Educational Psychology* 62, 5: 395–399.

Bransford, J., T. Hasselbring, B. Barron, S. Kulewicz, J. Littlefield, and L. Goin. (1987). "The Use of Macro-contexts to Facilitate Mathematical Thinking." In *Teaching and Evaluating Mathematical Problem Solving*, edited by R. Charles and E. Silver. Reston, Va.: National Council of Teachers of Mathematics.

Bransford, J., C. Kinzer, V. Risko, D. Rowe, and N. Vye. (In press). "Designing Invitations to Thinking: Some Initial Thoughts." Paper presented to the 1989 National Reading Conference, San Francisco.

Bransford, J., R. Sherwood, and T. Hasselbring. (1988). "The Video Revolution and Its Effects on Development: Some Initial Thoughts." In *Constructivism in the Computer Age*, edited by G. Forman and P. Pufall. Hillsdale, N.J.: Lawrence Erlbaum.

Bransford, J. D., R. D. Sherwood, T. S. Hasselbring, C. K. Kinzer, and S. M. Williams. (1988). "Anchored Instruction: Why We Need It and How Technology Can Help." In *Technology and Education*, edited by D. Nix and R. Spiro. Hillsdale, N.J.: Lawrence Erlbaum.

Bransford, J., and B. Stein. (1984). *The IDEAL Problem Solver*. New York: W. H. Freeman and Co.

Bransford, J. D., N. Vye, C. Kinzer, and V. Risko. (In press). "Teaching Thinking Content Knowledge: Toward an Integrated Approach." In *Dimensions of Thinking and Cognitive Instruction*, edited by B. F. Jones and L. Idol. Hillsdale, N.J.: Lawrence Erlbaum.

Brown, J. S., A. Collins, and P. Duguid. (January–February 1989). "Situated Cognition and the Culture of Learning." *Educational Researcher* 32–42.

Cognition and Technology Group at Vanderbilt. (In press). "Anchored Instruction and Its Relationship to Situated Cognition." *Educational Research*.

Chase, W. G., and H. A. Simon. (1973). "The Mind's Eye in Chess." In *Visual Information Processing*, edited by W. G. Chase. New York: Academic Press.

Kouba, V. L., C. A. Brown, T. P. Carpenter, M. M. Lindquist, E. A. Silver, and J. O. Swafford. (1989). "Results of the Fourth NAEP Assessment of Mathematics: Number, Operations, and Word Problems." *Arithmetic Teacher* 35, 8: 14–19.

Lesh, R. (1985). "Processes, Abilities Needed to Use Mathematics in Everyday Situations." *Education and Urban Society* 17: 330–336.

Paulos, J. A. (1988). *Innumeracy: Mathematical Illiteracy and Its Consequences*. New York: Hill and Wang.

Porter, A. (Summer 1989). "A Curriculum Out Of Balance: The Case of Elementary School Mathematics." *Educational Researcher* 9–15.

Sherwood, R., C. Kinzer, T. Hasselbring, and J. Bransford. (1987). "Macro-contexts for Learning: Initial Findings and Issues." *Journal of Applied Cognitive Psychology* 1: 93–108.

Silver, E. A. (1986). "Using Conceptual and Procedural Knowledge: A Focus on Relationships." In *Conceptual and Procedural Knowledge: The Case of Mathematics*, edited by J. Hiebert. Hillsdale, N.J.: Lawrence Erlbaum.

Simon, H. A. (1980). "Problem Solving and Evaluation." In *Problem Solving and Education: Issues in Teaching and Research*, edited by D. T. Tuma and R. Reif. Hillsdale, N.J.: Lawrence Erlbaum.

Slamecka, N. J., and P. Graf. (1978). "The Generation Effect: Delineation of a Phenomenon." *Journal of Experimental Psychology: Human Learning and Memory* 4, 6: 592–606.

Sternberg, R. (1987). "Teaching Intelligence: The Application of Cognitive Psychology to the Improvement of Intellectual Skills." In *Teaching Thinking Skills*, edited by J. B. Baron and R. J. Sternberg. New York: W. H. Freeman and Co.

Thompson, C. S., and E. C. Rathmell. (1988). "NCTM's Standards for School Mathematics, K–12." *Arithmetic Teacher* 39, 9: 17–19.

Van Haneghan, J. P., and L. Baker. (1989). "Cognitive Monitoring in Mathematics." In *Cognitive Strategy Research: From Basic Research to Educational Applications*, edited by C. B. McCormick, G. Miller, and M. Pressley. New York: Springer-Verlag.

Van Haneghan, J. P., L. Barron, S. M. Williams, M. F. Young, N. J. Vye, and J. D. Bransford. (In preparation). "The Jasper Series: An Experiment with New Ways to Enhance Mathematical Thinking."

Vygotsky, L. S. (1978). "Internationalization of Higher Psychological Functions." In *Mind in Society: The Development of Higher Psychological Processes*, edited by M. Cole, V. John-Steiner, S. Scribner, and E. Souberman. Cambridge, Mass.: Harvard University Press.

Whitehead, A. N. (1929). *The Aims of Education and Other Essays*. New York: Macmillan.

29

How Do You Choose a Thinking Skills Program That Is Right for You?

Richard D. Sholseth and Diane Y. Watanabe

Man's mind, stretched to a new idea, never goes back to its original dimensions.

—Oliver Wendall Holmes

Considering the many thinking skills programs available, and the many more being published, it's no wonder that educators have trouble when they go in search of "the best" thinking skills program. In order to lead the searcher to "the best" program, descriptions and data about the existing educational programs should be collected to determine the thinking skills and strategies that are important and appropriate to the educational community. Helpful information would assist in answering questions such as:

• Are any thinking skills being overlooked or taken for granted?

• Are any thinking skills being overtaught?

• Which thinking skills are found in the instructional materials?

• Which thinking skills are found in the tests?

• How are the students scoring on tests?

• Do the classroom teachers promote a positive classroom climate for thinking?

• Do the teachers practice question and response behaviors that encourage students to think better?

• Do the teachers have a repertoire of instructional strategies for the thinking skills that need to be taught?

Many people begin by looking at the published thinking skills programs themselves; however, if one is serious about finding a "good match" to the existing educational program,

a thorough needs assessment is the logical place to begin. It will provide the necessary data to guide the curriculum leaders in determining which thinking skills and instructional strategies are important.

One of the most thorough needs assessments is a curriculum alignment. This process begins with the existing district curriculum, which is what teachers are already responsible for teaching in the classrooms. The state recommended/mandated curriculums, such as state frameworks, are reviewed to be sure they are a part of the district curriculums. Then the various testing programs such as proficiency, norm-referenced, state, and district criterion-referenced tests are aligned.

Analyses of student performances on the tests provide answers to questions such as: How well are our students doing on the skills tested? Where are they excelling? Where are the weaknesses? Analyses of test data, together with the alignment of curriculum and tests, help to answer questions such as: Are we testing thinking skills not covered in our curriculum? Are we testing out of sequence? (e.g., 3rd grade testing of a skill that is not taught until 4th grade).

Analyses of test data may also provide other important information. For example, school personnel may discover that even though *main idea*, *analogies*, and *extrapolation* are important in the district curriculums, test results may show that schools already do a wonderful job on these skills. The thinking skills program, therefore, should provide skill maintenance and emphasize those areas where student performance is low. An anecdote illustrates this point:

Five principals and two board members went to a reading conference. They discovered a reading program that was foolproof! They could be assured that their number one reading objective, *understanding the main idea*, would be successfully learned. The committee went to the assistant superintendent and said that they wanted to buy this foolproof program. The survey of all of the teachers, the principals, and district staff showed that there was 100 percent agreement that the purchase should be made. Additionally, the assistant superintendent reviewed the district curriculum and found *understanding the main idea* as part of the continuum for every grade, 2–12. The skill was also stressed in every norm-referenced test. "Indeed, it's an important skill," he said. Who could fault the assistant superintendent for purchasing the $70,000 program?

In reality, if the assistant superintendent continued his investigation and did an item analysis on the test results, he would discover that student performance on the skill was already outstanding. Why spend another $70,000? Moral: What is important may not be a priority for more spending, because it may already be done well.

Instructional material, especially texts, should also be brought into alignment. Generally, textbooks are the major vehicle for delivering the curriculum. Curriculum leaders should discover what is adequately covered, what is missing, and what needs more emphasis in the match/mismatch of what is taught and what is tested, making certain that all that is tested is a subset of all that is taught. One of the purposes of an alignment is to ensure that local and state curriculum frameworks, district and state testing programs, and instructional material fit together, and to ensure that educators can identify which thinking skills need priority attention.

Other factors such as budgets, school climate, instructional practices, principal leadership, and staff development should also be considered in the alignment process. (For detailed information on this process see English 1987.)

The curriculum alignment document, along with the analyses of student performance data, becomes a needs assessment that can help schools select the thinking skills program(s) that may best serve their school or district.

Another question that the curriculum alignment will answer is "To what degree are thinking skills already part of the existing curriculum and testing program?" One of the questions most frequently asked by school personnel in the implementation of a thinking skills program has been "How will thinking skills fit into an already crowded curriculum?" One answer is "They are there now." The job is to identify them, prioritize them, and then focus on the appropriate instructional strategies to bring them out and provide instructional materials that are needed.

Art Costa advocates restructuring the curriculum because it would be unlikely that texts and other instructional materials are, or will ever be, designed that sufficiently include the three areas of teaching *for*, *of*, and *about* thinking. Richard Paul also advocates restructuring the local curriculum to ensure that vaguely stated objectives and ambiguous learner behaviors are reworded to explicitly emphasize critical thinking. The program(s) chosen should be the best match for the curriculum alignment. Thinking skills are an existing subset of the district curriculum, but often they are taken for granted and not identified. The curriculum alignment process is the ideal first step in choosing a program. Realistically, and unfortunately, most districts do not take the time or provide the resources to begin here.

Once the thinking skills components that need to be a part of the program have been identified, most districts and schools turn to published programs rather than develop a program from scratch. Educators have tough decisions to make and few have the time to thoroughly investigate all the programs. This leads to another question: "How do programs differ?"

How Do Programs Differ?

1. **Skills are presented differently.** Many programs, for example, include *cause and effect*, an important skill identified in almost all norm-referenced tests—e.g., the Illinois Test of Basic Skills (ITBS), California Achievement Test (CAT), Metropolitan Achievement Test (MAT), Stanford Achievement Test (SAT), and Comprehensive Test of Basic Skills (CTBS-4). A quick comparison of several programs shows how the skill differs in each. In Project Impact, the skill is called *inferring causes and effects*, and it is presented in terms of multiple causality and multiple consequences, along with the chaining of causes and effects (Figure 1).

FIGURE 1

Project Impact: Inferring Causes and Effect

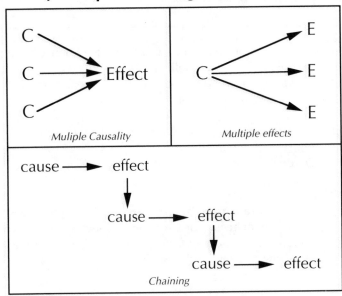

Muliple Causality

Multiple effects

Chaining

In Tactics, cause and effect is a subset of the tactic *elaboration* (inferring meaning from what is not stated). Similar to the skill in Project Impact, it includes multiple causes, multiple consequences, and chaining (Figure 2). In addition, the identification of explicitly and implicitly stated causes and consequences is required (Figure 3).

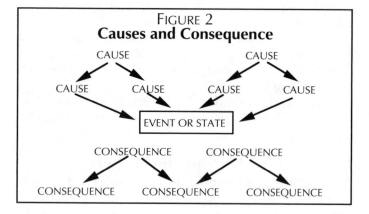

FIGURE 2
Causes and Consequence

Whimbey's presentation has a built-in sequence from easy to difficult for this skill in *Analytical Reading and Reasoning* (1983): stated reason and consequence; chains of causes; two independent reasons and a consequence; stated reason, implied reason, consequence; and premise conclusion. An example of "stated reason, implied reason, consequence" is shown in Figure 4.

De Bono treats cause and effect differently in his "tool" Consequences and Sequel, where he includes the implications of time (Figure 5).

2. **A program may be very strong in some areas and weak in others.** For example, in one program the presentation on *deductive thinking* may be strong; the same program, however, may include spelling but omit *analogical reasoning*.

FIGURE 3
Elaboration of Causes and Consequences

1. Identify important states or events

2. Using your frame, identify causes and consequences that are explicitily stated.

3. Justify your inferences.

FIGURE 4

If an idea is suggested but not actually stated, we say it is **implied.** Here is a sentence with a stated reason, implied reason, and a consequence:

The refrigerator was empty, so Shelly went to a restaurant to eat.

Your mental analysis of this sentence might look like:

STATED REASON: The refrigerator was empty
IMPLIED REASON: Shelly wanted to eat
CONSEQUENCE: Shelly went to a restaurant

Note that the implied reason is not directly stated in the sentence, but it is suggested by the stated reason and the consequence.

Spatial relationships are part of many programs. The "Cadillac" programs in this skill area are Instrumental Enrichment and Structure of Intellect (SOI). To a lesser extent, Tactics addresses *spatial relationships* in the unit called "Non-Linguistic Patterns." Spatial relationships are excluded, by design, from CoRT and Philosophy for Children. This omission does not negate these two programs; their power can be measured in part by the rich classroom discussions that are fostered by the materials.

Tactics' special forte lies in the "learning-to-learn" skills, which include metacognitive skills such as *goal setting* and *attention control* (paying attention and developing an internal locus of control).

3. **Terminologies are not consistent among programs.** For example, *synthesis* in Bloom's Taxonomy usually means to use the acquired data to create something new or original. In Tactics, *synthesis* is summarizing, as in outlines, flow charts, or Venn diagrams. Most educators are

---

FIGURE 5

C&S = Consequence and Sequel

The invention of the gasoline engine made possible automobiles, airplanes, the oil industry, and a great deal of pollution. If all the consequences could have been foreseen at the time, electric or steam engines might have been used in cars. A new invention, a plan, a rule, or a decision all have consequences that go on for a long time. In thinking about an action, these consequences should always be considered:

Immediate consequence

Short-term consequences (1-5 years)

Medium-term consequences (5-25 years)

Long-term consequences (over 25 years)

familiar with *evaluation* as used in Bloom's Taxonomy, where it is the highest level on a scale used to determine the complexity of intellectual activity. In SOI, evaluation is defined as the ability to make judgments, to plan, and to make decisions, and it is one of five intellectual operations that can be taught and for which lessons are provided. In Tactics, evaluation is applied in *evaluation of evidence*, *examination of value*, and *elaboration*.

There are other examples of inconsistency. For example, *divergent thinking* (SOI), *lateral thinking* (de Bono), *invention* (Tactics), and *application* (Bloom) are all terms associated with *creative thinking*. *Generalization* (or *inference*) and *extrapolation* also cross borders. Project Impact refers to a skill called *generalization* under a broader heading called *inference*. The *inference* skill in Tactics is found primarily in *elaboration*, though it is also in *evaluation of evidence*, *examination of value*, and *extrapolation*. Tactics' *extrapolation* would be the closest match to Project Impact's *generalization*.

4. **Programs vary in the amount of training required.** Training periods vary from a number of hours to a number of years. For example, Tactics requires approximately 15–20 hours of training, with an additional formal two-day trainer-of-trainer's program. At the other end of the scale is Instrumental Enrichment, which involves intensive training and directed practice over a period of several years (minimum training for this program is two to three weeks). CoRT requires little formal training, although eight to ten hours of training would be beneficial. Whimbey has not published a training program for *Problem Solving and Comprehension*, but the Thinking Skills Institute at the Los Angeles County Office of Education has developed one with input from Whimbey. The staff development component of Philosophy for Children requires about two weeks, while Project Impact requires three days of training for level one and another four days of training for level two.

5. **The adaptability of thinking skills content to subject areas varies among programs.** For example, in Tactics, *analogies* are easily adapted to all subject areas while *non-linguistic patterns* are more applicable to science, mathematics, and the arts. Project Impact includes the skills of *analyzing fact and opinion*, which may be appropriate in social sciences but may not be as adaptable to arithmetic or foreign languages. Similarly, a skill like *spatial relations*, which is exemplified in Structure of Intellect and Instrumental Enrichment, would be more aligned to geometry or art than to history or English.

6. **Most programs do not adequately consider how to teach "of thinking, for thinking, and about thinking**, as defined by Ron Brandt (1984). These three areas are well defined and described by Costa (1985); Figure 6 summarizes

their meaning. Most programs place all or most of the emphasis on teaching *of* thinking. Programs that rely on workbooks and blackline masters and have little or no teacher or group interaction generally fall into this area. This does not mean that these programs should be overlooked, but rather that teacher training should also be provided to ensure that there is teaching *for* thinking and *about* thinking as well.

If teaching *for* thinking is weak or nonexistent, strategies such as Whimbey's *paired problem solving* and *cooperative learning* strategies should be a part of the staff development program. Also, if *questioning strategies* (a subset of teaching *for* thinking) are not included, one may wish to look at one of the most powerful programs in this area, Philosophy for Children. Here, the use of the *community of inquiry* teaches students to ask questions. Instrumental Enrichment also provides an outstanding model for the transfer of learning. An excellent example in the area of teaching *about* thinking, specifically in the development of metacognitive thinking skills, is Whimbey's method that requires students to think out loud. Finally, the Odyssey program provides a detailed script for teachers that includes questions to ask students and responses to student answers.

FIGURE 6
Teaching FOR, OF, and ABOUT THINKING

1. Teaching FOR Thinking—Creating school and class-room conditions conducive to full cognitive development

2. Teaching OF Thinking—Instructing students in the skills and strategies directly or implementing one or more programs

3. Teaching ABOUT Thinking—Helping students become aware of their own and others' cognitive processes and their use in real-life situations and problems

---

The more skillful teachers are in the teaching *of* thinking, including *task analysis* of the strategies, the easier it is for them to develop ways to teach *for* and *about* thinking. A comprehensive thinking skills program requires teaching in all three areas, and it is the responsibility of the school or district to ensure that this occurs.

7. **Programs differ in their intended audience.** Some programs are designed specifically for teachers to use (e.g., Tactics), while others provide actual instructional material for students (e.g., CoRT, Instrumental Enrichment, SOI, Odyssey, and Project Impact). Some programs even have actual texts or workbooks (e.g., Midwest Publications and Philosophy for Children).

8. **Not all programs have assessment instruments.** Examples of some that do are Instrumental Enrichment, which uses sequential lessons requiring a level of mastery to proceed, with the level of mastery becoming the assessment; Philosophy for Children, for which many districts have used the New Jersey Test of Reasoning Skills; Whimbey's *Problem Solving and Comprehension*, which includes both the pre- and post-versions of the Whimbey Analytical Skills Inventory (WASI); and Structure of Intellect, which has an alternate form of the SOI Learning Abilities Test for retesting.

9. **Not all programs are supported by research.** When choosing a program, schools should be aware of how the program was validated. Has research been conducted? What do the studies indicate? Robert Sternberg cautions users that research studies of many programs lack consistent research data, and he calls for more formal research on all programs. Tactics was based on cognitive research and developmental psychology. The program that probably has the most research studies over a long period of time is Instrumental Enrichment. The benefit of Whimbey's work has also been studied, and reports show that students improved significantly on their SAT scores (110–150 scale scores) even long after the project ended. It has been reported that there is a significant difference between those who take the training and those who do not (Carmichael 1982).

10. **Programs may be used across the curriculum or in specific content areas.** Tactics and SOI are intended to be used across the curriculum. Examples of programs applicable to certain subject areas are *Problem Solving and Comprehension* (reading and mathematics), CoRT (social sciences and humanities), Philosophy for Children (language arts or philosophy), and Project Impact (reading, language arts, and mathematics).

11. **Programs may address a certain age or level or be comprehensive K–12 programs.** Tactics is a K–12 program. CoRT does not easily fit the early primary levels but has been adapted for the early grades by Sidney Tyler. Whimbey's program can be taught in grades 5–12.

The *hm Study Skills* programs published by the National Association of Elementary School Principals (NAESP) and the National Association of Secondary School Principals (NASSP) are intended for grades 1–12, while Project Impact is generally used at the middle or junior high school level and addresses minimum proficiency skills in reading, math, and social science.

12. **Programs may provide a written demonstration of the lesson with accompanying script.** For example, Odyssey provides a careful script along with student responses, and Instrumental Enrichment and Philosophy for Children have teacher's manuals that provide extensive support materials in the questioning and response behaviors for teachers.

What Are Some Typical Ways to Go?

Even after a careful search, rarely will a district or school find just one program to do the job. It is more likely that several programs need to be included in long-range planning, even though some of these programs will not be used in their entirety. Here are some brief descriptions of the progrsm we have touched on so far.

Tactics for Thinking. Many schools that have limited resources but want a program that will have broad application begin with Tactics. The materials are simple for teachers to understand and staff training averages less than an hour each for any of the 22 tactics.

The first six tactics are "learning-to-learn" tactics, and they address such skills as *attention control*, *power thinking*, and *goal setting*. Typically, a school begins with one or two units from this section and chooses several tactics from the 14 remaining, which are divided into "content application" skills such as *concept development*, *synthesis*, and *proceduralizing*, and "reasoning skills" such as *analogies*, *extrapolation*, and *examination of values*. The program represents a prudent use of funds, since the Teacher's Manual ($15) all that is required. It contains many practical suggestions for different grade levels and subject areas.

One advantage of Tactics is that it includes only tactics that are easy for teachers to learn and that are broadly applicable across the curriculum.

CoRT. This program fits neatly with Tactics. Particularly suitable for humanities and social sciences, CoRT gives more detailed techniques (called "tools") in the areas of *decision making* and *problem solving* than does Tactics. Tactics is a good place to begin; CoRT lessons are a fine complement: they give a fuller repertoire of skills for students to employ. The CoRT materials have been adapted by some teachers for primary grades, but the lessons are designed for upper elementary through high school. Students are taught from lessons contained on ten teacher-used "tool" cards. Hypothetical situations are given, and students learn techniques for "considering all factors" (CAF) and developing a "plus, minus, or interesting" (PMI) chart before they make decisions about the situation. Like Tactics, the program is a prudent investment. Materials cost approximately $20, and the same materials are used in teacher training and in classroom work with students. No additional purchases are necessary. Training for teachers on all ten "tools" can be accomplished in less than eight hours.

Problem Solving and Comprehension. Equally usable to supplement Tactics, especially for the skills of *everyday problem solving, academic problem solving, synthesis,* and *analogy,* is Whimbey's *Problem Solving and Comprehension* (1986). Another inexpensive investment ($16), this book supplies the teacher with numerous problem-solving activities to share with students. Particularly powerful techniques are (1) the paired problem-solving activities that emphasize metacognitive skills and (2) the verbal reasoning problems, each with an easy interpretation for teachers to share with students. The book is also useful for teacher training. The lessons are designed to strengthen the skills of all problem solvers, and they are especially adaptable for grades 5–14.

Philosophy for Children. Many districts complement their thinking skills curriculum with this program, especially in the areas of language arts and humanities. Materials are available for grades 1–12; they consist primarily of novels (adapted for various grade levels) that the entire class reads, plus teacher materials to foster reasoning skills. The program is somewhat more costly than those previously discussed because student materials must be purchased. Also, teacher training requires approximately two weeks in a special workshop.

SOI. This is a program for districts that prefer a more specialized program tied directly to individual student needs as profiled on a pretest. SOI is intended for individualized instructional activities based on a student's profile of strengths and weaknesses. The program requires two days of training to understand and interpret the pretest and profiles. Hand scoring is possible by trained personnel, but computer scoring services can be arranged with the Institute.

Tests and a master set of activities manuals must be purchased for SOI. These materials are usable *only* by staff members trained in the program, so ongoing training must be provided to ensure a knowledgeable teaching staff. School personnel who are willing to commit staff training time, to purchase the tests and activities manuals, and to ensure that a modest amount of time is regularly devoted to the SOI activities can have an effective program.

Some of the SOI materials are now available in Spanish as well as English, and student ability profiles can be developed for career counseling and preparation.

Instrumental Enrichment. This program has been validated by numerous research studies. Rigorous training and commitment is required for teachers, and materials cannot be purchased without the training. Sternberg ranks Instrumental Enrichment "among the best of the programs that emphasize thinking skills training." Schools must be willing to commit the time, staff training, and monetary resources necessary to implement the program.

Can We Implement Programs for Long-term Change, not for a Quick Fix?

Thinking skills programs chosen to implement long-term changes are more likely to yield success. Articulation between and among grade levels and subjects is a major consideration. A program dependent upon just one person or isolated at one grade level or subject area will be piecemeal. A program planned over a span of years and across subject areas is more likely to have depth and substance. Such programs require staff development training and the involvement of many staff members in all three areas of teaching thinking: teaching *for* thinking, teaching *of* thinking, and teaching *about* thinking.

An elementary school that wants to raise student achievement in the skill of *identifying the author's point of view* will plan a continuum that ensures that the skill is introduced uniformly at a grade level, and that it is reinforced at regular intervals with appropriate degrees of difficulty.

A secondary school that wants to raise student achievement in a reasoning skill such as *extrapolation* will conduct staff development and introduce strategies for presenting the skill in various subjects. As important as the initial staff development or dissemination of instructional materials is the follow-through by department or grade chairpersons or administrators; peer coaching can also help to ensure that skills are being taught. And test-item analysis of student achievement is one way to validate the degree of success.

A program that can serve several grade levels or be blended with other programs to address specific needs at specific grade levels or subject areas is advantageous. Such a program requires commitment—from the district administration as well as the principal—and is widely supported by the teachers. That commitment is engendered by involving as many staff members as possible in choosing the program and by offering staff training in a timely, sequential manner. There is no surer way to doom a program than by compacting the staff training into hurried sessions held late in the school day and then assuming that the new materials and procedures will take root—or by doing training for one or two days without subsequent follow-up or establishment of such supportive practices as peer coaching.

BIBLIOGRAPHY

Adams, M. J., et al. (1986). *Odyssey: A Curriculum for Thinking.* Watertown, Mass.: Mastery Education Corp.

Black, H. and S. Black. (1985). *Building Thinking Skills.* Pacific Grove, California: Midwest Publications.

Bloom, B., and D. R. Krathwohl. (1977; reprint of 1956 edition). *Taxonomy of Educational Objectives, Handbook I: Cognitive Domain.* New York: David McKay Company.

Brandt, R. (September 1984). "Teaching of Thinking, for Thinking, About Thinking." *Educational Leadership* 42, 1: 3.

Chance, P. (1986). *Thinking in the Classroom*. New York: Teacher's College Press.

Costa, A. (1989a). "Foreword." *Toward the Thinking Curriculum* (1989 ASCD Yearbook), edited by L. B. Resnick and L. E. Klopfer. Alexandria, Va.: Association for Supervision and Curriculum Development.

Costa, A. (1989b). "Restructuring Lesson Plans to Enhance Thinking." Unpublished Paper.

Costa, A., ed. (1985). *Developing Minds*. Alexandria, Va.: Association for Supervision and Curriculum Development.

de Bono, E. (1986). *CoRT Thinking Teacher's Notes*, 2nd ed. New York: Pergamon.

English, F. W. (1987). *Curriculum Management for Schools, Colleges, Business*. Springfield, Ill.: Charles C. Thomas.

Feuerstein, R. (1980). *Instrumental Enrichment*. Baltimore: University Park Press.

Marzano, R. J., and D. E. Arredondo. (1986). *Tactics for Thinking Teacher's Manual*. Aurora, Colo.: Mid-continent Regional Educational Laboratory.

Meeker, M. (1969). *The SOI: Its Uses and Interpretation*. Columbus, Ohio: Charles Merrill.

Meeker, M., R. Meeker, and G. Roid. (1984). *The Basic SOI Test Manual*. Los Angeles, Calif.: WPS.

National Association of Elementary School Principals. (n.d.) *The hm Study Skills Program Level B*. Alexandria, Va.: NAESP.

National Association of Secondary School Principals. (n.d.) *The hm Study Skills Program*. Reston, Va: NASSP.

Nickerson, R. S., D. N. Perkins, and E. D. Smith. (1985). *The Teaching of Thinking*. Hillsdale, N.J.: Lawrence Erlbaum.

Paul, R. W., A. J. A. Blinker, K. Adamson, and D. Martin. (1988). *Critical Thinking Handbook: High School*. Rohnert Park, Calif.: Sonoma State University.

Presseisen, B. Z, ed. (1988). *At-Risk Students and Thinking: Perspectives from Research*. Philadelphia, Pa.: National Education Association and Research for Better Schools.

Presseisen, B. Z. (1986). *Critical Thinking and Thinking Skills: State of the Art Definitions and Practice in Public Schools*. Philadelphia, Pa.: Research for Better Schools.

Sternberg, R. J. (1983). *How Can We Teach Intelligence?* Philadelphia, Pa.: Research for Better Schools.

Whimbey, A., and J. Lochhead. (1986). *Problem Solving and Comprehension*. 4th ed. Hillsdale, N.J.: Lawrence Erlbaum.

Whimbey, A., and E. L. Jenkins. (1986). *Analyze Organize Write: a Structured Program for Expository Writing*. Hillsdale, N.J.: Lawrence Erlbaum.

Whimbey, A. (1983). *Analytical Reading and Reasoning*. 2nd ed. Stamford, Conn.: Innovative Sciences, Inc.

Contributing Authors

Marilyn Jager Adams, Senior Scientist, Bolt Beranek & Newman Inc., BBN Systems and Technologies Corp., 10 Moulton St., Cambridge, MA 02238.

John D. Baker, President, Midwest Publications, Critical Thinking Press, P.O. Box 448, Pacific Grove, CA 93950.

Linda Barron, Research Assistant Professor of Mathematics Education, Peabody College, Vanderbilt University, Nashville, TN 37203.

John Bransford, Professor of Psychology, Learning Technology Center, Box 45, Peabody College, Vanderbilt University, Nashville, TN 37203.

Penelope Brooks, Professor of Psychology, Vanderbilt University, P.O. Box 9, Peabody Station, Nashville, TN 37203.

Susan Burns, Assistant Professor of Education, Dept. of Education, Alcee Fortier Bldg., Tulane University, New Orleans, LA 70118.

Geoffrey J. Comber, Creator of The Touchstones Project, 48 West St., Suite 104, Annapolis, MD 21401.

Arthur L. Costa, Professor, California State University, Sacramento, and Co-Director, the Institute for Intelligent Behavior. Send correspondence to: 950 Fulton Ave., Suite 245, Sacramento, CA 95825.

Anne B. Crabbe, Director, Future Problem Solving Program, St. Andrews College, Laurinburg, NC 28352.

Edward de Bono, Director, International Center for the Development of Thinking Skills, L2 Albany, United Kingdom, Piccadilly, London W.IV 9RR.

Margarita A. de Sánchez, Director, Developing Thinking Skills Program, Instituto Tecnologico y de Estudios Superiores de Monterrey, Campus Eugenio Garza Sada, Dinamarca #451, Co. del Carmen, C.P. 64710, Monterrey, N.L. Mexico.

H. Carl Haywood, Professor of Psychology and of Neurology, Vanderbilt University, P.O. Box 9, Peabody Station, Nashville, TN 37203.

Marcia Heiman, Co-Director, Learning to Learn, Inc., 28 Tenniman Rd., Allston, MA 02134.

Deborah E. Hobbs, Instructor, Elementary Education, Elementary Education Dept., Utah State University, Logan, UT 84322.

David Hyerle, Director of Curriculum and Development, 77 Pemberton St., Innovative Services, Inc., Cambridge, MA 02140.

Scott G. Isaksen, Associate Professor and Director, Center for Studies in Creativity, State University College at Buffalo, Chase Hall, 1300 Elmwood Ave., Buffalo, NY 14222.

Frances R. Link, President, Curriculum Development Associates, Inc., 1211 Connecticut Ave., N.W., Suite 414, Washington, DC 20036.

Matthew Lipman, Director, Institute for the Advancement of Philosophy for Children, Montclair State College, 210 Chapin Hall, Upper Montclair, NJ 07043.

Nicholas Maistrellis, Creator, The Touchstones Project, 48 West St., Suite 104, Annapolis, MD 21401.

Robert J. Marzano, Senior Program Director, Mid-continent Regional Educational Laboratory, 2550 S. Parker Rd., Suite 500, Aurora, CO 80014.

Mary N. Meeker, Founder, SOI Systems, P.O. Box D, Vida, OR 97488.

Anne H. Nardi, Codirector, Center for Guided Design, West Virginia University, 137 Engineering Sciences Building, Box 6101, Morgantown, WV 26506.

Carol Booth Olson, Project Director, UCI Writing Project, University of California, Irvine, CA 92717.

Sidney J. Parnes, Professor Emeritus of Creative Studies, SUNY at Buffalo, and Trustee, Creative Education Foundation. From November 1 to June 1, send correspondence to: 8535 Via Mallorca, La Jolla, CA 92037; from June through October: 214 Wedgewood Dr., Williamsville, NY 14221.

Stanley Pogrow, Associate Professor of Educational Foundations and Administration, College of Education, University of Arizona, Tucson, AZ 85721.

Carol L. Schlichter, Professor and Chair, Program for Gifted and Talented, University of Alabama, Box 870231, Tuscaloosa, AL 35487.

Richard D. Sholseth, Consultant, Thinking Skills Institutes, Divison of Curriculum and Instructional Programs, Los Angeles County Office of Education, 9300 E. Imperial Highway, Downey, CA 90242-2890.

Robert J. Sternberg, IBM Professor of Psychology and Education, Department of Psychology, Yale University, Box 11A Yale Station, New Haven, CT 06520.

Shari Tishman, Associate, Project Zero, Graduate School of Education, Harvard University, 313 Longfellow Hall, Appian Way, Cambridge, MA 02138-3752.

Donald J. Treffinger, Director, Center for Creative Learning, 4152 Independence Court, Suite C-7, Sarasota, FL 34234.

Sydney Billig Tyler, Author and Program Design Specialist, Thomas Geale Publications, Inc., P.O. Box 370540, Montara, CA 94037.

James Van Haneghan, Assistant Professor of Educational Psychology, Department of Educational Psychology, Counseling and Special Education, Graham Hall, Northern Illinois University, DeKalb, IL 60115.

Nancy Vye, Research Associate, Learning Technology Center, Box 45, Peabody College, Vanderbilt University, Nashville, TN 37203.

Charles E. Wales, Co-Director, Center for Guided Design, P.O. Box 6101, West Virginia University, Morgantown, WV 26506-6101.

Diane Y. Watanabe, Consultant, Thinking Skills Institutes, Divison of Curriculum and Instructional Programs, Los Angeles County Office of Education, 9300 E. Imperial Highway, Downey, CA 90242-2890.

Howard Will, Vice President, Great Books Foundation, 40 E. Huron St., Chicago, IL 60611.

Susan Williams, Research Assistant, Learning Technology Center, Peabody College, Vanderbilt University, Nashville, TN 37203.

S. Lee Winocur, National Director, Center for the Teaching of Thinking, 21412 Magnolia St., Huntington Beach, CA 92646.

Elena Dworkin Wright, Managing Editor, Charlesbridge Publishing, 85 Main St., Watertown, MA 02172.

Michael Young, Assistant Professor of Educational Psychology, 249 Glenbrook Dr., Box U-4, University of Connecticut, Storrs, CT 06269-2004.

Howard Zeiderman, Creator, The Touchstones Project, 48 West St., Suite 104, Annapolis, MD 21401.

Index to Authors

Windsor Farm Elementary
Media Center